A Fly Fisher's
Reflections

A Fly Fisher's Reflections

JOHN GODDARD F.R.E.S.

Foreword by Lefty Kreh

THE LYONS PRESS
GUILFORD, CONNECTICUT
AN IMPRINT OF THE GLOBE PEQUOT PRESS

The Lyons Press is an imprint of The Globe Pequot Press

ISBN 1-58574-698-3

Typeset by Derek Doyle & Associates, Liverpool

Printed in Canada.

First published in Great Britain by Robert Hale Limited.

10 9 8 7 6 5 4 3 2 1

Library of Congress Cataloging-in-Publication data is available on file.

Contents

Acknowledgments

Many of the articles reproduced in this volume have been culled from back numbers of the following magazines or journals: *Trout & Salmon, Fly Fishing & Fly Tying, Anglers Mail, Salmon Trout & Sea Trout, Trout Fisherman, Sea Angler, Ahlan Wasahlan, Fly Fisherman* (USA) and the journal of the Fly Fishers' Club. I would like to thank the owners and editors of these publications for allowing me to reproduce them. It should also be mentioned that some have been taken from old publications including *Angling, Salmon & Trout, Creel, Anglers World, Fisherman*, and others that are no longer with us.

Foreword

If you are a fly fisherman and you want to enjoy both reading about the sport as well as learning how to become a better fly fisherman, read *A Fly Fisher's Reflections.* I promise you it will deliver in both areas.

The first time I fished with John Goddard was on the River Kennet, my personal favorite among all the English chalkstreams. Stepping from the car, we began rigging tackle, and I learned the first of a number of useful things from John. In his soft-spoken way, he looked at my fly jacket and asked, "Do you have a jacket that is a little more subtle in color?"

At first I thought he was joking, but looking at him I realized he was serious. I had worn this same khaki-colored jacket for years in many parts of the world where I had fished, and no one had ever questioned it before. Almost apologetically, John explained that we would be fishing with green trees behind us, and that the trout might notice the brightly colored jacket I wore. The next day I borrowed one of John's dark green jackets, and for the rest of the days we fished there, I found it made a huge difference.

It was just one of the many neat things I have learned over many years from John Goddard, who has become a very good friend.

Many fly fishermen have fooled thousands of trout with the celebrated Goddard Caddis, which John created. But he has developed many other patterns that are just as effective, though perhaps not as famous. Unfortunately, most of John's brilliant, original fly patterns are little known in the United States.

John Goddard is one of the most innovative and creative fly fishermen I have ever known. Some of his research on how trout see flies came about from observations he made in an aquarium that was made with angled, see-through ends. John could stand below and peer up at actual insects floating on the surface. This afforded him a trout's eye view of the bugs, and this knowledge in turn has helped him to develop his original patterns. Often these seem to fly in the face of tradition—but they certainly catch fish!

John was one of the first tyers in the world to develop effective midge suspender flies, and he popularized the upside-down dry fly years ago—a highly effective tying style that is only now catching on in this country.

Few anglers in the world have ever had the breadth and depth of fly-fishing experience that John Goddard offers in this priceless volume. He first fished the Seychelles Islands during a pioneering trip to the Indian Ocean for bonefish and other tropical flats denizens in 1974—and the Seychelles have recently become a "hot" destination for traveling saltwater anglers. Decades ago he fished sailfish off Africa's west coast. Our own western US rivers, in Montana, Idaho, California, and elsewhere, are nearly as well known to him as his home waters in Britain. John has made numerous angling trips to Chile and Argentina, and annually for years caught trout in New Zealand as well. For many years he has hosted expeditions to the Bahamas in search of the wary and elusive bonefish.

John Goddard has now published *A Fly Fisher's Reflections.* Here he shares with readers his many wonderful fly-fishing adventures around the globe. It all makes for fascinating reading. But this book is more than just a great read. The chapter on flies and how to tie and fish them will come as a revelation to many already skilled fly rodders, and will doubtless help them to catch more fish, no matter where their own adventures may take them.

I cannot think of a fly fisherman on the planet who has had more experience fishing in both salt and fresh water. I consider John Goddard to be the finest trout fisherman I have ever fished with—and I have been very fortunate to fish with many fabulous—and famous—trout anglers around the world. None of them approaches John's skill level.

John shares both his experiences and his knowledge in this book. Turn the pages, and let John Goddard share with you a rich harvest gleaned from a lifetime of learning about the great sport of fly fishing.

Lefty Kreh
August 2002

Illustrations

Between pages 144 and 145

Colour section:

ILLUSTRATIONS

Introduction

After much deliberation I originally decided to give this book the title 'The Golden Years of Angling' as I sincerely believe that the post-war period up to around the mid-eighties encompasses the most exciting and revolutionary period in angling history. At the last moment, however, I had second thoughts as both I and my publishers felt that the title it has now been given was more indicative of the contents. This volume contains a selection of articles that I have written for various angling publications and many of them cover this most important period.

Some may argue that the first half of this century was more important as much progress was made in this period. First of all, by the turn of the century, dry fly fishing had become firmly established and this was followed within a few years with the first developments in nymph fishing. During this same period many new coarse fishing records were achieved with bigger and bigger fish being caught, mainly due to the many new techniques that were established over this period. At the same time, deep sea fishing was undergoing a quiet revolution with the introduction of more powerful rods and new types of big game reels and lines that were, at long last, able to cope with the huge size and weights of the larger species of marlin and tuna. However, in my opinion, all this pales into insignificance when compared to the huge advances made in all aspects of our sport since the late fifties.

Let us now consider some of the more important advances made in this latter period on the various branches of our sport.

Coarse Fishing

Apart from anything else two huge advances were made in the post-war period. The completely new and revolutionary fixed spool reels were introduced, which for the first time made it possible to cast light baits enormous distances. This was followed a few years afterwards with the introduction of much lighter and stronger rods made of glass fibre and eventually carbon and graphite, which in turn led to the introduction of pole fishing which, again, was a highly revolutionary method of fishing. Some of these poles today are of an unbelievable length. During the first half of the last century the average coarse fisher's kit was confined to a rod and reel, a tackle bag, and possibly a rod rest and a stool. Furthermore he had to obtain and mix his own bait and groundbait. Today he has a complete range of angling luggage to choose from, as well as plastic seat and tackle carriers, along with the many hundreds of accessories now available including tents to sleep in, umbrellas for wet weather and even bite alarms. In addition to this it is now possible to purchase a bewildering array of both baits and groundbaits.

Despite all this it is a moot point as to whether the actual fishing in our rivers and lakes for the various species of coarse fish (apart from carp) has improved over this period.

Sea Fishing

Like the coarse fisherman the sea angler now has a vast range of accessories and baits to choose from, and has also benefited from the introduction of fixed spool reels as well as more efficient and sophisticated multiplying reels. These, together with new and powerful graphite rods, have enabled beach and shore fishers now to cast baits incredible distances. Deep sea and big game anglers have also benefited enormously from the introduction of new graphite or carbon rods and more efficient big game reels, as well as nylon monofilament lines, which are far superior to the old braided lines.

Another aspect to be considered, particularly by big game fishers, was the opportunities offered to them when the last great war ended. During this period little commercial fishing throughout the world was possible, so the seas were literally full of all species of fish just waiting to be caught. Consequently from the early fifties through the seventies many, many records were broken. Sadly, since then the seas have been literally plundered by commercial operators using more and more sophisticated equipment with no regard for the future, which has now resulted in many sought-after species of fish becoming endangered.

Fly Fishing

Without doubt, this branch of our wonderful sport has benefited more dramatically than any other, mainly due to the vast array of new materials and technology that has been developed in this period. We are now able to purchase rods that are incredibly efficient, made from space-age materials that are unbelievably light, weighing less than a quarter of the old split cane rods. Furthermore, these are available in a vast array of sizes and lengths to suit all styles and methods of fly fishing. We also have a vast range of fly lines to choose from which, compared to the old silk fly lines which were the only ones available prior to the fifties, have literally opened up completely new horizons for fly fishers, enabling them to perfect many new techniques that were just not possible before. In addition to this we now have monofilament tapered leaders and also new tippet materials such as fluorocarbon and copolymer, which are incredibly thin and strong when compared to the old horse hair or gut tippets that had to be kept constantly wet.

So far as fly reels are concerned there have been fewer advances in this direction than in many others, although they are now much lighter. There are also reels now available with very large capacities for backing and with very sophisticated breaking systems, which offer huge advantagees to salmon fishers and which also allow salt water fly fishers to subdue fish weighing upwards of two hundred pounds. We also have a far larger range of hooks available, many of these with chemically-sharpened points.

Finally, one of the biggest advances has been made in the range of artificial flies now available to us. Before the last war there were but several hundred patterns of flies, whereas today there are many thousands. In fact many fly fishers now consider there are far too many. This huge increase has come about partly due to the many new techniques that have been developed, and partly due to the huge range of new materials now available to the fly dresser.

Let us now look at the actual fishing over this same period of time. So far as salmon are concerned there is little doubt that they are now an endangered species. There has been a steady decline in Atlantic salmon stocks over the past century, which has accelerated to an alarming degree over the past twenty years or so, mainly due to commercial netting at sea. Sadly it has now reached a stage where many UK rivers have few, if any, salmon running up them.

Consequently many dedicated salmon fishers are now turning to other branches of our sport. However, since the late fifties fly fishing for trout has really taken off. Prior to the last war stillwater fly fishing was mainly confined to the lochs of Scotland and the loughs of Ireland, where the fishing was practised usually from boats using traditional loch-style methods of fly fishing. So far as fly fishers in the Midlands and the South were concerned, the only other option available to them was Blagdon reservoir in Somerset, which opened in the early part of the last century. Over the years the fishing proved to be so popular that in 1957, when a new reservoir nearby Chew Valley was formed, they also decided to stock this with trout and open it to the public. The trout fishing at this new venue in the first two or three years can only be described as spectacular, so consequently it was not long before some other water authorities followed suit. The big break-through in stillwater fishing occurred in the early sixties, when the government of the day decreed that in future all reservoirs throughout the country should be made available for leisure pursuits. Up to this time most reservoirs were off limits to the public, but due to this decree most were opened up for fishing, sailing or other water sports within a very short period of time. This, in turn, resulted in many landowners all over the country jumping on the bandwagon and stocking their lakes or ponds with trout, and also selling day tickets to fish them. Today there are many hundreds of small stillwaters through-out the country stocked with trout, which has now resulted in still-water fishing becoming a major branch of our sport. In this same period many completely new methods, techniques and fly patterns have been perfected to fish these new stillwaters both from boat and bank.

The other big advance made in fly fishing during this very exciting period was the introduction of a completely new and novel form of fishing, which started not in lakes or rivers, but in the sea. This occurred shortly after the last war one bright and windless morning in 1947, when the late and great Joe Brooke – fly fishing out of Islamorada in the Florida keys – took the first two recorded bonefish on flies specifically dressed to catch them. This set the angling world alight, and within a relatively short time fly fishers all over America were vying with one another to take part in this exciting new sport. The bonefish that frequent the shallow sand flats in many tropical areas are, without doubt, the most exciting of all fish to take on a fly. The first run of a bone after it has taken your fly has to be experienced to be believed. Averaging four to six pounds, even a relatively small fish of a little over three pounds can take over fifty yards of backing before you dare try to stop it. Little wonder that the sport is becoming increasingly popular.

Before long this new breed of saltwater fly fishers was looking to other species of saltwater fish to test their skills, By the early seventies heavy-duty fly rods were being produced to take ten and twelve weight lines, and great Tarpon close to two hundred pounds were being subdued. In latter years sailfish and even great marlin were being taken regularly on the fly, while today there are dozens of different species that can be taken in the salt on a fly. While the sport was slow to take on in the UK (probably due to the travel distances involved) it has, with the introduction of cheap air travel, rapidly increased in poularity over the last twenty years or so.

During mv formative years of fly fishing in the mid-fifties my time was divided between local rivers, the newly opened Weir Wood reservoir and monthly trips to Blagdon and Chew. This was followed in recent years (and up to comparatively recently) by regular visits to them and also other big reservoirs such as Grafham, Rutland Water and Bewl Bridge. I have never been particularly keen on fishing the many small stillwaters available, which I tend to look upon as put and take fisheries. On the other hand, I do often enjoy a day on these where the water is clear and one can stalk individual trout. I also became very keen on deep sea fishing and, during the late fifties and early sixties, made many annual sorties after blue sharks off Looe in Cornwall. Due to the publicity attracted by some of these forays, I was very privileged to be asked by the Portuguese Tourist Board to undertake a survey of the deep sea fishing around the coasts of Portugal. This eventually led to many offers from other tourist boards and also to my great friendship with the late Leslie Moncrieff, often described as the gentle giant of sea angling, who eventually accompanied me to many of these facinating venues around the world during the seventies and early eighties. Since my retirement fifteen years ago, with more time on my hands I have specialized in leading groups of fly fishers to many exotic locations all over the planet to fish for both trout and the many species of saltwater fish.

My first and most lasting love, however, has been with fly fishing on rivers for trout and in latter years also for grayling which are now, of course, one of our only true wild fish. Most of my fly fishing has been confined to the many chalkstreams and other rivers in the South of England and West Country, where on some streams it is still possible to catch truly wild trout.

Since then I have fished many waters all over the world for trout, particularly in America from the East coast to the West coast where I have made very many fly fishing friends, including some of the country's top fly fishers such as Gary Borger, Darrell Martin, Mel Kreiger, Len Wright, Larry Solomon, Dick Talleur and many others including my great buddy Lefty Kreh, that doyen of American fly fishers with whom I shared many adventures both over here and also in the salt.

Despite my passion for river fly fishing I also made time to fish many stillwaters during this same period and it was in the summer of 1957– the year that Chew Valley lake opened for trout fishing – that I first met the late Cliff Henry, who was to become one of my closest fishing friends for many years. Cliff was a master stillwater fisher and also a very accomplished fly dresser, from whom I learned much in those early years. At the time he had rarely fished rivers for trout, but in the early sixties I managed to obtain membership of The Piscatorial Society for him, so in a comparitively short time he mastered the very different techniques required for fishing in this medium. By this time I was reasonably happy with my approach to dry fly fishing, but had only recently taken up nymph fishing on rivers, which to start with I found very demanding. It was around this time that I was very fortunate indeed to be introduced to Major Oliver Kite by my good friend Preben Torp Jacobsen, one of Denmark's top fly fishers, I soon became very friendly with Ollie, as he was known to his friends, and we fished together for many years until his sad and untimely death on the banks of the River Test. In my opinion he was the greatest exponent of modern nymph fishing that ever handled a fly rod, and over a period of time he handed on to me many of the finer techniques that he had learnt over the years the hard way. As a result of his teaching I eventually became a dedicated nymph fisher. However, within a few years I came to realize with experience it was easier to catch trout on the nymph than in some cases on the dry fly. So these days I prefer (at least for trout) to fish the dry fly in preference as I find it much more of a challenge, because if you find a really educated trout rising he is usually much more difficult to take on a dry than on a nymph.

Like many fly fishers, in my early days I was only interested in catching as many trout as possible, but within a few years as I became more proficient I became more interested in seeking out only the larger fish. This in time led me to the challenge of trying to catch the most difficult trout, those 'Aunt Sallies', as we call them, that no one has been able to tempt. The clock eventually turned full circle, so for several years now I have been more than content just to be on the water with the ever-changing landscape as the season progresses, and observe the many interesting facets of the wild creatures so often found beside rivers and lakes. In addition to this, very extended lunches (often by the water) are now the order of the day, where socializing and often lengthy discussions with many of my old and also current friends with whom I regularly fish. These include such luminaries as Brian Clarke, Neil Patterson, Peter Lapsley, Tom Saville, Ron Clark, Dave Steuart, Bernard Cribbins, Tony Hayter, Eric Williams and Max King, all of whom are great exponents of the gentle art.

On the other hand, to be perfectly truthful, even today, if someone were to point out a truly big fish and ask me to try for it my hands would still tremble as I tried to tie on a fly he may accept. Apart from anything else, one of the greatest aspects of angling is that no matter how old or experienced you become, you never stop learning. I sincerely hope that some of the techniques and observations made in the following chapters will not only assist the tyro, but also the more experienced fly fishers, for, although much of the book was written many years ago it is all as relevant today as it was then.

A Fly Fisher's Reflections

PART ONE
FLY PATTERNS

Observations on Chironomids 1968

Over the years much has been written about the aquatic life on which river fish feed. On the other hand, apart from one or two books published comparatively recently, little reading is available on the aquatic organisms that inhabit lakes and reservoirs.

Most still waters contain a greater variety of aquatic creatures than rivers and, therefore, the subject is more complex and the lack of angling literature adds to the difficulties facing the student observer. During the past three seasons, in conjunction with that well-known angler and entomologist David Jacques, I have made some interesting observations and as a result of raising various insects in tanks under controlled conditions, combined with observations in the field, we have made many enlightening discoveries.

The 'hatching midge pupa'
artificial representing a
surfacing chironomid

As far as possible we have confined our observations to the same species or family but in the course of this past year I went off at a slight tangent and started a personal study of the Chironomidae.

I find these insects quite fascinating and without a doubt they are responsible for a large proportion of the stillwater trout's diet, particularly when they are in their pupal stages. Before I proceed further I should like to make it clear that my study of the family which comprises nearly 400 species has been restricted to a few particular types.

Chironomid species vary in size from adults with a wing length of less than 1 mm to those with a wing length of nearly 8 mm. Both the pupae and adult winged flies also vary considerably in colour, with bodies ranging from orange to brown, green or black. Therefore, for simplicity's sake from the fly fisherman's point of view, they can be classified by the aforementioned colours and by their sizes which may be described as small, medium and large.

The Chironomids, buzzers or midges, as some anglers prefer to call them, are part of the extremely large Diptera order. The females have fairly stout cylindrical bodies while the males are slimmer and both have two semi-transparent wings usually shorter than their bodies. Many species hatch in vast numbers early in the morning or late evening, others at any hour of the day.

Little is known about their life cycle but personal observation of certain species has revealed that the adult females lay their eggs on the surface in clusters in the form of beads. The small larvae which eventually emerge swim to the bed of the lake where they remain for a considerable period, living either in small tunnels in the mud or forming cases of such things as decayed vegetable matter and silt. They vary in size according to species, the largest I have seen being nearly an inch long. During this period some species are found browsing or moving with a characteristic figure-of-eight lashing movement along the bed of the lake or immobile in weed, particularly blanket weed.

The colour of these larvae varies from a pale brown or green through to a brilliant red and it is thought that this latter colour is due to haemoglobin in the blood. This substance has the property of absorbing oxygen and distributing it through the body of the larvae, thus enabling them to live in waters or areas of waters that have a low oxygen content.

It is worth recording that even in well-oxygenated water many specimens which, in their larval stages are often a dull, brown-red colour, become a brilliant red shortly before pupation.

It is fairly easy to tie a lifelike representation of these larvae by using size 12 or 14 fine-wire, longshank hook and merely tying a body of red or green maribou silk mixed with a judicious amount of fluorescent floss of the same colour and ribbed with a fine silver tinsel. Unfortunately, it is a difficult pattern to fish, owing to the virtual impossibility of representing the laboured movements of the larvae along the mud bottom. However, I have had a certain amount of success by retrieving such artificials exceedingly slowly along the bottom.

The pupation period of the Chironomids I have observed has been between 12 and 24 hours. In its final stage the pupa ascends into the surface film where it remains hanging in a vertical position with the filaments on top of its head just breaking the surface. It remains in this position for anything up to an hour, wriggling at constant intervals.

The pupae, when at rest in the surface, have a strongly-curved body with a slightly bulbous thorax. The top of the thorax is covered with fine white filaments which, no doubt, assist respiration, and the tails of most specimens I have handled have small appendages usually of a distinct whitish colour. As transformation to the adult approaches, the movement of the pupa gradually decreases until it ceases completely. The pupa, now as stiff as a poker, slowly swings upwards and assumes a horizontal position in the film. Within seconds the skin of the pupal case splits along the thorax and the adult winged fly emerges on the surface.

It is during this final stage of pupation when the pupae are hanging in the film that the trout feed on them avidly with the familiar slow head-and-tail rise. As most anglers know, it is when a widespread rise of this nature is in progress that the fish are often most difficult to catch. I am, therefore, of the opinion that it is most important to observe the following points if one wants to increase one's chances of success.

The artificial must be a reasonably accurate representation of the pupa. The size and colour of the natural on the water at the time should be simulated. The artificial should be fished either without movement or exceedingly slowly in small jerks and it must be fished in the surface film.

Since adopting the above points my catches have increased considerably and for those of my readers who are interested, the dressings that I have developed to represent these midge pupa are given below:

Hatching Midge Pupa – Hook: D/E Wide Gape Fine Wire 12 to 16. Silk: As body colour. Tag: White fluro floss. Tie a sparse bunch well round bend of hook. Body: Black, brown, orange, or green maribou silk, rib sparsely with narrow silver lurex and then cover with opaque PVC. Thorax: Green or purple peacock herl. Filaments: The fine fluffy down from base of white hen feather.

The body should be continued well round the bend of the hook to represent the strongly-curved shape of the pupa, and the filaments should be tied through the thorax but facing forward and upward over the eye of the hook.

I have also had considerable success fishing this pattern in midwater in tiny jerks during the day when no surface feeding fish have been observed. It seems reasonable to suppose that these pupa do spend some time in midwater, although I have so far been unable to substantiate this. I have, however, caught many trout during these periods that have been full of the pupae.

I should add that some species may conform to a different pattern in regard to the final stage of pupation, but my research in this direction is not yet complete.

NB This pattern could be looked upon as the father of all modern midge pupa or buzzer patterns that are today so popular. Prior to this dressing the only other popular buzzer pattern was the black buzzer by Dr Bell of Blagdon, but this pattern, unlike the author's, had no tail filaments and the white feather was tied in sloping back down body not sloping forward over the eye as the white breathing filaments do in the natural.

Some New and Effective Fly Dressings 1968

I had the feeling that the 1967 trout season, in terms of catching fish, had been a little better than the previous two, despite the fact that many fellow fly fishermen I had spoken to during the course of the summer had expressed varying opinions about it.

On referring to the fishing diary of my colleague, Cliff Henry, and to my own, it soon became apparent that my initial thoughts were quite correct. Not only had more trout come to the net per days fished but the average size had been larger. Many of these trout were over two pounds and, in view of the fact that in hard-fished club waters such as ours the fish stocked do not exceed 16 inches, we had reason to be pleased with our personal results. As many of our more accomplished fly-fishing members had not been particularly successful, I wondered why we had fared better.

Now, I can only assume that it may have been due to some of the new patterns we have developed and which assisted considerably in providing an acceptable answer to what the fish were feeding on at the time.

The past season has been difficult and easy fish have been less evident than in previous years. Why this should have been so is difficult to decide. So far as our own waters are concerned, it could be due to two factors – heavier rod pressure due to members fishing more frequently, and many of our trout now being reared in natural conditions, making them more difficult to catch than hatchery-bred fish.

I also learn from fishermen in many other areas of the country that the trout fishing generally seems to have been poor, so there must obviously be other reasons as well. At the start of the season we had an exceptionally wet spring, with resultant high water for several weeks. This meant more food being swept down to the fish, and this, combined with coloured water, caused reluctance among many trout to rise for surface food. Finally, we had a hot, sunny period lasting through June and July and, in these bright conditions, fishing is always difficult. As a consequence of this bright weather, weed growth was phenomenal and, in many cases, river keepers had little alternative but to attack weed in a wholesale manner. As a result, many stretches of river were practically denuded of surface and sub-surface weed and this, of course, led to an inevitable shortage of fly life.

Because of all this I found that in many cases the old accepted patterns of artificial flies were of little avail. On the other hand, some of the new patterns that Cliff Henry and I had developed over the past few years came into their own. In retrospect, I am inclined to look upon last season as the final testing period for many of these creations, some of which now appear beyond any reasonable doubt to be killing artificials when used on the appropriate occasions. Up to now, apart from giving a few of the dressings for them in my book *Trout Fly Recognition*, I have not publicized them, being a little wary of recommending new patterns until they had been thoroughly tested.

The first of these patterns, which I call the 'Hatching Nymph', is one we use when the fish are feeding in the surface film and taking the various nymphs as they are drifting preparatory to hatching out. When trout are so feeding they are usually exceedingly difficult to catch, as they often ignore both the surface fly and the ascending nymph. During this season we have found more trout preoccupied feeding in this manner than in previous seasons, no doubt due to the hot weather.

In these conditions the adult winged flies leave the surface rapidly, and obviously the trout find it easier to concentrate on the nymph which drifts in the film for some distance. When fish are feeding in this manner the rise form is very similar to the rise to a surface fly and it requires careful observation to spot the difference. This fly pattern is designed to rest in the film with the head and hook eye just protruding and, to achieve this, it is necessary to keep the cast slightly greased. It is presented in a similar way to a dry fly but it is a little more difficult to fish, as the strike has to be made on the estimated position of the artificial.

In most cases, as we all know, drag is fatal with a dry fly but with this pattern it seldom puts a fish down and this can be a distinct advantage on many occasions. I have often had trout charge at my Hatching Nymph when the current has imparted a slight drag. I tie this pattern in two sizes, medium and small, alternated with light and dark bodies, to represent the various species of nymphs.

The second pattern is a dry fly developed by Cliff Henry to represent the Medium Olive, either *B. vernus* or *B. buceratus*, and on waters where these species occur it is a useful pattern during May and June and often again in September when the naturals are most in evidence.

This is not, of course, a very revolutionary pattern as there are many well-known dressings of a similar appearance. We are, therefore, inclined to think that the success we have had with this over the years is due to the combination of colours in the dressing, combined with the pale edging on the hen hackle stalk which forms the basis of the body and imitates the pale-coloured ringing on the body segments of the natural to perfection. This pale edging is provided when the flue is stripped from the olive-coloured hen hackle stalk.

The next pattern which we have used with much success over the last two seasons is another developed by Cliff Henry. On our waters, one of the most common naturals that is seen in the evenings from mid-June to the end of August is the Small Dark Olive, *B. scambus*. The artificial is tied to represent the female spinner and even during the evenings when this is not the predominant species, the trout seem to have a distinct preference for it and will often pick it out from other natural spinners.

We tie two variations of this particular pattern, one with a fairly sparse hackle which is fished in the surface film, the other with a *very* sparse hackle fished just under the film. The reason for this is that the small red spinner is one of the species that is believed to crawl under water down weeds or posts to deposit its eggs. It sometimes fails to break through the film on its return to the surface, hence the need for the two methods of fishing the artificial. Whichever method is used, it is essential that it is dressed on a very tiny hook, as, of course, this species *B. scambus* is often exceedingly small and is by far the smallest of our upwinged Olives.

If I were to restrict myself to one pattern only throughout the season I would have no hesitation in naming this next pattern as my choice. I call it the 'Last Hope'. Although tied specifically to represent either the Pale Watery, *B. bioculatus*, or the Small Spurwing, *C. luteolum*, it is a very killing pattern when any small fly is on the water, but its most valuable application will probably be found in its use as a last resort. I have lost count of the number of difficult trout I have grassed using this pattern when all others have failed.

The Last Hope. A pin head indicates the fly's size

It is a very simple fly to dress and requires little in the way of materials, but I must emphasise the importance of adhering rigidly to the dressing details and colour. It will be noticed that I give two hackle colours in the dressing, cream and honey, the former being my original specification. I have now found in practice that the fly with the cream hackle is most effective early in the season, whereas the darker honey hackle is to be favoured as the season progresses. I also particularly specify a hackle very short in the flue. I appreciate that hackles in this category are now very difficult to obtain and, as an alternative, a hackle may be trimmed.

The final pattern is my PVC Nymph. The basic material is copper wire as used in Frank Sawyer's Pheasant Tail Nymph and due credit for the original idea must be accorded to him, and also to Major Oliver Kite who brought this pattern to perfection.

Over the years. I have used, and still use, this PT nymph with considerable success, but five or six years ago I decided I felt far from happy with the general appearance and coloration, particularly when fishing it as a representation of the various species of Olive nymphs. My dressing is, therefore, very much lighter in colour. The body is basically olive condor herl covered with colourless PVC and, in most cases, I tie a sparse rib of silver tinsel over the herl but under the PVC. This gives that translucent appearance to the body that is characteristic of many of the natural nymphs.

Any weighted nymph, no matter what colour, will take fish on occasion if fished by the induced-take method which, of course, imparts movement to the nymph. It is therefore as an imitation where movement is not advocated that I recommend this new pattern. In the early days when testing this pattern, I and my colleagues fished side by side to the same nymphing fish, presenting the PT and the new PVC nymph alternately in the same manner without movement, and the number of takes came down heavily in favour of this new pattern.

Most of these patterns are tied to represent specific natural flies and, therefore, may only prove effective on waters where the naturals are found in reasonable quantities.

Hatching Olive Nymph: Hook – 13 to 16 d/e.

Tying silk – Brown.

Body – Olive green condor or alternate colour, three fibres, leave tips projecting to form tails, rib with narrow silver Lurex and cover body up to thorax with one-sixteenth-inch wide strip olive PVC.

Thorax – Three dark pheasant tail fibres doubled and redoubled.

Hackle – Two turns of pale honey tied in front of thorax.

Hatching BWO nymph: Dark as above but substituting pheasant tail fibres in place of condor and dark honey hackle in place of pale honey.

Medium Olive Dun: Hook – 15 or 16 u/e.

Tying silk – Green.

Tail – Grey-blue whisks.

Body – Hen hackle stalk from light olive cape sharply tapered.

Wings – Mallard duck wing feather.

Hackle – Pale gingery olive.

Small Red Spinner: Hook – 16 or 17 u/e.

Tying silk – Red.

Tail – Light blue-grey, six to twelve fibres, three only for the sub-surface pattern.

Body – Rusty red cock hackle stalk.

Wings – Pale blue-grey mottled cock hackle tips tied spent.

Hackle – Pale ginger, short in the flue, two or three turns, one turn only for sub-surface pattern.

Last Hope: Hook – 17 or 18 u/e fine wire.

Tying silk – Pale yellow.

Body – Two goose primary or condor herls, buff colour.

Hackle – Cream or dark honey cock very, very short in flue.

Tails – Honey dun cock, six to eight fibres.

PVC Nymph: Hook – 16 to 12 d/e.

Tying silk – Yellow.

Body – Cover shank of hook with fine copper wire, forming hump near eye to represent thorax. Tie in silk at bend and tie in body materials; first of all, three strands of olive condor herl, leaving the

A Male Spinner of an upwinged fly

A Female Spinner of an upwinged fly

The PVC Nymph, the basic material of which is copper wire as used in Frank Sawyer's Pheasant Tail Nymph. The John Goddard dressing is very much lighter in colour

fine tips protruding to represent the tails. Follow with silver tinsel if required, and then a one-sixteenth-inch wide strip of colourless PVC. Take herl up to eye and tie in. Wind silk back over herl to rear of thorax, bring tinsel and then PVC up to this point, and tie in. Continue back to eye with silk and, finally, tie in three blackish pheasant tail fibres doubled and redoubled over top of thorax.

The Fall of the Ant and the Rise of the Snail
1968

In the early part of the season I was discussing trout fishing with editor Brian Harris, and he mentioned he had recently spent a successful April day on Darwell reservoir in Sussex when many other rods had poor results. The reason for his achievement on this occasion was mainly due to his powers of observation. He described how most other anglers were fishing the deeper water from the dam, which early in the year usually offers the best chances. He got bored with fishing a sunk line, which meant the fly constantly caught the stones of the dam and as a breeze was blowing off the north bank he decided to see if any fish were moving in the shallows as they had on previous occasions. He walked to the selected bank and settled down to watch. Within a few moments he had seen several trout moving, so he walked to the water's edge to see if he could find out to what they were rising. At first he was unable to see any life in the water in sufficient quantities to account for the rising fish, but after a little while he spotted several small black beetles crawling in the weeds in the margins. The breeze blowing offshore sent one or two of these beetles out into the body of the reservoir on the surface film. Suspecting that it was these little creatures that the trout were feeding on, Brian followed one with his eye as it drifted out into the reservoir, and sure enough, about 20 yards from the shore it disappeared in a swirl as a hungry trout accepted it. Mounting a size 12 Black Beetle (thick black ostrich herl body, short black hen hackle tied in the *middle* of the body) with the leader greased to fish the fly high in the surface film he commenced fishing very slowly. He consequently netted several nice trout and it was really the subsequent discussion we had that prompted me to write this article.

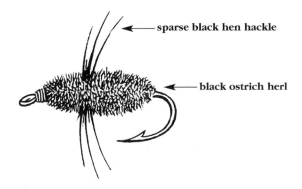

sparse black hen hackle

black ostrich herl

Black Beetle (Harris)

It is probably not generally realized that there are many opportunities such as this throughout most seasons when the observant angler may catch fish where others fail. I will now describe two other instances that occur occasionally and usually bring about a heavy rise of fish. The first is brought about by insects of a terrestrial nature, while the second is caused by aquatic fauna.

There are many creatures of a terrestrial origin that will often bring trout up to the surface to feed when they fall or are blown on to the water in sufficient quantities. The fish are sometimes a little slow on the uptake, but once they start feeding on whatever species it may be, they probably look upon them as manna from heaven and commence feeding avidly, usually to the exclusion of anything else. Among these, to mention just a few, are several fauna of a seasonal nature such as the Hawthorn, the Black Gnat, the Heather Fly, the June Bug and several other beetles. However, the particular insect I am about to discuss is certainly not seasonal in the accepted sense so far as the fisherman is concerned, as some years it may not be observed at all while in others it may be encountered on several widely-separated occasions in the one season. This is the ant, or rather the ant in its winged form. As most people are aware, at certain times of the year, usually on hot sultry or thundery days during July, August or early September, many species of ants develop wings for their annual nuptial migration. It seems that they are often attracted by water in this winged state and should there be a breeze blowing to take them out over the lake, being poor fliers they invariably finish up struggling in the surface film, thereby making a tempting target for any hungry trout. There are, of

A special pattern to represent the black ant in its winged stage

course, many species of ants but the two most common and likely to be encountered are the small Black Ant (*Acanthomyops niger*) and the Common Yellow Ant (*Acanthomyops flavus*). The former is black while the latter is usually brownish, varying between red-brown and yellow-brown. An artificial pattern is fairly easy to tie and should be fished in the surface film with an occasional twitch to animate and represent the struggle of the natural as closely as possible. A fall of ants is not a frequent event, but when it does occur the lucky angler present is likely to have a day to remember all his life, providing he has remembered it is essential to carry the requisite artificial in either brown or black – the trout are unlikely to accept a substitute.

Apart from terrestrial forms of life there are also many aquatic insects or other fauna that at some stage in their life cycle provide food for the trout in or on the surface. It is probably not generally realized that at certain times of the year the common aquatic snail may be included in this category. Most anglers are aware that snails – where they exist in quantities – form a major part of the diet of still-water trout. These are normally browsed off the weed or bed of the lake by the fish in their search for food, but it is unfortunately virtu-ally impossible to represent successfully with an artificial, the snail in its natural aquatic abode. However, on occasions, usually during the hot weather of mid or late summer, there takes place on many still waters a mass migration of snails to the surface. This phenomenon is most interesting and although I have personally observed it on many occasions I have so far been unable to ascertain the reason for it. I have also discussed this with one or two people who have made a study of the life history of snails but with nil results. Therefore, one can only hazard a guess and the most likely explanations seem that it is either due to a migratory instinct coupled with mating, or alternatively slight deoxygenation of the water due to high temperature causing the snails to rise to the surface. Snails are very much more sensitive to the oxygen content of the water than many other forms of underwater life, including fish, and this slight depletion of the oxygen content could well be the cause. To favour this latter theory it is interesting to note that snails put into a tank of water that many hours before has been boiled, thereby removing the oxygen, will immediately rise.

When snails rise to the surface in this manner they float with their shell below the surface but their foot or pad adhering to the underside of the surface film. In this manner they can move quite rapidly along this underside of the film or alternatively be carried along in the film by current or wind. When one of these mass rises to the surface happens the snails will often remain on the surface for several days and on at least one small lake I know of, the snails were to be found over a period of nearly three weeks. This is probably unusual though. From the angler's point of view this is a golden opportunity, although this is probably not realized by the majority of trout fishermen. When the snails are up the trout are most selective as they are then presented with one of their favourite foods in a very accessible position on the surface, and are unlikely to be caught with anything other than an artificial pattern to simulate these floating snails. However, providing you have an imitation with you at the time this phenomenon occurs wonderful sport is usually assured. My colleague, Cliff Henry, has perfected an excellent cork-bodied pattern which floats beautifully in the surface and has provided us with many good fish in the past.

Without doubt the most difficult aspect of this rise to the snail is to know when it is taking place. The rise of a trout to a floating snail is a typical head and tail rise usually associated with trout feeding on midge pupae, nymphs or *Caenis* spinners, all of which are common during mid-summer. Apart from the difficulty of recognizing the rise one would assume that it would be an easy matter to spot the snails in the surface, but in fact they are extremely difficult to see, and it is often only by looking directly down into the water that they will be observed.

Finally, I should like to recount a little story in connection with the snail that happened to my friend Cliff Henry in August last year at

Grafham. Having fished all morning from the south bank with the wind in his face, with little success, he decided to join the majority of anglers on the north bank fishing with the wind behind them. Upon arrival there was little space left to fish so he engaged one or two anglers in conversation. He was promptly informed that the fishing was terrible and despite the fact that numerous trout were rising none had been caught. His curiosity aroused, he walked to the water's edge to observe and try to decide what the fish could be taking. There at his feet was the answer; snails in profusion floating along the margin. The wind was gradually blowing these out into the lake a few at a time and odd trout being aware of this were patrolling near the shore awaiting their arrival. Mounting the appropriate snail artificial my friend was fortunate to get his limit of trout in a very short time, much to the amazement of the many anglers in the vicinity. Questioned as to the successful fly he was very happy to furnish this information but, unfortunately, none of the fishermen had such a pattern or even a near approach.

Cliff Henry's dressing for the floating snail

Ant, Black or Brown, (John Goddard): hook – 14 u/e; tying silk – black, brown or orange; body – two small cylindrical pieces of shaped cork split and bound round shank of hook, one near bend other near eye. Cover with dubbed fur from bend to eye; wings – two white hackle tips tied spent fashion but at an angle to rear; hackle – black or Rhode Island Red cock hackle tied in at eye.

Snail, (Cliff Henry): hook – 10, 12 or 14 d/e (according to size of snail); tying silk – black; body – a flat-topped, tapered section of cork, partly split and bound lightly on to shank of hook with flat section facing eye. This is then covered with stripped peacock quill except for a last two turns near flattened top representing pad of snail for which bronze peacock herl should be used.

The late Cliff Henry with three lovely
brown trout from the River Kennet

Chironomid Pupae 1970

The Chironomids or 'buzzers' as they are commonly referred to by many anglers form one of the most important sources of food for trout in still water. Despite this fact little is known about this particular family of insects, and it is only comparatively recently that their importance to the angler has been fully realized.

Pupa of orange-silver midge enlarged from a John Goddard transparency

During the last four years I have undertaken fairly extensive research on them and have made many interesting discoveries. The family is a large one containing over 380 different species, most of which are aquatic. Fortunately for the angler many of these are uncommon or extremely localized and accurate identification is rarely necessary. So far as I have been able to ascertain the very common species can be confined to quite a small number, although I would not be dogmatic about this as they are an extremely difficult group to identify. The following list would seem to cover most of those that are of interest to the angler.

Angler's name	Entomological name	Wing length
Large Green Midge	*Chironomus plumosus group*	6.5–8mm.
Large Red Midge	*Chironomus plumosus group*	6.5–8mm.
Orange-Silver Midge	*Chironomus plumosus group*	6.5–8mm.
Golden Dun Midge	*Chironomus plumosus group*	6.5–8mm.
Ribbed Midge	*Chironomus plumosus group*	6.5-7mm.
Black Midge	*Chironomus anthracinus*	5–7.5mm.
Blagdon Green Midge	*Endochironomus albipennis*	4–6mm.
Small Brown Midge	*Glyptotendipes paripes*	4–6mm.
Small Red Midge	*Microtendipes pedellus*	4–4.5mm.
Small Black Midge	*Polypedilum nubeculosus*	3.5–4mm.

In a short article such as this it is not possible to give full details of location and season of all species mentioned in this list, so I have picked two at random. *Orange-Silver Midge.* This appears to be the most common species likely to be encountered early in the season; the adults are seen on the wing in the late evening from April to early June, and occasionally in the early morning too as the weather turns warmer. They are extremely widespread and up to now I have come across them on every still water I have fished. A large species, the adults have a wing length of about seven millimetres and their bodies have a most distinctive colouration, the segments being silver-grey with orange rings where they join. The pupae are quite fascinating and if one is captured and held up against the light in a glass jar, the junctions between the body segments show up as a bright crimson, while the segments themselves appear as if formed from wide bands of silver Lurex. During late May or June a smaller medium-sized species of the same colour and appearance will often be observed hatching in the late morning or afternoon.

Small Brown Midge. This is one of the smaller species, the adults having chestnut brown bodies with a wing length of about five millimetres. The bodies of the pupae are a similar colour although they often have a distinct orange tinge. They are also a common and wide-spread species, usually hatching from deeper water during the warmer summer months. Emergence of the adults sometimes extends over a long period, mainly during the day between 11 a.m. and 5 p.m. On some waters the trout seem particularly fond of them, feeding on the pupae or emerging adults in the surface film. When trout are feeding on these small pupae the rise form is most distinctive; in a flat calm the fish rise repeatedly in a semi-circular pattern as they rapidly sip down the pupae. In a ripple they nearly always feed upwind in a dead straight line.

The Pupa. Although trout will occasionally feed on the adults resting on the surface after they have hatched, it is on the pupae that they mainly concentrate. Most of the larger species hatch either during the very early morning, shortly after dawn, or during the late evening. The trout have several opportunities to feed on the pupae at various stages in their comparatively short life, and to appreciate this it is necessary to describe this phase of their existence in more detail. My experiments to date lead me to believe their pupal life extends over a period varying between 36 to 72 hours.

As the pupae reach maturity they partially emerge from their burrows or tubes of mud and undulate rapidly back and forth for all the world like miniature hula hula dancers; this is apparently necessary to assist respiration. They rapidly retreat into their burrows at the first sign of danger; even so trout often feed on unwary ones at this stage. When conditions for emergence are right the now-adult pupae emerge from their retreats and swim slowly to the surface, and it is at this time that the trout have their first good opportunity of feeding on them. My research seems to indicate that the pupae swim directly to the surface and spend little or no time in midwater, as do the pupae of some other aquatic species of Diptera. When they reach the surface they adopt the typical pupae position, hanging tail down with their respiratory filaments on top of their heads just piercing the surface film; within seconds the transformation to the adult winged fly takes place, and almost immediately they fly off.

The above sequence of events usually happens under breezy conditions when there is a good ripple, as due to this broken water there is little surface film or tension and therefore the pupae transform rapidly. When these conditions apply the trout tend to feed on the ascending pupae rather than in the surface and consequently the rises of trout are rather spasmodic.

On the other hand when there is a flat calm the situation is very different, as in these conditions there is nearly always a comparatively thick surface film. The ascending pupae then seem to have considerable difficulty in breaking through this to emerge, and on many occasions I have observed them for upwards of an hour or more hanging under this film before they have found a weak spot in which to break through. Naturally under these conditions their behaviour is very different; this is important to the fisherman endeavouring to imitate them. When the ascending pupae find a heavy surface film like this, they spend much of their time swimming along with a strong wriggling action in a horizontal position immediately under the film, obviously endeavouring to locate a weak spot. At frequent intervals they stop, probably to rest and adopt the more typical vertical position. It is at these two stages that they are most vulnerable to the depradations of the trout. When these circumstances apply it usually results in a very heavy widespread surface rise of trout which will often extend until it is too dark to continue fishing.

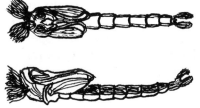

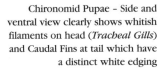

Chironomid Pupae - Side and ventral view clearly shows whitish filaments on head (*Tracheal Gills*) and Caudal Fins at tail which have a distinct white edging

I am sure most of us are only too familiar with this type of rise, when every trout in the water seems to be rising at the same time, yet none of them seems to be the least interested in the pattern one is offering them. At this time I am convinced it is essential to offer them a good imitative pattern in the right colour and size, and fished in the correct manner, to achieve success. Even so, fishing under these conditions is always difficult, as it appears that some trout become preoccupied, only feeding upon those pupae swimming along horizontally, while others will only accept those hanging stationary in the film. Furthermore, should the hatch be a large one, within a short time there will be so many pupae in the surface that the chances of a fish accepting your artificial are much reduced.

So far as the fishing technique is concerned it will now be obvious from the above sequence of events that to ensure maximum success it is necessary to fish the artificial pupae at the correct depth and also in the right manner. Up to now the accepted and, as far as I am aware, only method of fishing a buzzer rise, is with an artificial pupa on the point, perhaps with one or two others on short droppers. These are then fished in the surface film with a lightly greased leader, very slowly with frequent pauses. While this method will often account for several fish there are many occasions when it proves quite useless; at the best it is only a compromise as the pupae on the point and droppers sometimes will probably be fishing too deep. *An inch below the surface can at times be too deep.*

I have therefore evolved the following new techniques to imitate as closely as possible the varying stages in the life cycle of the pupa.

Method one: To imitate the pupae ascending to the surface. An artificial is mounted on the point and also on the first dropper if desired with a large heavily greased dry sedge on the top dropper. This selection should be fished when a buzzer rise is anticipated – before the actual rise on the surface commences – as follows. Using a floating line the artificials are cast into the desired area and allowed to sink until the pupa on the point and first dropper are hanging in midwater directly under the floating sedge on the top dropper. During a flat calm a very slow sink and draw retrieve is required, but when there is a good ripple on the water it is often unnecessary to retrieve at all, the floating sedge bobbing on the surface waves imparting sufficient movement to animate the pupae below. When fishing this team it is essential to watch the floating sedge closely and at any suspicious movement an immediate strike should be made.

Method two has been designed to represent the pupae in the surface film, either hanging vertically or wriggling along horizontally. With this method it is necessary to dress or buy your artificials on straight-eyed hooks; these are then mounted directly on to the leader between two blood knots. Two or more of these artificials may be mounted at about 12-inch intervals, and again a heavily greased sedge is utilized, but this time it is mounted on the point, leaving at least 30 inches before tying in the first pupa. The leader between each artificial pupa is lightly greased, and fished in this manner without movement they will remain hanging vertically in the film in a most lifelike manner for a long time. It will be found that to imitate the naturals wriggling along horizontally it is only necessary to make a slow retrieve, and the artificials will immediately assume the same position. Again, with both these styles of fishing it is necessary to watch the floating sedge on the point for indication of a take. Later in the year when the natural sedges are about this artificial will often provide an occasional bonus fish. In a heavy rise I usually fish the water, but in an indifferent rise I like to cast in the path of a rising trout.

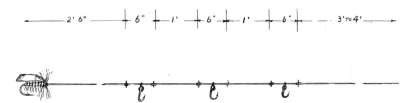

New method of mounting midge pupa artificials for fishing a 'buzzer' rise. Blood knots should be as close to the fly as possible, six inches maximum

Method three is a compromise between the two previous methods. In this case I also use artificial pupae tied on straight-eyed hooks, mounting them direct on to the leader between blood knots. However, for this method I tie a pupa on the point and mount the heavily greased sedge on the top dropper, again lightly greasing the leader. In this case it will be found that the pupa on the point will commence sinking after a few seconds, closely followed by the next one in the leader. If a yard or so of line is retrieved every two or three minutes it will in effect allow you to present your artificials at varying levels between midwater and the surface. During a spasmodic surface rise this is a useful technique to adopt, as at this period trout are most likely to be feeding at all levels. Again it is of course essential to watch closely your floating sedge for any evidence of a take.

I feel that a lifelike artificial is particularly necessary to represent these relatively slow-moving pupae, consequently several seasons ago I developed a pattern that has since proved to be very successful. I am pleased to give the dressing herewith, and it will be noted that I suggest a coloured body with a narrow silver Lurex rib covered with opaque PVC. While this provides for a wonderfully translucent body, I would emphasise that the outline of the artificial is of equal importance.

It is also important to note the dressing includes the materials to represent the white tail or caudal fins of the natural pupa, and also suggests that the materials used to match the white filaments (tracheal gills) on the head are tied into the thorax facing *forwards* over the eye of the hook. Up to the time when I first included this dressing in an article I wrote two years ago, most midge pupa patterns were dressed without the former and with the latter tied in over the thorax facing the bend, which I feel must give the artificial a very unnatural silhouette. Finally I would mention I dress this artificial in five different patterns to match the five different colours of the naturals.

Hatching Midge Pupa

Hook: straight-eye round bend 10 to 14; silk: as body colour; body: black, brown, red or green Marabou silk, ribbed with silver Lurex or tinsel and then covered with opaque PVC. The red pattern tied to represent the Orange-Silver Midge pupa should be ribbed with wide Silver Lurex, leaving only a narrow band of red showing between each turn of Lurex; tag: white hen hackle fibres projecting about $1/8$ in. from tail and tied in well round bend of hook; thorax: green peacock or buff condor herl; head filaments: loop or bunch of white hen hackle fibre tips tied through thorax but facing upward and forward over eye of hook.

N.B. For tag and head filaments strands of white glassfibre cloth may be used as an alternative, and these certainly give the fly a longer life.

Trout on Winged Midges 1974

A few years ago I remember reading a report in one of our fishing journals, which I viewed with some scepticism, about trout feeding regularly on adult winged Chironomids, or 'buzzers' as they are popularly referred to by many anglers.

For a long time now I have made a special study of this fascinating family of insects and until last season it had been only on very rare occasions that I have personally observed the odd trout feeding upon these adults on the surface. However, I now feel that I owe the writer of the article an apology for my doubts, as during the early part of last season, for a period of two or three weeks on our local reservoir, the trout started feeding on these in the evenings and were not interested in any other form of food. This phenomenon was also observed at this time on other reservoirs in the area, according to reliable reports I received.

First of all I should like to make it quite clear that the reason for this appeared to be an unusual behaviour pattern on the part of the 'buzzers', not of the trout; after all, it is a natural reaction of the fish to feed on the form of food that is most easily accessible and that is what was happening at this time. Let me explain. As I have reported in previous articles on these particular insects, trout feeding on them are influenced by the natural life-cycle of the chironomids, plus weather conditions appertaining at the time. To start with, the trout usually commence feeding on the ascending pupae as they slowly swim to the surface to transpose into the adult. On windy mornings or evenings when the surface is rough and broken, the pupae hatch at the surface very quickly indeed and almost immediately fly off. The trout, being wise in the ways of nature, find it easier to feed upon these ascending pupae at this time and only occasionally chase one and take it at the surface. However, on calm, still days when there is a relatively thick film present on the surface of the water, the ascending pupae often have difficulty in breaking through to hatch, and the trout quickly realize it requires much less effort to feed upon the pupae hanging in the surface, which is more often than not the cause for those splendid evening rises we sometimes encounter on calm, warm evenings. It is also under these conditions that I have sometimes seen the odd trout also taking the newly hatched winged adult, but in my experience this is the exception rather than the rule.

Last season started quite normally with some good evening rises to the midge pupae and plenty of trout were taken on midge pupae artificials, but by about the third week of May the position altered dramatically. The evening rises were still as good, if not better, but very few fish were being caught, and the normally highly successful midge pupa patterns were steadfastly refused. After a couple of evenings with very poor results my fishing companion Cliff Henry and I decided to make a closer study of the feeding pattern of the trout. First of all we noticed that the trout were feeding higher out of the water and, furthermore, instead of the normal, rather slow head and tail rise associated with fish feeding on the pupae, the movement was more hurried and closer allied to trout feeding on sedges or similar surface flies. We were extremely puzzled by this as despite careful observation the only insects hatching in sufficient quantities were 'buzzers'. The next calm evening we therefore concentrated on studying the surface of the water and it was only then that we noticed that there appeared to be considerable numbers of adult winged 'buzzers', or midges actually flying low over the water surface.

They flew relatively slowly with their legs actually trailing in the water, and once we became used to spotting them their flight could easily be observed as they left a very faint V-shaped trail on the surface; in most cases the wake would suddenly cease as the insect disappeared in the swirl of a rising trout.

We studied this phenomenon closely over the ensuing three weeks and after catching many of these adults we ascertained the following facts. To start with we had never previously seen adult midges flying for long periods over the surface in this manner, as normally as soon as they hatch they fly to the nearest land, where mating takes place at a later period. The egg-bearing females then return to the water, usually at dusk, to drop their egg clusters over or onto the water. Most anglers will be familiar with the swarms of these females that gather round a boat just as it is getting dark, emitting an audible buzzing sound from which, of course, they obtain their common name. We caught many dozens of these adults on the surface, and for the first week or 10 days they were the familiar orange-silver midge, but during the last few days of June and early July, a few large red midges were observed, although the majority were a medium sized green midge. These were very similar to the common green midge normally to be seen a little later in the season, except that they had a distinctly yellow thorax as opposed to the normal greenish colour. Finally, and of particular interest, in each and every case they proved to be females, but their gyrations over the surface seemingly had nothing to do with oviposition as in no case were there any traces of eggs.

Now what can we deduce from these facts? The answer I am afraid is very little. Our first reactions were that this peculiarity could be accredited to a species with which we were unfamiliar, but this theory was quickly dispelled when we found that many we caught were the common orange-silver variety. Secondly, we thought it might have something to do with distribution of the eggs onto the surface, but this idea was also quickly discarded as there was no trace of any eggs at all. Could it be due to weather conditions, as up to this time we had had one of the driest springs on record?

Apart from our very interesting study of the natural insects involved, we also tackled the problem of evolving a suitable pattern and technique to catch the trout that at this period were preoccupied in feeding exclusively on these adults. So far, sad to relate, we have only met with mediocre success. After some experimenting we perfected a dressing that floated well and in appearance closely approximated the natural in flight. The method of fishing this pattern, however, proved to be the most difficult problem. Fished without movement it brought negative results. Fished along the surface with either a slow or fast retrieve resulted in far too much wake, which apparently scared the trout. A compromise of giving an occasional slow pull on the line did result in the capture of a few fish, but apart from this the only real success we attained was in the latter part of the evening when the light was fading and the odd trout rose extremely close. When this happened, by dapping the artificial lightly on the water close in front of the trout, it was immediately accepted without hesitation. Perhaps readers may have some thoughts on this most difficult problem but, in the meantime, in case it should prove to be of assistance another season, I am pleased to give details of this relatively simple dressing as follows:

Hook: No. 12 up-eye.
Tying Silk: brown.
Body and Thorax: orange or dark green seal's fur.
Rib: narrow silver Lurex.
Wings: white hackle fibres tied spent.

An adult male winged midge
(Chironomid)

Instant Sedges 1976

The first of the two new flies I want to look at here is, strictly speaking, a modification of an existing pattern developed by Kenneth Bostrom, the well known Swedish fly dresser, in 1981. I was introduced to the pattern the following year by my good friend Preben Thorp Jacobsen, one of Denmark's leading fly fishers. I must admit I was very unimpressed when he first showed me this new artificial, as it looked just like a lump of dark brown wool thrown on a hook.

At the time we were fishing together on the Kennet, and he quickly dispelled any doubts I may have had about the fish killing properties of this pattern by promptly catching four fat brown trout in less than an hour.

The following season I caught a lot of trout on this nondescript pattern although at the time I must admit I was really puzzled why the trout were accepting it so readily. So far as at a casual glance I could tell, it really bore little resemblance to any form of natural food. But it seemed to be very much more effective, later in the season, and that provided the clue I was looking for.

On many of the waters I fish, Sedges form a predominant part of the trout's diet from July onwards, and it seemed that the fish were accepting this new offering as some form of Sedge adult or pupa. Subsequently, underwater observations removed any doubts I may have had, as in or on its natural medium the fly certainly looks very different. Beneath the surface it could easily pass as a Sedge Pupa while on, or rather in the surface, and viewed from below it bears an astonishing resemblance to a hatching Sedge.

Having proved its killing potential, I proceeded to modify it for my own use on the particular water I was fishing. The original pattern was called the *Rackelhanen*. This is a bit of a mouthful for the average English fly fisher, and I have taken the liberty of re-naming my modified pattern the *Poly-Pupa* after the polypropylene yarn used to dress it. The original pattern had a body, separate wings and a thorax all formed from the same dark sepia brown poly yarn. My modification is even more basic as I form both body and wings from the one length of poly yarn and I have dispensed with the thorax altogether. I don't know whether the original inventor intended his pattern to represent any particular stage in the life of a Sedge or not, but I am quite sure that my modification has improved it in this respect, as with the thorax removed and the wings further forward it certainly has a more lifelike appearance. Apart from that I have little doubt that this must now surely qualify as the easiest fly in the world to dress.

On rivers I use this as a dry fly, casting it to drift down over rising fish. It can be fished by two methods, both equally effective. (a) Treat it with floatant so it sits on the surface and fishes as a dry fly. (b) Use it untreated and after a couple of casts you will find the polypropylene will absorb a certain amount of water, when it will float down to the rising fish actually in, or even partly under, the surface. When fishing it this way I will often give a slight tweak on the line as it comes into the vision of the trout, which seems to prove irresistible. On many occasions I've had trout move over three or four feet for it after a bad cast. For river fishing dress this pattern on hooks size 12 to 16.

I've not fished it so much on stillwater, but when I have, I've found it most effective fished very slowly on the point, degreased to fish partly beneath the surface. On the big stillwaters, dress the pattern on size 12 or 10 hooks. Last season I started dressing it in various colours, olive green, dark green, pale brown, and even white, as well as the original dark brown. It is a little early to say yet whether certain colours are better than others under varying conditions, so there is obviously further room for experiment in this direction.

Poly-Pupa dressing

Take a length of polypropylene yarn of your chosen colour and tie it in at the bend. Then wind it back and forth along the shank to form a nice fat looking body. Tie the yarn in just behind the eye and form a loop back over the top of the body with the same piece of yarn. Tie in and whip finish. It is then only necessary to cut the loop with a pair of scissors and spread the yarn over the top of the body to form the wings. I suggest you soak the piece of yarn in water before you wind the body, as you will then get a smoother finish and nicer shape.

Poly Caddis – John's latest
Sedge pattern

Polypropylene yarn is one of the few modern synthetics I really like. It is obtainable in a wide variety of colours; it ties in very well, and for fly bodies it seems to provide a lifelike sparkle. In addition it's very buoyant, particularly when treated with floatant. It seems an obvious choice for the body of a Sedge dry fly which as it is often fished with a bit of movement, quickly drowns and is rendered virtually useless. I therefore used this material for the body of a new Sedge pattern I have developed which I now refer to as my Poly-Caddis. Since 1982 it has accounted for hundreds of trout. It floats beautifully and looks extremely lifelike, and the trout, particularly on rivers, just love it. On the few occasions I have used it on stillwater it has been equally effective, although on the big stillwaters I still feel that my sheet anchor, the G and H Sedge may still have the edge.

However on rivers I definitely prefer the new pattern, as apart from the fact that it is extremely simple and quick to dress, it can be tied in small sizes on tiny hooks if required, which is all but impossible with the G and H.

To date I have only found it necessary to tie two colour combinations in the new pattern. The first has a green body, brown wings and a natural red (brown) hackle, while the alternative has a grey body, brown wings and a grizzle hackle.

Poly-Caddis dressing

Form a cylindrical shaped body from green or grey polypropylene yarn, on an up-eyed size 10 to 16 hook. It should taper at each end. Secure behind the eye. Then take two short lengths of brown polypropylene yarn, spread and tie in at eye, sloping back over the body and trim to the 'V' shape silhouette of the adult Sedge's wings.

Finally, tie in behind the eye, but in front of the wings, three or four turns of hackle, either natural red (brown), or grizzle.

This new Sedge pattern has accounted for several large and very difficult trout that would not even look at any other pattern so I am now absolutely convinced this is a winner. A further big plus is that they are virtually indestructible, and very quick and simple to dress, even on very tiny hooks.

Private Lives – The Damsel Fly 1977

The Order Odonata embraces both the dragonflies and damselflies and while the former are of doubtful value to the angler, the latter particularly in their nymphal form are of considerable importance.

This has not always been realized, as it is only in the last two decades or so that fly fishers have recognized their value in the feeding cycle of trout.

The damselflies can be readily distinguished from the dragonflies as they have very slim bodies and two pairs of wings of equal size which are folded together over the body when at rest. There are seventeen different species in the family and the predominant body colours of the adults are green, blue or red.

While the adult flies may be represented at certain times it is the nymphs that are of prime interest to both fish and fishermen. The life cycle of the nymph lasts approximately twelve months and during this time it undergoes about twelve moults (instars) rapidly increasing in size. They are long and slender in proportion to their size and the mature nymphs vary according to species from 20mm to over 30mm. They all have three pronounced tails (which are in reality gills), a body composed of nine segments, a pronounced thorax and six legs. The wing cases project along the top of the body and are dark brown in the fully mature nymph. The colour of the body varies tremendously from grey through brown to a very pale green, and in some cases the bodies are mottled.

It has been suggested by many authorities that their colour is an aid to identification of the species, but as a result of my personal research I am now more inclined to believe that this nymph like the fabled chameleon can change its colour according to its habitat.

These nymphs are strongly carniverous, feeding mainly at night. During the hours of daylight they seldom leave their habitat of weed beds or detritus on the floor of the lake, so I think it is extremely doubtful as has been suggested recently that trout feed on the immature stages in the early part of the season.

When the mature nymph is ready to change into the adult, they swim towards the surface, and then travel shorewards just under the film looking for emergent vegetation in order to dry out before transforming into the adult. It is during this shoreward migration that they are most vunerable to the trout. It is worth noting this is more likely to take place in the morning or early afternoon, rather than the afternoon or evening. The peak period is during late June through July to early August.

On those days when good hatches occur, the trout will feed on them avidly, often pursuing them into quite shallow water where the bank is undisturbed. The artificial damsel nymph should be cast out on a floating line utilizing as long a leader as you can manage – the retrieve should then be in long steady pulls.

Over the years the pattern I have enjoyed most success with is one developed by Cliff Henry, but latterly my own wiggle nymph pattern has accounted for a lot of fish. I developed this in an effort to simulate the pronounced wriggle of the natural as it swims along just under the surface film. With this pattern the retrieve should be made with a shorter retrieve and frequent pauses to animate the hinged tail each time it begins to sink.

There is considerable scope here for the amateur fly tyer to develop a pattern that can be retrieved slowly without pauses but with a built-in wiggle, and to this end I have recently been experimenting with a small angled plate tied in under the head of the wiggle nymph to achieve this effect. I would add that artificials to represent these nymphs may also be fished successfully at all levels in the water, utilizing sink tip or at times even sinking lines, as at this time of the year the trout also feed on them underwater as they often leave the shelter of weeds etc. several hours prior to hatching.

The adult egg laying female damsel climbs down emergent vegetation or other projections sticking out of the water such as decaying tree branches or posts in order to oviposit her eggs. She will sometimes remain underwater for upwards of half an hour existing on the oxygen trapped under her wings.

During this time she will often travel along the bottom or over weed for a considerable distance to find suitable egg laying sites. When oviposition is completed she swims to the surface where the attendant male who has been quartering the surface all the time literally plucks her out of the water. I am satisfied that trout do feed on the female as she returns to the surface, as I have on several occasions found partly digested adults in the stomach contents of trout. I have since fished a pattern to represent these female adults with some success. It should be fished in the sink and draw style in areas where the copulating flies are observed.

Top: Author's Damsel Wiggle Nymph, *Bottom:* Cliff Henry's Damsel Nymph

A mature Damsel Nymph

A fine fat rainbow taken on a Wiggle Nymph

Damsel Wiggle Nymph by John Goddard

Dressing
Hook D/E size 8 to 12
Silk Brown
Tail Tips of three olive cock hackles to extend ¼ inch
Body Olive seal's fur
Rib Flat silver tinsel
Thorax Dark olive seal's fur
Wing Cases Three strands from a brown dyed turkey tail feather, doubled and redoubled
Legs Bunch of olive hen hackle fibres

Damsel Nymph by Cliff Henry

Hook Down eye long shank 8 to 12
Silk Green
Tail Tips of three olive cock hackles
Body Medium olive seal's fur
Rib Flat gold tinsel
Thorax Dark olive brown seal's fur
Wing case Brown mallard shoulder feather fibres doubled and redoubled
Legs Bunch of six fibres from grouse hackle

The Unsinkable Buzzer 1980

How best to present a midge pupa artificial so as to hang tail down and head up in the surface film is an age old problem. Until now, using grease or floatant on the leader has been the most usual answer.

A much better solution, however, is a revolutionary new pattern which I call The Suspender. And to tie it you will need, among other things, a small square of fine nylon mesh cut from new or old ladies' stockings!

Last season Neil Patterson, a constant fishing companion on the Upper Kennet, introduced me to a new floating nymph pattern with which he was experimenting. The original concept of this unique dressing had been noticed by Neil in an American book, *Nymph fishing for larger trout*, by Charles E. Brooks.

The author called this new pattern the 'Natant nylon nymph'. The basic dressing of the pattern and materials used were purely traditional, as it was intended as a general pattern. However the originality of this nymph lay in the addition of a small ball of polypropylene fibres enveloped in a small square of fine nylon net or mesh.

This little ball was tied on top of the body of the nymph well back from the eye, and was intended by the author to represent the emerging

Two of the new patterns suspended in the surface film in the classic head up, tail down position

wings bulging up through the split nymphal chuck. If desired the little ball could be anointed with grease to hold the pattern in the surface film where the natural is usually found.

Now Neil immediately realized the potential of this pattern but soon found that even with the ball well greased there was insufficient floatation either in the grease or the polypropylene fibres within, the nylon mesh to float the pattern for more than a few seconds, particularly if the water was fairly turbulent.

We then hit upon the idea of replacing the polypropylene fibres with a small square of foam trimmed into a ball shape and then enclosed in the mesh.

It was at this stage that we tried it on the water, and I must admit I was most impressed as it floated extraordinarily well, although not quite as high in the film as I would have liked. After much trial and error I eventually hit upon the idea of using ethafoam as this relatively new closed cell foam is the most buoyant of all. We now had a pattern that floated high up in the surface and would float all day, even in the roughest of water.

From then on it was but a short step to produce an imitation pattern to represent the hatching olive nymphs that were so prevalent on our stretch of river. This olive Poly-nymph proved a great success and during the season accounted for many nice trout from our stretch of river.

What has this new river pattern got to do with stillwater trouting? We could say that dressed on a slightly larger hook this would probably be most effective on stillwaters to represent the emergent nymphs of Pond or Lake Olives, but we have not had time to try it. However, I can now divulge details of a new stillwater pattern that derived directly from the river pattern I have been describing.

Towards the middle of the season I was sitting at my fly dressing bench enjoying a leisurely cup of tea, and at the same time idly studying our new poly-nymph to see if I could think of any further improvements. It just so happened that one of the nymphs happened to be a pattern I had dressed the day before and omitted to colour as usual with a felt tip pen. Therefore the little ball of nylon mesh looked distinctly white, due to the white ethafoam showing through. It immediately reminded me of the bunch of white breathing filaments on the top of the head of the average midge pupa.

Excited by now I asked myself, could the new pattern be adapted to represent an emerging midge pupa? If so, it would surely solve that age-old problem of presenting properly an artificial in the surface film without the aid of any grease or floatant on the fly or the leader.

I suggested to Neil we dress some midge pupa patterns but position the ball of ethafoam on top of the shank immediately behind the eye. And lo and behold we had a pupa that simulated the natural hanging down from the surface almost to perfection. I eventually simplified the original dressing and also found that by tying the white net ball of ethafoam out over the eye of the hook an even better silhouette viewed from underwater was obtained. It was also difficult at a quick glance to pick out the naturals from the artificials, as in the mirror of the under surface, only a portion of the ball could be seen.

We have now proved beyond doubt that this is an exceptionally killing pattern during a surface rise of trout to the midge pupa, or buzzer as it is affectionally known. Last August, I and two very experienced stillwater fly fishers, Stewart Canham and Max King, tested this new pattern on a local lake where by repute the trout were extremely difficult to catch. Soon after our arrival that evening the trout started to rise, obviously to midge pupa, so the three of us took up a position on the bank about ten yards apart.

My companions used standard pupa patterns of various types while I used the new patterns. Within the next 30 minutes I landed six trout and they had not even an offer. Stewart then took my rod and flies and promptly proceeded to pull in four trout, while Max and I continued casting hard to no avail. Finally, just before dusk descended, Max took over the new patterns and broke his luck with a couple of nice fish.

The difference between a standard pupa, on a dropper, and The Suspender hanging in the surface film

I have since used these new patterns on several stillwaters in America and found they were equally effective over there. I mount two or three of these Poly-Pupa on droppers about 30 inches apart, which is much closer than I normally mount my patterns. I like to cast them in the path of a rising trout and if they are closer together there is a better chance he will see at least one of them. They should be fished either with no movement at all, or alternatively a particularly productive method is to give the line a small twitch when you estimate they are within the trout's vision.

This slight pull on the line causes the artificials to lift up slightly and take up momentarily a horizontal position before dropping back to the vertical. This simulates to perfection the natural pupa lifting up to search for a weak spot in the film in which to break through. The slight animation with the artificial seems to be irresistible and is only possible with these new patterns. On standard patterns the floatant one has to use on the leader will only serve to scare the trout rather than attract when movement is imparted.

First take some white nylon filaments or several strands of white fluro wool and tie them well round the bend of the hook. Then tie in a length of silver lurex with which to rib the body. Next wind on the body material of seal's fur, or the new seal's fur substitute, of the appropriate colour two-thirds of the way up the shank, rib and tie off.

From a sheet of ethafoam cut a small square between one-eighth and three-sixteenths of an inch in diameter according to the hook size being used. With practice you will soon be able to judge the desired size, but it should be no larger than required to float the pattern. The square should then be trimmed into a ball with your hackle scissors.

We then come to the difficult part, as you now require one white ladies' stocking which you will have to beg, borrow or purloin. From this cut a small square of nylon about one inch in diameter and wrap the ethafoam ball in it, so that it forms a pouch. Tie the base of the pouch in front of the thorax and behind the eye, and when it is well secured with your tying thread trim off the excess of nylon mesh and finish with a dab of varnish.

This is followed with a thorax formed from three strands of brown dyed turkey herl.

Like standard midge pupa you may dress these with different coloured bodies and on different sized hooks. We also had some success with a small white bodied pattern, with the little ball coloured orange with a felt tip pen. This was a good match for the pupa of the phantom fly, and although these naturals are seldom found right in the surface film except possibly late at night the trout did not seem to mind.

Queen of the May 1983

Some fly patterns stick, and others fall by the wayside. If a fly is an exceptionally killing pattern over a wide variety of waters, is of completely new design, is simple to dress, and tied from easily available materials, it's more likely to attract the attention of commercial and amateur fly dressers.

The Poly Mays fit this criteria. They've been developed to represent our largest upwinged fly, the Mayfly (*Ephemera danica*), and I dress them in two slightly varying styles to represent both the dun and the spinner. Both get their names from the material involved, polypropylene yarn.

Over the last five seasons of development the pattern has accounted for hundreds of trout. The final versions have been so effective that I feel no need to use any other pattern, even for the most difficult of trout. They are extremely good floaters, and exceptionally durable - a big plus for any artificial. One of the dun versions took 35 trout over two days, all of which I returned, before I lost it in a tree.

The basic idea for the new fly came to me about six years ago, during one day on the River Kennet with Stewart Canham. It was a very pleasant day with a good hatch of Mayfly duns. Stewart was using a very bushy fly with which he was rapidly taking more than his fair share of trout. Eventually I could contain myself no longer, and asked to have a closer look at it.

It was apparently a pattern given to him by Terry Griffiths which I rapidly tagged the Haystack. I dressed a few to try, and although it was extremely durable it became less effective as a hatch progressed, and the trout became more selective.

The dressing, however, was very simple - buff coloured seal's fur for the body, dressed very thickly, and cream coloured calf's tail for the V-shaped wings.

With my new patterns I retained the calf's hair wings (and the durability), but went for a closer copy of the natural.

Trial and error, and concentrating on the right colours, brought about the following pattern.

Poly May Dun

Hook: Up eyed wide gape medium shank sizes 8 to 12.
Silk: Yellow.
Body: Polypropylene dark cream yarn.
Wings and Tail: Good calf's tail.
Hackle: Black cock.

Cut a bunch of hair from a calf's tail of sufficient length to form both wings and tail. Whip this down along the top of the hook, leaving about a third of the body length projecting beyond the bend in the form of the fine tips to make the tag or tail. (This should represent the remains of the shuck as the natural fly hatches on the surface.)

The cut end of the bunch of hair forms the wings, which should be secured into a narrow V shape with a figure of eight whip finish.

Take the silk back to the bend and tie in a length of cream polypropylene yarn to form the body. Take the silk back up to the eye, and follow it with tightly wound polypropylene. Trim the poly at the eye. One tip for a smoother neater finish with this material - thoroughly wet it first.

Finally tie in a substantial black cock hackle at the eye, and wind one or two turns in front of the wings, and three behind. When it's complete soak it in Permaflote, and you will then find you can fish it for a long time before it needs treating again in floatant.

With a little practice this pattern is simple and quick to dress, and almost indestructible.

The *Poly May Spinner* is slightly more sophisticated. Trout get far longer to look at the spinner as it floats along either dead or dying. If you study the behaviour of the natural you may be surprised to see that at least 70 per cent drift along with one wing flat on the surface, and the other pointing up at ninety degrees.

This spinner pattern is supposed to float in the same manner. The idea is to increase the V shape of the wings to ninety degrees so that when the fly lands on the water, it will invariably tip over on to one wing. Coupled with a fairly short-fibred hackle you'll find this happens fairly consistently.

If you don't, try clipping one wing a little, ensuring that the fly is unbalanced.

Poly May Spinner

Hook: As dun
Silk: Black
Body: White poly yarn
Tails: Three black dyed pheasant tail fibres
Wings: Mixture of white and black calf's tail
Hackle: Black cock fairly short in the fibres.

First tie in the black dyed PT fibres to form the tails, spread wide. Then cut two bunches of calf from a white and a black tail. These need not be as long as those from the dun pattern, as of course they don't form the tails. Mix the two bunches really well by rolling them together – there's no short cut to this job.

Whip the mixed bunch along the top of the hook as for the dun but with no tail, then turn up the ends and whip them into an exaggerated V as described. Then use a short fibred black cock hackle, two turns before and behind the wing.

The Curse of the Smutting Trout 1987

If we delve deeply enough into some of the older books on angling we are likely to come across a section titled the 'Anglers' Curse', which referred to hatches on rivers of small black flies so tiny that it was impossible to imitate them.

In later years writers have elaborated a little and often refer to hatches of tiny black flies as the 'Black Curse', and hatches of tiny pale-coloured flies as the 'White Curse' while still others use the term 'Anglers' Curse' in a general sense to apply to any extremely small species of insects upon which the trout may be feeding, including some of the very small species of chironomids.

As this chapter is directed towards the river fly-fisher, let me now look at some of the problems facing him when he comes across such a trout selectively feeding on tiny insects. To start with I should point out that in the USA they seem to have overcome this problem to some extent by matching the hatch with tiny artificials mounted on ultra-light tackle. Today many American fly-fishers seem to carry a large selection of these from size 20 down to 26 and in some extreme cases even down to size 28, and fish them on very light leaders sometimes as low as 1 lb test.

Some of their more experienced fly-fishers regularly land very big trout well over 4 lb, but how they do it is still a mystery to me. During the past 20 years or so I have on several occasions experimented with such tackle on our rivers with a lamentable lack of success, for the following reasons.

I find it extremely difficult to set such small hooks in a trout, and even when I am successful I invariably break the very light leader on the strike. On those few occasions when I have been successful, if it has been a trout much over 2 lb I have been unable to apply enough pressure with the very light tackle being used to keep it clear of snags or heavy weed and have consequently lost it. So is there another answer to this problem, apart from using special patterns on normal size hooks - which are rarely accepted by the trout? First of all, let me take a closer look at some of these minute insects and at precisely how trout feed upon them.

While the various species of caenis are important on stillwater, they are of much less interest to the river fisher, where hatches are more often than not confined to the very early mornings before the dry-fly fisherman is on the water. So we shall ignore the so-called 'White Curse'.

If you observe a trout feeding avidly close to or on the surface on apparently invisible flies, you are probably looking at a trout feeding on the 'Black Curse'. These are any extremely tiny black or dark-brown flies such as the reed smuts or various other tiny species of the chironomids (buzzers).

Reed smuts, often referred to as black flies, will often be seen swarming in huge clouds close to the surface of the water. In Britain 35 different species have now been identified in this family, with the adults varying in overall colour from dark brown to black. Rarely exceeding 5 mm most are very tiny indeed - between 2 mm and 3 mm. The larvae live and also pupate on river weed and when they hatch the pupal case splits and the fully winged adult ascends to the surface in a bubble of gas or air, where it rapidly becomes airborne. The trout, when feeding on these tiny hatching insects, usually lies a few inches below the surface, where he can feed either on the ascending fly or on the fly as it breaks through the surface. The actual rise-form is similar to a trout rising to small duns.

At times - particularly on many of our chalkstreams from late June onwards - the trout will often feed throughout the day on adults lying on the surface. These are probably smuts resting during or after the mating process. In this latter instance if you study the surface carefully you can see these tiny black specks drifting along on the surface.

Hilara, a species of the diptera order, are also referred to as black flies and this family contains many species, several of which are attracted to water and swarm over it in a similar manner to the reed smuts. They are a little larger - between 5 mm and 9 mm - and in some areas the larger species may be looked upon as black gnats rather than black flies. The trout take these on the surface in a similar way as they take the smuts.

Chironomids, or buzzers, are certainly better known to the stillwater angler, where they form a major diet for the trout. On rivers they are hardly ever mentioned and I very much doubt that even one river fly-fisher in a hundred carries any artificials to represent them. This is very strange, as on some rivers, or certain stretches of rivers, they are abundant. While they will thrive even in the purest of streams they are more likely to be found in quantities in slightly polluted streams or stretches below fish-farms or large towns as well as in stretches that have a reduced flow.

In the previous issue of *Trout and Salmon* Timothy Benn wrote a very interesting and informative piece on buzzers on rivers and emphasised that they were ignored by most anglers. It may be of interest to hear that in 1984 a scientific survey on the aquatic insects in a stretch of the Winterbourne stream was completed and this showed that chironomids outnumbered the ephemeroptera by more than four to one.

Unlike buzzers in most stillwaters, those in rivers are usually the smaller species, the pupae rarely exceeding 5 mm. The most common colours seem to be various shades of olive or brown. So far as rivers are concerned I think we can safely ignore the adult buzzers as in my experience most trout seem to feed on the pupae hanging in the film prior to hatching. While I agree with Timothy Benn that most trout seem to take these buzzers with a distinct head-and-tail rise I cannot agree with the conclusions he reached. He states, 'Blow across a water butt full of pupae and at the first ripple all the pupae will instantly flip down one, two or even three feet.' In my experience this is not typical behaviour as the pupae of chironomids are rather poor swimmers and, once they reach the surface, rarely descend again.

I would respectfully suggest that the pupae he observed were not chironomids but probably the larvae of mosquitoes, as this is typical behaviour for them. My observations indicate that a trout feeding on the pupae of chironomids lies at last six to 12 inches below the surface, looking into the mirror for the approaching pupae, which hang vertically below the surface film prior to hatching, when they then adopt a horizontal position. He then arches upwards to intercept the pupa and with a single stroke of his tail returns to his lie. If the trout were lying as Mr Benn suggests, with his dorsal fin all but awash, I doubt whether he would ever show his tail as he would only have to raise his head slightly and open his mouth to intercept. Indeed, trout adopting this position are commonly observed during a very heavy hatch of surface fly or fall of spinners resulting in the 'sip' or 'kiss' rise, which barely breaks the surface as the fly is sucked in as the trout opens his mouth.

During the past season I have spent a great deal of time not only studying trout feeding on these tiny flies and pupae but also experimenting with various new patterns in an effort to solve the dual problem of devising an artificial small enough to be accepted but on a hook large enough to ensure success. While I would not be so bold as to suggest that I have completely solved the problem, I do now have a pattern that has proved to be highly successful against smutting trout.

Like many killing patterns it is very simple to tie. I use a size 18 hook with a wide gape and, with a single black ostrich or triple black crow herl, form a body less than half the length of the shank. In front of this body and immediately behind the eye I tie in 1½–2 turns of black cock hackle. This hackle should be very short in the flue, but as these are normally found only on high-quality capes an alternative is to clip the hackle after it is tied in.

Tied in this way, this pattern presents a silhouette small enough to be accepted by the fish, on a hook of sufficient size to be used with a 3 lb leader. For those trout feeding on the ascending smut or chironomid pupa I present it just under the surface film, or for trout feeding on smuts or small black fly on the surface I present it dry and well treated with floatant. In addition I tie it with a honey hackle and a

brown or olive-green ostrich-herl body for those trout taking pupae. However, I must admit it has been less successful with pupae-feeding fish so this season I intend to try some of my Suspender midge pupa patterns tied in this new way.

Timothy Benn with a nice trout that took the new smut pattern

Enter the Super Grizzly Emerger 1991

In the late 1970s I developed a new dry-fly which was designed not as a specific imitation of any natural, but more as a general pattern to be tried when one was unsure about which particular fly the trout were feeding on. I dressed it on hooks between size 12 and 14 (occasionally size 16) and it proved highly effective when any of the medium or large upwinged flies were hatching. The fly quickly gained quite a reputation and has since proved very successful as far afield as New Zealand and the USA.

I decided to call the new fly the Super Grizzly, because the main hackle used for the wing came from a Metz super grizzle cape.

In the summer of 1988 I spent a couple of weeks in Montana, based in West Yellowstone. One of the larger tackle shops in the town is called Blue Ribbon Flies and through earlier visits I had become quite friendly with the owner, Craig Matthews. During my stay I paid him a visit and after a lengthy chat he happened to mention that together with John Juracek he had perfected a new dry-fly which was proving incredibly effective. Knowing that they were both top-class fly-dressers, I asked to see it.

Usually you can tell at a glance whether or not a pattern is going to take fish – and this looked very good indeed. Dressed on a size 18 hook with a grey dyed beaver fur body, and wings formed from splayed deerhair, the most interesting aspect of this fly was the tail, which was formed from a pale brownish sparkle material almost the length of the body. Craig told me that this was tied to represent the shuck of an upwinged fly emerging at the surface, so it was classified as an emerger pattern. The fly was dressed with various body colours to represent different species of small olive duns that proliferate on many Montana rivers. The name they had bestowed upon this new pattern was the 'Sparkle Dun' and as I said to him I liked the look of the grey-bodied pattern Craig kindly insisted that I accept a dozen of these to try out during the remainder of my holiday. I found them very killing and took some good trout on them.

Halfway through the following season I was fishing my favourite stretch of the Kennet when I came across a really good trout rising regularly under the far bank. He had refused all my usual patterns and I was glancing through my flybox to decide what to offer him next when I came across a few of these Sparkle Duns. Tying one on, I was surprised when he rose and took it first cast. He turned out to be a lovely wild trout of just over 3 lb.

For the remainder of that season I fished this pattern pretty regularly when any small olives were hatching – and very effective it proved to be. However, the most surprising thing I discovered about this artificial was that the grayling seemed to find it irresistible. It has now become established as my favourite dry-fly for grayling.

That winter I was dressing some flies for the coming season, including some Super Grizzlies, when it suddenly struck me that this pattern without the tails and its grey body looked very similar to one of Craig's Sparkle Duns, so I immediately proceeded to tie one with a tail in a similar manner. I did not have any of the Sparkle Poly material that Craig used to represent the shuck, so decided to use half a dozen strands of pale yellow Krystal Flash. When I finished dressing this it looked so good that I tied a further dozen and so the Super Grizzly Emerger was born. I have used this fly for the past two seasons with great success; and for trout, at least, it does seem to have the edge over the Sparkle Dun. It seems equally effective on both the Kennet and Test and other rivers I have fished – particularly from July onwards when the smaller olives are hatching – and has accounted for well over 200 trout, most of which I have returned.

Super Grizzly Emerger

Hook: Size 18 Roman Moser Arrowpoint
Silk: Purple
Tail: Pale-yellow Krystal Flash, three-quarters the length of the body
Body: Grey heron herl
Wing: Red and grizzle hackle, short in the flue, tied in together.

Suspenders on the River 1988

The importance of midges to the river fisherman is something that has greatly intrigued me over the past three seasons and I have spent considerable time both observing the naturals and experimenting with new patterns.

However, it was only last season that the breakthrough occurred, and as a result I am now prepared to put my reputation on the line and suggest that midges and their artificial imitations are of far greater importance on many rivers than most fly-fishers have previously suspected.

The smaller species of non-biting midges – those up to about 5 mm long – abound on most of our alkaline rivers, including the chalk-streams of the south. Whether or not they are of any importance on the faster upland rivers and streams I do not know, although it is rather doubtful that they would occur in the same abundance, as the environment is unlikely to be suitable.

The first question that many fly-fishers will ask is how do we know when the trout are feeding on midges, as most are so small as to be all but invisible from any distance? The answer is really quite simple, for any trout lying and feeding close to the surface are likely to be feeding upon them and, even when they may be feeding on other small species, will certainly accept one if it drifts within range. The position of the trout in relation to the surface film, as detailed above, is of paramount importance to the observer. In fact, during the latter half of last season I had reached the stage where usually I could tell from a trout's position and behaviour whether or not it would be likely to take my artificial Midge Pupa.

The other most interesting discovery concerned those infuriating trout that seem to spend most of the summer feeding on tiny reed smuts – and usually proving to be impossible to catch. Since the middle of the last century, when the cult of the dry-fly started to gather momentum, the distinctive rise-form of trout feeding upon small gnats, smuts, or 'the curse' as they used to be described, has been well documented. The trout lies all but in the surface, tilting up slightly to open his mouth often at very short intervals and rarely deviating from side to side – as he does so often when feeding on other species.

Such trout have always posed a problem for the dry-fly fisherman. At the turn of the century F.M. Halford, the father of the dry-fly, perfected two patterns to deal with these trout – his male and female Black Gnat patterns – and, although he experienced a modicum of success with these flies, they never truly solved the problem. Over the past two seasons I have enjoyed quite a high success-rate with a new smut pattern that I devised, but on occasions even this has been completely ignored. In early June last year I spent over an hour casting in vain to a smutting trout until, in desperation, I decided to try him with a Midge Pupa. To my astonishment he took it first cast! Having spooned him, I found his stomach was packed with a mass of tiny green chironomid pupae. Subsequent catches of these smutting trout now prove beyond reasonable doubt that many of them are not only feeding upon smuts etc., but also various species of midge or chironomid pupa as well. Since that day in June smutting trout no longer pose such a problem for me!

John Goddard's Suspender Midge Pupae, dressed on size 16 and 18 hooks

Now, dear reader, you are doubtless wondering about the identity of this new pupa pattern that is achieving such astonishing success. Well, you will probably be surprised to hear that it is not a new pattern at all! Those of you who read my article on smutting trout in *Trout and Salmon* two years ago may have noticed my statement that next season I intended to try my Suspender Midge Pupa, which has proved to be so successful on stillwater, dressed on very small hooks for those trout that I suspected were feeding upon chironomids in rivers. The result was over 120 trout (mainly brownies), many of which weighed between 3 lb and 5 lb. I hasten to add that most of them were returned. Several of my friends are now using these tiny pupa patterns with phenomenal success and towards the end of the season John Ketley said to me, after catching five trout before lunch, 'They ought to be banned'!

I don't know why this Suspender pattern has proved to be so killing, for in the past I have tried various emerger or buoyant dressings with indifferent results. It may be due to the fact that, as in my stillwater pattern, I dress this tiny river pattern with a white tail and the white ethafoam ball covered in a white or colourless mesh, to match the whitish tail and breathing filaments on top of the head of the natural pupa. Whatever the reasons, I have rarely before known trout take an artificial pattern with such confidence.

Accurate casting with this pattern is essential, as with the trout lying so close to the surface their range of vision is limited. Initially I dressed these small Suspenders with four different body colours – red, black, green and brown – but in practice I found the latter two colours to be adequate on most occasions. I tie them in sizes 16 and 18 on Partridge Roman Moser arrow-point hooks as these are very strong and have a nice wide gape. While the smallest size is most readily accepted by the trout I tend to use the larger size most often as I seldom lose a trout on this size of hook.

Fishing with the Suspender has also produced a couple of very useful advantages. As serious dry-fly fishermen know only too well, unintentional drag when fishing any surface pattern is normally guaranteed to put down even the most foolish trout. Not so with a Suspender! If the drag occurs before the artificial reaches the trout, and when the fly is still visible, the trout will often follow it for some distance yet still take it very confidently. The probable explanation is that the fly is behaving in a manner that the trout expects. Most chironomid pupae in both still and running water rest briefly upon reaching the surface film, and remain hanging in a vertical position until they are ready to hatch, at which time they adopt a horizontal position, often swimming for some distance – and this action is simulated by the drag of the artificial as it is pulled into the same horizontal position.

The other advantage is even more significant, as it greatly assists in a problem that has bedevilled the dry-fly fisherman since the inception of this branch of our sport. How do you present your dry-fly to a rising trout in the late evening, when it is too dark to see where your fly lands on the surface? At this time, when using a Suspender, forget all about delicate presentation and cast it as you would a nymph – to achieve a quick entry through the surface film. You will find that it creates a highly visible 'plop' which, provided you are fishing into the last of the dying light in a westerly direction, can be clearly seen, even on the darkest of nights. Last season this ploy enabled me to catch many trout that had been rising far later than I have ever fished before. However, I found it essential at this time to lift the rod-tip slowly as the pattern drifts towards the trout, in order to keep in touch with your fly. The takes are so gentle that most will be missed if you don't do this. Apart from this, the lifted rod-tip obviously imparts a very slight drag on your fly, which seems to prove very attractive to trout as darkness falls.

I have also established that, as darkness approaches, hatches of these small midges often increase – and many trout will switch their attention to them. I am sure that most of you will be only too familiar with those maddening evening rises when, as dusk approaches, the trout became harder and harder to tempt. I am now sure that in many instances a midge-hatch is the reason. On the other hand this is not always the case, as I found out to my cost one evening last August. When the evening rise started I quickly established that the trout were on caddis and by the time the light started to fade I had caught and released four nice fish. As often happens at this time I found that they had suddenly lost interest in my Caddis/Sedge pattern and at the same time I noticed that the rise-form had changed, as the trout were now rising much more gently, their mouths barely breaking the surface. This indicated a change to either small fly or spinners. After a few minutes of careful observation I mistakenly concluded that the trout must have switched to small midges as I could see no sign of any duns or spinners, either on or above the surface.

Quickly mounting a Suspender Buzzer I wasted the next 20 minutes covering fish after fish, with no response at all. Eventually I stopped fishing and after further observation realized that the trout were taking blue-winged olive spinners that were drifting down on the surface from somewhere further upstream, but by then it was too dark to see to change my fly.

Finally I must pose the question to which I am sure many fly-fishers and fishery managers will want an answer. Should the Suspender Midge Pupa be treated as a nymph or a dry-fly? I am quite sure that many fly-fishers will have different views on this, so I can only put forward my own opinion. I consider that the Suspender Midge Pupa should be treated as a dry-fly as, first, I cast only to rising trout with it and, second, nearly two-thirds of the ethafoam ball is always above the surface. It can usually be seen as clearly as a tiny dry-fly. The dressing for the Suspender Midge Pupa is as follows:

Hook: Partridge Roman Moser arrow-point, sizes 16 and 18
Silk: Fine midge – dark brown
Head: Ball of plastazote or ethafoam enclosed in fine white nylon mesh
Tail: White fluorescent wool
Rib: Fine silver wire or lurex
Body: Seal's fur or similar of required colour
Thorax: Brown dyed turkey herl or natural peacock.

To form the ball for the head one can purchase a set of coarse-fishermen's bread punches from most tackle-shops and if these are then sharpened they can be used very successfully to cut the required size ball from any sheet of foam of suitable thickness. They will then require little trimming.

A steady riser, this big brownie took a tiny Suspender Midge Pupa

Trout lying as close to the surface as this will usually take a Suspender Midge Pupa without hesitation

As a postcript I feel I should point out that the original concept of enclosing buoyant material in a much of nylon mesh must be credited to Charles E. Brooks of the USA. This concept was then further developed in conjunction with Brian Clarke and Neil Patterson prior to the publication of our book *The Trout and the Fly*. I should also like to emphasize that fishing for trout feeding on midges as described above is but a branch of dry-fly fishing and in no way replaces more traditional methods.

A Caddis for All Waters 1990

The G & H Sedge or Goddard Caddis as it is now known in America is one of my earlier patterns that was first perfected in the early sixties, and since then has steadily grown in popularity. Originally developed for fishing on the big English reservoirs and lakes, we required a pattern that would literally float like a cork as at the time – particularly during the summer when big hatches of various species of Caddis occurred late in the evening – a favourite method when there was a good ripple on the water was to skate a big bushy Caddis pattern over the surface. At this time none of the standard patterns available even when dressed with floatant would stay on top for very long. So the search began for a pattern dressed with materials that would provide this extra floatability. At this time suitable plastic foam was yet to be invented and cork proved unsuitable. The breakthrough occurred when I was presented with a new pattern from America which at the time was proving popular with a lot of our fly fishers that fished lures – this was called a Muddler Minnow.

A semi-buoyant pattern, the buoyancy was provided by the collar of deer hair behind the eye, so I wondered if this could be extended along the shank to provide the maximum floatability that I required for a Caddis pattern.

It was at this stage that I called upon the expertise of my late very good friend Cliff Henry. One of the top fly dressers of this period, Cliff very quickly assisted me in producing a spun deer hair body of the required shape.

This new pattern proved an instant success, and when I decided to publicize it I gave it the name the G & H after the initials of our surnames.

Not only did this prove to be a very killing pattern on the big reservoirs, but also proved very effective dressed on smaller hooks for river fishing. Now you may wonder how this pattern came to be called the Goddard Caddis in America – so let me explain.

In the mid-sixties a well known American Fly tyer by the name of Andre Puyance visited England for the first time, and I was chosen to host him for three days' fishing on our English chalk streams. The first day was spent on the River Test where good sport was enjoyed during the morning and afternoon, so we retired early in the evening for a good dinner at a local inn.

The remaining two days we fished on a stretch of the upper River Kennet, and as sport was a little slow during the day decided to stop and fish the evening rise. This proved to be a good decision as it turned out to be a perfect balmy summer's evening with sufficient trout rising to keep us interested. After netting my sixth nice trout a fishless Andre approached and said, 'What the devil are you taking all those trout on, I have hardly had an offer'. I explained that I was using a relatively new Caddis pattern, recently perfected, and gave him a couple to try. Now even in those days Andre was an excellent fly fisher and within minutes he was into his first fish, and before the rise was over had taken a further four trout – one of them being well over twenty inches. The next evening proved equally successful, so the following morning before he departed he asked me to write down the dressing for the new pattern. At the time he was trying to build up a fly dressing business from the large fly shop he owned just to the north of San Francisco. Upon his return he decided to put this pattern on the market, initially through his shop, and for some reason known only to himself marketed it under the name the Goddard Caddis. I was completely unaware of all this and it was not until many years later on my first visit to fish the Western States of America, that I was amazed to find this pattern on sale in nearly every fly shop I visited.

I subsequently met Andre again in the late seventies and he then admitted that after he decided to put it on the market he had forgotten its original name.

Since those early days when we were using this mainly on stillwaters as a wake fly dressed on size No. 8 or 10 hooks we quickly realized its potential dressed in smaller sizes for rivers and even small streams.

While its biggest potential when dressed on size 10 or 12 hooks is for large brawling rivers, like so many found on the west side of the USA where good floatability is of the essence, I have over the years now fished it successfully in many countries throughout the world, finding it particularly effective on many of the lovely rivers in New Zealand. In the smaller sizes 14 and 16 it has proved to be an excellent standby on many small rivers and tiny streams. In addition to this, more recently I have found it to be very effective on many of the spring creeks I have fished in America and elswhere. Many of these have undercut banks and a long cast upstream tight into the bank with a size 10 or 12 has produced many big trout. Last year a friend of mine fishing for salmon in Russia on the Kola peninsula used a size 8 with great effect, raising many fish and finally landing several. In conclusion I would add that only this year, during a six-day visit to fish the Rio Grande river in Tierra del Fuego for its fabled sea trout, I hooked and released over a four-day period nearly fifty of these magnificent fish including several specimens between 15 and 19 lbs all on my Caddis dressed on size 10 hooks. I would therefore like to suggest that this is truly a Caddis for all waters.

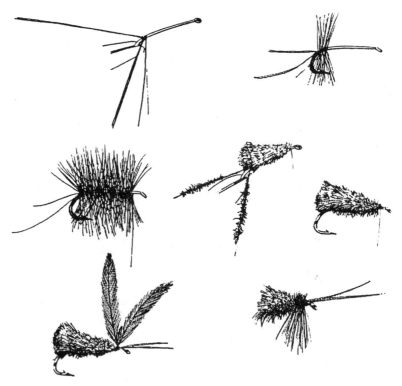

The Goddard Caddis

The dressing for the Caddis is as follows.

If you have mastered the technique of spinning deer hair on a bare shank this is a simple pattern to tie, although it is rather time consuming as up to 12 turns of hair have to be tightly applied to achieve the correct silhouette. The first stage is to apply the deer hair, each turn being pressed firmly up against the last starting at the bend of the hook. The last turn should be within about 3/16 of an inch of the hook eye, leaving sufficient room to tie in the hackle. The hair can then be trimmed to shape as shown. It is then only neccessary to apply the two hackles of the desired colour and trim. The original pattern had seal's fur of the required colour spun on thread tied in at the bend and then drawn along under the body and secured at the eye as shown in the illustration. However I now dispense with this underbody as I find it just as effective and more practical to colour the base of the seal's fur, if desired, with a waterproof felt tip pen.

A superb brown trout taken by the author from the River Kennet
on a Goddard Caddis

Down to the Wire 1998

When our book, *The Trout & The Fly* was published in 1980, Brian Clarke and I included details of several new patterns that we had perfected in an effort to overcome some of the problems detailed in the text. One of these was a rather revolutionary dry fly pattern that we called a USD (UpSide Down) Dun. This was dressed in such a way that it would land and float with the hook uppermost, as opposed to more traditional dry fly patterns where the bend barb and point hang below or pierce the surface. Mind you, the main object of the exercise was to create a dry fly that would keep the body and tails clear of the surface, so that only the hackles of the fly would make contact with the surface, and to achieve this it was purely coincidental that it had to be dressed with the hook uppermost. The thinking behind this new pattern was our endeavour to produce a dry fly where only the hackle points would indent the surface in a similar way to the legs of the natural duns which result in little 'footprints' of sparkling light forming in the mirror, often acting as a trigger to trout feeding upon the duns. At the time there were no other patterns capable of achieving this, so we were rather thrilled with the final result. In practice, this new pattern was phenomenally successful, particularly for those very difficult trout or 'Aunt Sallys' – as they are often called – that are to be found on most waters. Despite its

The parachute hackle on the original USD Dun required a special gallows tool to tie it.

Despite proving highly effective on very difficult trout, it never became popular due to the intricate nature of the dressing. Now, the originator has simplified the pattern . . .

success it has never proved popular, as it is difficult and time consuming to dress and also necessitated the use of a gallows tool which apparently few fly-tiers possess.

Dressing for the new USD Dun

Hook: Up-eye dry fly 12 to 16.
Thread: To match natural.
Tail: Microfibbets.
Hackle 'post': A short length of 10 lb BS saltwater trace wire in the form of a small vee, secured on to the shank by the thread.
Wing: Two bunches of grey calf tail, splayed to form a vee.
Body: Polypropylene yarn to match natural.
Hackle: Sharp and stiff genetic cock hackle (colour to match natural) wound around the wire hackle post.

For several years I continued to carry a small selection of these flies with me, but due to the time they took to tie, I only used them very occasionally for particularly difficult trout. Three years ago I was confined to the house for two or three weeks with a pulled muscle in my back, so spent considerable time at the fly tying bench. Consequently, it was during this period after much experimentation that I finally perfected several modifications to this USD pattern which have not only made it more effective but, more importantly, much quicker and easier to dress. It is now not necessary to use a gallows tool, and I have replaced the cut hackle wings with V-shaped calf's tail wings, which are much more durable, effective and simpler to dress. Finally, I now use polypropylene yarn to form the body, which is available in a large range of colours to match the varying body colour of the natural duns.

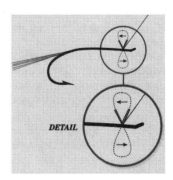

Fig. 1. Tie in six Microfibbets to form tails, ensuring they are taken just around the bend. For the parachute hackle 'post', form a vee shape in the length of stainless steel trace wire and bind it on to the top of the shank with figure-of-eight turns to secure it about one quarter of the way down the shank from the eye

Fig. 2. Now invert the hook in the vice and tie in your bunches of calf tail so they project forwards and to either side of the hook eye

Fig. 3. Tie in a length of polypropylene yarn and wind it forwards to form the body before catching in at the root of the wing

Fig. 4. Now re-set the hook in the vice in the usual fashion and tie in a hackle at the base of the wire vee. Wind a few turns of hackle round the vee before tying off and whip-finishing. The stiffness of the wire allows for a parachute hackle to be wound without fuss and it holds the hackle securely without fear of slippage and without adding a significant amount of weight

P.S. I have recently found that by making a single post with this wire in place of the V shape, a neater parachute hackle can be formed. The wire can then be cut off level with the hackle and a spot of superglue applied to stop the hackle coming off the post.

Golden Nuggets 1999

Like many very popular and killing patterns before them, the simple idea of adding a brass bead to the head of many standard patterns proved to be a real winner. One of the most popular of these standard patterns that has been improved beyond all measure and today is to be found in nearly every fly fisher's fly box is that old standby the Gold Ribbed Hare's Ear Nymph. Depending upon the depth and speed of current it can be dressed on hooks from size 18 down to even 8 with corresponding sizes and weights of gold beads from 2 mm up to 5 mm.

I have been using this Gold Head GRHE nymph with great success both for trout and grayling for the past three or four seasons. I now carry it in a full range of sizes and look upon it as one of my premier nymph patterns together with my own PVC and Shrymph nymphs and Sawyer's PT Nymph and grayling bug patterns. These five patterns now form the basis of my nymph armoury so I rarely find it neccessary to use any others. Since I have been fishing this relatively new nymph pattern I have had the best results when using the smallest size possible according to the depth of the water and the speed of the current. Consequently, I would hazard a guess that I have caught far more trout and grayling on hook sizes 18 and 16 with 2mm and 3mm beads than I have with any of the other sizes. I have also found that in many situations, this pattern dressed with a copper bead is more effective than dressed with a gold bead. On the other hand I have found that the copper beads eventually become less effective after they become dull and tarnished with age. The gold (brass) beads do not seem to be affected in the same way. Since I started using these GRHE goldheads I kept wondering why they were so effective. Obviously the fish were associating them with some form of aquatic food, and after much thought I decided that the only item of food that they vaguely resembled were various species of caddis larvae.

However it was not until early in the last season that I gave this further thought and came to the conclusion that if I dressed these on long-shank hooks instead of the standard length hooks that were currently being used by everone, I would then have a pattern that much more closely resembled the average caddis larvae in silhouette.

During the remainder of last season I therefore tested my theory by using alternately patterns dressed on standard length hooks and long shank. As a result of these tests, although they are far from conclusive, I certainly seem to be getting even better results. I also found that this pattern dressed on a red long shank Drennan UV Rainbow hook was particularly effective for grayling.

The longer the shank, the more effective the bead head Hare's Ear Nymph

Finally, I feel I should point out that I did have problems finding long shank hooks in sizes 16 and 14 that were small enough to use in conjunction with 2 and 3mm gold heads. Apart from this, it is also necessary to find these long-shank hooks with a round bend similar to a Model Perfect as with a sneck or a similar bend of hook it is impossible to thread the bead around the bend. Another annoying factor is that on a lot of these small long shank hooks the eyes are so small that the bead cannot be retained by the eye, so the shank behind the eye has to be built up with thread to retain it – a time wasting operation . . . but ultimately worth the effort!

The Negative Nymph 1999

During the past few years I have done less and less stillwater fishing as most of the large lakes and reservoirs which I love to fish are now, with my advancing age, a little too far for a comfortable drive. While I have a multitude of small stillwaters within easy driving distance of home, I have never been a lover of these what I term 'artificial' waters, as most of them are put-and-take fisheries with murky water where it is difficult – if not impossible – to see any trout.

However, four seasons ago I was introduced to a water but a short distance away that has three lakes, two of which – although quite small – are always crystal clear. Since then, I have been fishing this water on a fairly regular basis, as I find it great sport to stalk individual trout in clear water. Unfortunately, both of these small lakes are usually unfishable by the middle of the summer due to heavy weed growth and accompanying algae encouraged by too much sun. This past season was different, as with much less sun large areas have been fishable throughout the season. Consequently, with a lot more fishing pressure, the trout became harder and harder to catch as the season progressed. These lakes are well stocked with good quality trout that put on weight rapidly throughout the summer so that by the end of July there were plenty of trout in the six to seven pound range to be seen, but by then most of the rods fishing the water had all but given up trying to catch them. The few that were still persevering were catching the odd trout, but it was very hard going.

While I had enjoyed considerable success during the early part of the season, I also found the trout almost imposssible to catch by mid July. Up to then I had taken most of my fish on small nymph or Midge Pupa patterns in sizes 14 and 16, but by July even nymphs dressed on hooks size 18 were not only ignored, but in fact caused panic. Time and time again I would intercept a cruising trout with a delicately placed size 18 nymph, and invariably as the tiny nymph hit the surface the trout would turn to intercept, but as soon as he saw it he would depart at speed.

I must admit this situation intrigued me as in this very clear water you could see that the trout were still feeding. If you watched carefully you could see them turning and intercepting food and very often you would clearly see the mouth open and close. During this period there seemed to be very little hatching on the surface, so I assumed they were probably feeding upon tiny nymphs or chironomid pupae.

Following this theory I dressed some Pheasant Tail and P.V.C. Nymphs on size 20 hooks and, although I did catch a few trout on these, the majority still spooked as they approached the artificial. Not only did I try placing the nymph very delicately in front of them but I also tried the often so successful method of ambushing cruising trout, and then lifting the nymph up in front as they approached . . . but all to no avail.

After a further long period of frustration, I eventually came to the conclusion that it was the movement of the artificial that was spooking the trout. I therefore decided to make a further study of the feeding fish and it was then that I noticed most of them seemed to be cruising and feeding between one and three feet below the surface. In view of this, I decided a possible answer may be to develop a pattern that would have a slight negative buoyancy so that it would sink very slowly down through the water column and remain in the feeding area of the trout with but little movement. It would also have to be dressed on a very tiny hook, either an 18 or 20, and look vaguely like a tiny nymph or pupa. In my experience, theories – particularly in fly tying – rarely seem to work, but on this occasion I hit the jackpot. During the latter part of last season many of the larger trout succumbed to my tiny nymph, although I must admit only on sunny days when there was little wind to disturb the surface.

For this style of fishing, clear water with good visibility is essential, as you have to be able to see your quarry fairly clearly. I found that the best technique was to cast the nymph about ten to twelve feet in front of a cruising trout which gave it time to sink to his level before it came within his vision. This of course depends upon him staying on roughly the same course. Now such a tiny nymph is all but invisible once it sinks below the surface; furthermore it is no good watching the leader for any sign of movement as these cruising fish usually swim fairly slowly and intercept and eject the nymph pretty quickly. I therefore concentrate on the area where I think the nymph should be, and then tighten if I suspect he has taken it. Any slight movement by the trout either up or down, or from side to side, or the opening and closing of the mouth, usually indicates he has intercepted something. When this happens and I tighten the line I'm still most surprised when I feel the weight of a good fish on the other end . . . but I'm getting used to it!

The pattern, which is simple and quick to dress is based upon the Suspender principle, but its success does depend upon choosing the correct size of plastazote or ethafoam ball. This must be of a size where it will not quite support the size of hook being used. The ideal sink rate is about four to five seconds per foot.

For want of a better name I decided to call this pattern the *Negative Nymph*.

The Negative Nymph: an adaptation of the author's Suspender Nymph – with an ethafoam ball that is just not big enough to support the hook, so the Nymph sinks very slowly

Hook: Size 16/18 Karnasan No.B983 (wide gape).

Thread: Fine brown.

Head: Small white foam ball wrapped in cut square of ladies' white nylon stocking, then coloured brown.

Body: Olive green or brown polypropylene yarn.

Rib: Fine silver tinsel.

Thorax: Two fibres of peacock herl.

Optional: One or two turns of grizzle cock hackle tied round base of ball.

Suspender Secrets 1999

This is the second pattern that I have recently modified, and like the USD Paradun was originally introduced by Brian Clarke and myself and featured in our book *The Trout & The Fly* (1980). Since its inception all those years ago it has proved to be extremely popular and has accounted for many thousands of trout particularly on stillwater when dressed in the larger sizes. Dressed on a smaller hook such as a size 18, it has also proved to be very effective indeed on rivers when trout are holding close to the surface and sipping down tiny smuts or midges.

When fishing these Suspender patterns it is essential to watch the fly carefully at all times as rises are often gentle and easily missed unless one really concentrates. This can often be a problem, particularly if you are fishing the fly at any distance, as the only part of this pattern that shows above the surface is a quarter of the tiny white ethafoam ball which assists to float the head of the pattern in the surface film – where the trout expect to find the natural pupa.

Apart from the problem of visibility on the surface, some fly fishers seem to have reservations regarding this little white ball at the head of the pattern when it is viewed by the trout from below, as they feel it may alert the trout to possible danger. Personally, I rather doubt this is much of a problem as the natural pupae have dense white filaments growing on their heads which often pierce the surface. However, I must admit that the artificial Suspender would probably look more natural and be more acceptable to the trout if less of the white ball was showing below the surface.

With these factors in mind I have, I think, now overcome both the problems with a very simple solution. After completing the pattern, I now tie in a parachute hackle of the appropriate colour and size underneath the little white ball of ethafoam, using the base of this as a pillar around which to form the hackle. In practice, this not only floats the head of the Suspender higher in the water so that it is much more visible to the angler, but it also means less of the little ball is visible to the trout looking up from below. Another plus is that I think it gives the artificial more realism, as the hackle fibres may well look like the legs of the natural pupa as it begins to emerge from its case. Vary the body colour and hook size when tying these. I usually dress these in five different body colours - black, brown, green, red or orange as these seem to cover the body colour of most natural pupae. On rivers, I usually dress these on hook size 18 and fish just the one Suspender on the leader in either brown or green.

The hackle is added by tying it in last and using the ethafoam ball encased in stocking material as the 'parachute hackle post'

Suspender Hatching Midge Pupa

Hook: Limerick bend, or Drennan Sedge hook, size 10-18.
Thread: Tying silk colour to match natural.
Floatation ball: White ethafoam enclosed in a square of white nylon stocking and bound in just behind eye.
Tag: White nylon filaments.
Ribbing: Oval silver tinsel.
Body: Polypropylene yarn.
Throax: Peacock herl or brown dyed turkey herl.
Hackle: Natural red or grizzly hackle tied parachute style.

On stillwater, I tend to favour hook sizes either 14 or 12 and mount one on the point and two on droppers about five feet apart on as long a leader as possible. To start with, I always mount different colours and only change if I find the trout favour one particular colour. Should one experience one of those wonderful morning or evening rises that used to be quite common on many stillwaters I would suggest that you mount the three Suspenders much closer - as little as 18 inches, because during a heavy surface rise to the natural pupae the trout are swimming very close to the surface with their vision restricted to around 18 inches on either side.

Note: When fishing artificial Pupae patterns, such as the above Suspender, they should always be fished on the dead drift – never retrieve apart from occassionally giving the rod tip a slight lift to provide a little animation.

Sitting Pretty 2000

Many years ago, when I first started to fish the chalkstreams of southern England, I found that so far as fly patterns were concerned, one of the most frustrating periods of the season occurred early on, in the so-called 'Duffers' Fortnight'.

This is the period when the biggest of all our upwinged flies, *ephemera danica*, was hatching. Traditionally, it is a silly time on any river or lake in the UK, where big hatches of either *e. danica* or *e. vulgata* occur. During the early stages of the hatch, practically any big pattern will take trout consistently, but this is not the case when the hatch intensifies and the trout become choosy.

Hatches on most rivers and lakes usually extend over a period of about three weeks, and towards the end of this time the fish often become even more difficult to tempt, so an effective pattern is of paramount importance.

In my early days of fishing, I experimented with most of the popular patterns of the time such as Greendrakes, Fan Wings, Straddlebugs and Shadow Mayflies. I even tried a Walker's Mayfly later on. It wasn't until much later when I started using a Grey Wulff that I began to enjoy a modicum of success in the later stages of the hatches. In retrospect, it now seems significant that this is the only pattern out of all those mentioned above that actually sits in the water's surface, allowing the body of the fly to pierce the film.

During the late 1970s, Brian Clarke and I were engaged in extensive research on trout vision underwater and how they saw natural and artificial flies beneath and on the surface. This eventually led to the publication of our book, *The Trout and The Fly*, in 1980. During this period we discovered that, probably due to their size and weight,

Fooled by a Poly May emerger, this chalkstream brownie goes back

these big Mayflies drifted along the surface after hatching with their bodies actually piercing the film, as opposed to most smaller upwinged flies that were able to support the weight of their bodies above the surface, on their legs.

With this in mind, we produced a pattern called the PB Mayfly, incorporating one of Veniard's plastic Mayfly bodies. While this was quite successful, I still felt it could be improved. It wasn't until the early 1980s that I finally perfected (and was happy with) a pattern that represented both the dun and spinner. These two patterns – the Poly May Dun and the Poly May Spinner – have now proved to be two of my most successful patterns and are now used extensively by many fly-fishers on both rivers and the big Irish loughs.

For many years now, neither I nor any of my friends have ever needed to use any other pattern at this time, apart from the occasional evening when big falls of the spent fly occur. On windy evenings it was noted that a large percentage of dead and dying spent flies drift along with one wing stuck up in the air. My Poly May Spinner was designed with the v-shaped wings spread well apart, so it also drifts with one wing sticking up.

On windless evenings, a bigger percentage of spent flies seems to drift along with both wings flat on the surface. At this time, we would often switch to a more traditional spent-wing pattern such as Neil Patterson's Deer Stalker – an excellent fly.

Occasionally, however, one does come across a trout feeding avidly on duns but which constantly ignores your fly, no matter how well it is presented. A few seasons ago, with this in mind, I decided to take a further look at the Poly May to see if I could produce something close, yet different, that would at least give me an alternative to offer to these fussy trout.

This eventually resulted in the creation of a new pattern that used most of the basic materials as the previous fly, but actually represented a dun with most of its body below the surface struggling to remove itself from its nymphal case. Over the past two seasons, this new pattern, the Poly May Emerger, has exceeded all expectations. It's as effective as the Poly May Dun.

When dressing emerger patterns, there are several different materials one can use to represent the partially discarded nymphal shuck, but I must admit I have never been happy with any of them.

I was delighted, therefore, to come across a relatively old material that fits the bill admirably. This is a fine, pale-gold (blond) extra-long acrylic fur called Fly Fur (obtainable from Orvis or Mystic Bay Flies, Green's Farm, CT 06436 USA). It is now used universally for the wing of a famous bonefish pattern called the Gotcha. When wet and tied in sparsely as a tag, it appears extremely realistic and now forms the basis for my new Poly May Emerger.

I still use the same body material and black hackle. Alternatively, you can use grizzle hackle, which I now tend to favour for this new pattern. Finally, I still use the same pale-gold calf's tail for the wing (obtainable from Veniard's dyed to this colour).

Over the years, many fly-fishers have asked me why I use this colour for the wings of the Poly May. On close examination, they appear almost dark grey, with a faint tinge of yellowish green. However, if you observe the same fly, particularly in bright sunlight from a distance or even on the water surface, they do appear a yellowish gold.

The new pattern is dressed on a Drennan curved suspender hook, which assists the body and tag to sit well below the surface. To this end I treat only the wing and hackle with floatant, while soaking the body and tag in the water before starting to fish.

Poly May Dun

Hook: Size 10–12 wide gape
Thread: Strong white or pale brown
Tag: Tips of a bunch of calf tail dyed pale gold
Wings: Calf, as above, continued along shank and split into V to form wings
Body: Cream-coloured polypropylene yarn
Hackle: Black cock, two turns on each side of wing roots

Poly May Spinner

Hook: Size 10–12 wide gape
Thread: Strong black
Tails: Three or four Betts brown microfibbets spread well apart or black hackle fibres
Wing: Black-and-white calf tail well mixed and tied in a wide V
Body: White polypropylene yarn
Hackle: Black cock hackle short in flue, two turns each side of wing roots

New Poly May Emerger

Hook: Size 12–14 Drennan suspender
Thread: Strong pale brown
Shuck: Blond Fly Fur two-thirds of body length
Body: Cream-coloured polypropylene yarn or cream antron body wool
Wing: Bunch of pale-gold-dyed calf tail
Hackle: Black or grizzle cock tied parachute style around base of wing root

PART TWO

FLY FISHING TECHNIQUES

Softly, Softly, with Silk Lines and Long Leaders 1972

A couple of years ago I wrote an article titled 'Back to the Silk', outlining experiments conducted over a season's fishing by my colleague, Cliff Henry, and myself. I tried to explain how our tests had provided us with reasonable proof that under certain conditions the use of a silk line, as opposed to a plastic coated line, resulted in a higher proportion of takes.

Most of our experiments were carried out from a boat on stillwater, but we also found that, so far as we could tell, they appeared to be equally advantageous from the bank or when river fishing. On the other hand, I must admit that now, although I still tend to use silk lines more or less exclusively when I am boat fishing, the same does not always apply when I am river fishing.

I feel the time is now appropriate to give some further information on this subject in the light of recent experiments, and to reply to some of the points against the use of silk lines put forward by Barrie Welham in his article in 1970, called 'Back to Silk? Never!'

First, let me try to reply to some of the points made by Barrie Welham, refuting or minimizing some of the statements I made. He quite rightly suggested that the angler using the silk line during our tests consistently caught more fish on each outing than the angler using plastic, and that this does not prove the issue conclusively. With this, of course, I must agree up to a point, as these tests would have to be carried out over several seasons to prove the issue beyond doubt. However, I do feel it goes some way to proving their superiority under certain conditions. Let me qualify that last statement: I mean under relatively calm conditions, as on rough and windy days the advantage of silk is of less importance.

This brings me to the second point made by Mr Welham, refuting my statement that a silk line is less fatiguing to use and under windy conditions easier to control than the corresponding weight in a modern plastic line. He tells us that because the difference in thickness between the two lines is minimal – in fact only five-thousandths of an inch – the difference because of this is insignificant. But I fear I must adhere to my feelings in this matter, as apart from the fact that I am sure that the difference in diameter is more than he suggests, the feel of the silk in practice is better, and I am certain it cuts into or across the wind more efficiently.

Finally, Mr Welham tells us that, again because of this minimal difference in diameter, he does not believe that the thinner silk line will be significantly less visible on the water to a trout. I would respectfully point out that I made no such assertion in my article. What I said was: '. . . they can be presented on the water surface with far less disturbance'.

Last year, Mr Henry was given access to some delicate sound-testing equipment, and he was able to mount this in a very long tank filled with water. He then proceeded to carry out line-presentation tests on to the water surface with modern plastic bubble lines and corresponding weights in silk. The results of these tests were extremely illuminating as the decibels of sound produced by those lines hitting the surface was extremely high when related to their displacement. From these tests it seems quite apparent that it is the noise of the line hitting the surface that puts most trout down in calm conditions, and not so much any noise or movement the angler may be making.

The late Cliff Henry with
a fine rainbow

In addition, these tests seemed to show quite clearly that the silk lines produced an appreciably lower decibel rating than the plastic. We did intend to carry out a series of carefully controlled tests to prove the point with facts and figures, but unfortunately further access to this expensive equipment was denied as it was required for another use.

Following on from those rather revealing tests relating to the noise that all lines make when cast on to the water, we naturally wondered if there was any way of overcoming this. After considerable thought we came to the conclusion that a partial answer would be to use a much longer leader than those of 9–10 ft. commonly used. Our theory was that the longer the leader, the further the fly line from the trout, and the less noise the fish is likely to hear. Consequently, for most of last season we used much longer leaders – 16 to 18ft. Results indicated a higher percentage of takes, but I trust the reader will appreciate that it is all but impossible to prove or disprove.

Strange though it may seem, previous to these tests we had considered using longer leaders for a completely different reason. We had for some time felt that when a fly is used on the point in conjunction with one or two droppers for reservoir fishing, the flies may be too close together. For this reason alone a longer leader should be desirable, as there would be less likelihood of a trout seeing in his window two artificials at the same time, which might seem suspicious.

Finally, before anyone writes to say that the use of long leaders is not a new idea, it is a new approach so far as we are concerned, and I sincerely hope that our suggestions may give at least some anglers food for thought.

Incidentally, I still receive many requests regarding my special floatation treatment for silk lines. So let me again explain the procedure. A new line or an old line cleaned and then treated in the manner described will float without regreasing for several hours.

For treating or greasing, use at all times Barbour's waterproofing compound. First of all, fill a shallow tray with enough melted compound to cover the coiled fly-line. Then place the tray in a warm oven for about an hour, remove, uncoil the line and hang it in the garden on a warm sunny day. Thoroughly rub down the line with a felt pad of compound at least twice during the day. It is, of course, still necessary to transfer the line from the reel to a line winder to dry after each fishing outing, and as this is done it should be rubbed down with a felt pad and the same grease.

N.B. While the author was probably the first to publicize the advantages of long leaders which are taken for granted today, the advantage offered by the old silk lines has now and for many years been annulled due to the many great advances offered since then by modern plastic fly lines.

Trout Without a Net 1973

Have you ever arrived at the waterside and found to your consternation that you have left your landing net at home? If not, do not be too complacent, as it is sure to happen eventually. When it does I hope that the following information will prove of some value.

Let us first consider this situation when applied to still-water fishing, from the bank, as for this style of flyfishing I am now of the opinion that a landing net, on most waters, is not even necessary, and furthermore, at least for evening fishing, is actually undesirable. Let me qualify this rather controversial statement by saying this is not a conclusion I have reached overnight, but over many years of forget-fulness. In the early days of fishing Blagdon Lake in the south-west of England I often arrived minus a net, as in those days, when I had less room, I used to keep my tackle in various parts of the house, and in the rush to get away for the weekend, it was all too easy to overlook some item. As a result I quickly became proficient at landing trout without a net.

The technique I originally adopted is really very simple and even today, the method I use is basically the same. Whether you hook a trout from the bank or when wading well out from the bank, play it in the normal way until it is ready to be landed. At this juncture, holding the rod high and keeping a tight line on the fish, back slowly towards and up the bank, leading the trout into the shallow margins, where its struggles will assist you to pull it onto dry land, or into water too shallow for it to swim away. Still keeping the line taut, lay your rod down, walk down the line to the trout, and either kill or release it as the situation dictates.

This method can be adopted on most waters, so consequently for the past four seasons when bank fishing I have dispensed with a net completely, as even on waters with weedy margins, the trout can be worked over the top of the weed once you have established confidence in the method. The only exception I now make is when there is deep water right into the margins, a situation often found on small, artificially created waters. I have yet to lose even a big trout through lack of a net, and so far as evening fishing is concerned, when the light is poor, I think a net is a positive menace. Many times in the past, just when the light has been fading, I have netted a trout when using one or two droppers, and even after struggling to keep the line taut, by the time I have released the trout from the mesh, one or often both droppers have become entangled. On numerous occasions, by the time the tangle has been sorted out the evening rise has finished. This is no longer a problem.

Let us now consider the situation of the netless river trout fisherman. Up to this last season I really had no answer, as in the past on those odd occasions when I found myself with a trout on one end of the rod and no net at the other, I endeavoured, often, I may add, with disastrous results, to scoop the trout out and up on to the bank with my hands. Several years ago I saw one or two American-made films showing anglers fishing trout, and even large steelhead, nonchalantly 'gilling' fish, I believe they term it. This entailed pushing one's forefinger, or thumb, or both, under the gill-covers and lifting the fish out. Now, while this may be a simple matter for the expert, I have never mastered it, as the fish always seem to close their gill-covers at the crucial moment, and in any case it is only a feasible technique for the wading fisherman. On most of the trout rivers I fish, either wading is frowned upon, or the water is too deep.

Early last season I again found myself without a net, and no other angler on the river! Knowing this particular stretch of water held many a large trout, I was naturally undecided what to do. I considered driving into the nearest large town to buy a net, or trying to find the riverkeeper to see if I could borrow one, but as the surface of the river was dimpled with rising trout I decided to try to manage without. However, I must admit that the thought of even trying to land a large trout without a net filled me with foreboding.

They say that necessity is the mother of invention and so it was on this day, as by the time the rise finished in the early afternoon I had succeeded in landing a limit bag of 6 fine trout totalling 18 lb. I had a struggle with the first two fish, but by the time number six was safely grassed, I had, by trial and error, developed a method which seemed to work tolerably well. I have subsequently, mainly to test the method, landed a further 30 or so fish and I am confident it can be used under any conditions, even for landing a big trout from a boat on a reservoir which, incidentally, I have since accomplished. Let me make it clear, though: I am only suggesting this method for emergencies as from a boat it is certainly safer to use a net. The technique I adopted, which I do not doubt has been used by other anglers in the past, is as follows.

First of all it is essential to find a clear spot along the bank you are fishing, where one can play the trout right into the bank. Having located such an area, fight your fish as hard as possible and as soon as it shows signs of weakening lead it towards the chosen landing place. Now, either kneel, or sit down with your legs dangling in the water (wellingtons and waterproof trousers are a necessity) and once you have succeeded in getting its head above the surface and keeping it there, lead the fish towards you. At this stage, to bring the trout into your reach, it will be necessary to walk up the rod with your hands, pushing the butt up the bank behind you, simultaneously trapping the line under your fingers. On most occasions I finished up half-way along the rod, shortening the line as I progressed until the fish was near enough.

Still gripping the rod with the right hand, with the line held between the thumb and the rod (which can be immediately released if the fish makes an unexpected lunge for freedom) the left hand should be brought slowly down and slid along the back of the trout where it should be gripped firmly and then turned over and lifted out. When a trout is turned upside down it ceases to struggle. Finally, do not attempt this method if you are very old, or suffer from vertigo unless, of course, you are a very good swimmer in wellington boots!

To Grease or Not to Grease? 1975

I am surprised at the comparatively large number of stillwater trout fishermen I have encountered over the last two or three seasons who seem unaware of the importance of oil or grease, or the lack of it, on their flies or leaders. In fact, these floatants can often mean the difference between success and failure, and are vitally important under most conditions.

Several different brands of line grease are available, but my preference is for the plain Mucilin in the little green tin. This is supplied with a felt pad for application to the leader, but it should be used sparingly.

Oil or floatant for flies is offered either in bottles or aerosol-type sprays. Again, my personal preference is for Permafloat, the preparation first recommended by Richard Walker in *Trout and Salmon*. It is in liquid form and is best kept in a wide-mouth screw-top bottle, so that the whole fly, no matter how large, can be dipped, preferably some little time before use to allow it to dry out thoroughly. Flies treated with this oil float beautifully for several hours.

Several preparations can be obtained for degreasing leaders or flies, from ordinary liquid glycerine to thick mud from the edge of the water, which will suffice if nothing else is available. Liquid detergent is good, but I prefer glycerine mixed with Fuller's earth.

A basic error made by many anglers is to apply grease too liberally to the leader in an effort to ensure that the dry fly does not become waterlogged. You should always apply it lightly, and always leave the last 6 ins completely free of grease. Some fishermen do not realize the disturbance a greased line creates as it is retrieved on the surface. Under calm conditions this will be immediately apparent, but in rough water it is not noticeable to the angler, though it is to the trout.

The same applies when you are using wet flies or nymphs on a floating line. If you need to fish these at any depth, it is essential to degrease both flies and leader before you start to fish. It should also be appreciated that the application of grease to different sections of the leader can predetermine the depth at which the various flies on it will fish.

For example, from midsummer onwards when a lot of sedge-flies are about, an extremely effective method is to use in conjunction with a floating line a dry Sedge pattern on the dropper with a Sedge Pupa artificial on the point. In this case the leader above the dry fly is greased, while the remainder down to the point fly which must be retrieved just below the surface is thoroughly degreased. Or you may wish to retrieve a dry Sedge, Invicta or similar pattern in the surface film. This can be a killing method when trout are feeding on the adult sedge, for they will often ignore a dry Sedge fished on the surface, but readily accept the same pattern fished in the film. They seem to take this for a sedge-fly hatching. To ensure that your chosen pattern fishes in the correct position, you must degrease the leader and sparsely oil the artificial. Too much oil and it will float too high, too little and it will sink too far below the surface.

To illustrate the importance of this aspect of fly-fishing, let me recount an incident I was involved in last season. The time was early July and I had arranged to take a friend for a day's boat fishing on one of our larger reservoirs. Fairly new to this style of fishing, he asked me to guide him on which patterns to use and how to fish them. Few fish were rising and anglers were having most successes to deeply retrieved lures.

Observing several sedge-flies fluttering in the margins, I felt it should be possible to take a few fish on the surface despite the complete absence of rises. Under these conditions it would be necessary to attract the trout to our flies, so it was essential to use a large dry, well-oiled Sedge on the dropper with an Invicta fished just below the surface on the point. I explained this to my friend and advised him to grease the leader above the Sedge. We then started a nice drift over water not too deep, where the trout should be able to see the disturbance created by the Sedge on the dropper even if they were lying near the bottom.

Sure enough the method was successful, and during the next two hours I boated four nice trout and rose several others which came short. The disturbance created by the Sedge attracted them to the surface where most accepted the Invicta. Despite the fact that he was fishing the same method with similar flies my companion rose only one fish. I checked his flies, leader and even the distance between flies, but could not account for this. We also changed places in the boat, but all to no avail. Eventually I suggested we exchange rods, and the reason for his lack of success was immediately apparent. The flies were fishing incorrectly as he had greased the leader between the two flies instead of the section only above the Sedge on the dropper. I corrected this for him and within five minutes he was delightedly playing a fine plump trout.

This clearly demonstrates the extreme importance of this aspect of fly-fishing.

The Herringbone Effect 1979

Some time ago, I wrote an article on when to grease or degrease your leader or flies; since then, and no doubt before, many other writers have contributed to this particular aspect of still water fly fishing. Despite this, many of today's modern generation of fly fishers ignore this aspect entirely, which is of paramount importance when fishing with a floating fly line.

It is of little consequence when fishing with any form of sinking line, and it is probably for this reason that many fly fishers fail to appreciate its importance when changing to a floater. Many, many times during the past few seasons I have observed anglers fishing their fly or team of flies on a floating line leaving a wake behind each fly, or worse still also from each connecting length of leader which no self respecting trout would come near. They then wonder why they finish up with a blank. Had they taken the trouble to degrease their leader and each fly thoroughly before fishing, they would doubtless have taken their share of trout as then they would have been retrieving their flies just below the surface film where the fish were feeding on these occasions.

Conversely at other times I have watched anglers retrieving their flies and leader just below the surface (whether by design or not I do not know, as even if you fail to degrease the leader and flies they will after a time become waterlogged or degreased and sink below the surface of their own accord) when they should have been fishing with at least one fly in or even on the surface. To achieve this they should have applied a judicious amount of grease or floatant to their fly, although at the same time making sure their leader was still thoroughly degreased.

As time has passed I have become more and more convinced that any form of grease on your leader for any style of surface fishing

Seemingly unavoidable but a real problem none the less, line wake causes V-shaped waves and shadows on the surface of a calm lake

reduces your chances of success. Consequently today the only time I ever apply any to the leader, is on the butt section when drift fishing and bouncing the top dropper along the surface, or when fishing a single weighted nymph and looking for takes on the drop.

This whole aspect of surface disturbance or lack of it I find most intriguing, particularly as it has been one of the subjects of underwater research undertaken by Brian Clarke and myself over the past few years. As a consequence of some of our experiments I am now sure that the fly fisher should take a very hard look not only at the flies and leaders he uses and the positions these flies take up on the leader, but also the fly line itself.

Some time ago I instigated a series of experiments in an effort to find out what effect in terms of noise the fly line landing on the water may have on trout in the vicinity. I came to the conclusion at the time, that this did scare fish and this in consequence encouraged me to adopt the practice of using exceptionally long leaders, these facts I duly publicised and as long leaders are now an accepted tactic in the trout fisher's armoury it would seem that many other anglers agreed. However in the light of our more recent experiments it would seem that the surface disturbance caused by the fly line alighting on the surface would have an even more frightening effect.

Now where does this leave us? In the first place it confirms my original thoughts on the advantages of long leaders for most styles of fishing, as the further your flies are away from your line the better your chances of avoiding the dual effects of noise and surface disturbance. But what of the fly line itself?

This leads us to further intriguing possibilities. The colour of the fly line for a start. This can be of considerable importance as I think we have proved with photographic evidence in our book *The Trout and the Fly* so I will not dwell on this, but what about the effect of drag on the fly line? I think this could also have much more effect on our fishing than we may have realized in the past, and it is a subject that up to now I have done little research on. However after giving it much thought in the past few weeks I have now convinced myself it could for certain styles of fishing be the main cause on occasions of indifferent success.

Having observed from underwater the frightening disturbance caused by a greased leader being pulled across the surface I can just imagine the effect a bulkier fly line floating high in the surface would have. Let us now look at this situation a little closer. Except on those relatively few stillwaters that have high banks combined with clear water where you can see many of the trout, none of us really know how many trout we may be lining on each cast. On stillwaters under these conditions this is unavoidable, and although any trout between you and the end of your fly line will undoubtedly flee in panic the moment it alights upon the surface, any in the vicinity of your flies or leader (particularly if it is long enough) will be undisturbed and it is these trout that may rise to your flies or follow and eventually take. Now I am sure most anglers appreciate that in stillwater trout are constantly on the move and therefore it is a reasonable assumption that trout, other than those scared, will probably move into this area between you and the end of your line after the initial disturbance caused by your line landing. However these trout and any others that may swim into the area will rapidly depart as soon as the retrieve is commenced and the fly line starts to drag along the surface, giving off a herringbone ripple of light reflections that is most unnatural and frightening.

How can we overcome this problem? If those trout beneath the fly line were undisturbed our chances would be greatly enhanced as the more trout that see your flies on the retrieve, the greater the possibility of a take.

Obviously there is little one can do regarding the disturbance caused by your line alighting on the surface, but this in itself is not too much of a problem because other trout, as previously mentioned, may move into the area, particularly if you pause for a minute or two before commencing your retrieve. The main problem of drag on the fly line can be partly eliminated by using a sink tip line, but at the best this can be but a compromise as it still leaves the bulk of the line on the surface. On the face of it an obvious solution to the problem would appear to present itself in the form of a slow sink line. Unfortunately this immediately presents us with another problem because it means your flies will probably be fishing too deep for most surface feeding fish. Are there any other possibilities? Well I think for those that still possess one of the old type silk lines, it should be possible to degrease one of these partially so that it sinks just below the surface film. The only trouble though would be to ensure that the line balanced correctly: too much grease and it will float too high, too little and it will sink too quickly. The ultimate answer is of course a purpose-made low density line that would sink just below the film, but this could prove difficult to manufacture with any degree of accuracy.

Maybe there are other ways to solve the problem, as I am sure if we could find a solution to it we would all catch more trout. Finally I feel though I should point out that even if we could find a way to float a line consistently either in or just below the film, it would not be of assistance to the nymph fisherman. Most of the time he requires at least the tip of the line on the surface where he can see it for indications of a take.

Play Them Hard, and Play Them by Hand 1980

Many big fish – the very fish we want most to land – are lost because of inadequate technique, and because coolness is lost in the heat of the moment. An illustration will make the point. One day I had access to the Littlecote water on the Upper Kennet, and asked a friend to join me. The Littlecote water holds very large trout, and fish in excess of 6 lb are by no means uncommon.

While my colleague was a good and experienced dry-fly fisherman, and had caught in his lifetime many hundreds of trout, he had rarely been given the opportunity to fish for really large trout (I don't often get the opportunity either!). On the day in question, the first four trout that my friend hooked – all of them in excess of 4 lb – were either lost in heavy weed, or broken off when they gained too much line. After being shown the correct technique of handling such large trout, he took six big fish from the water without further loss.

The first decision that the fly-fisher must make on arrival at the waterside concerns the strength of leader tippet (point) to be used. Unless the trout in the water are known to be particularly shy, or it is intended to fish very tiny midge patterns on very tiny hooks, it is good practice to use a test of nylon of at least an equivalent weight of the larger trout known to inhabit the water, up to 5 lb or 6 lb breaking strain. It is rarely necessary to use leaders heavier than this, even for the largest trout in rivers.

Provided a leader of the correct test for the trout being fished for is chosen, it should be possible to contain any trout after its initial run, without giving much more line. The rod should be held high at all times to fulfil its main purpose as a shock-absorber and so to buffer any sudden lunges for freedom the fish may make. The tip should be lowered only in making a last-ditch effort to turn a fish from a snag.

Do not take the rod back past the vertical as this will not only reduce power, but may well lead to a ruined or even shattered rod. On the other hand, do not be afraid to hold the rod at the full stretch of your arm above your head. The most important aspect to concentrate upon once the trout has completed his initial run is to get him to the top, and to make every effort to keep him there during the rest of the fight.

Let a large trout get his head down and he will dictate the fight, but keep his head up and he cannot run effectively. You will quickly realize how much easier it is to control a fish on the surface, and to bring the battle to a rapid conclusion. At this time it is inevitable that a big trout – particularly one hooked at long range – will take a lot of line on its initial run, and make it impossible to exert pressure at a sufficiently high angle to bring its head up. Do not watch the fish go! Under such circumstances it is essential to move along the bank quickly towards the trout in order to recover line.

Once you have gained confidence and learned how much pressure can be applied to your tackle, it is surprising how tightly even a big trout can be held. I learned early on – and painfully! – that when fishing for trout of 4 lb-plus in weedy water, it is a question of holding on as soon as you set the hook, or the fish is as good as lost.

John Goddard practises what he preaches with a big Kennet rainbow

113

I learned also that the secret lies in the element of surprise. When a big trout rises to take your fly (provided he is at fairly close range) you must apply maximum pressure immediately the strike is made, and under no circumstances allow him to get his head back underwater for more than a moment at a time. The effect of this seems to disorientate a fish, and it is normally possible to contain him within a tight circle close to the bank.

There is one other golden rule for handling large trout: never attempt to play them from the reel. Many books go to great lengths to inform the fly-fisher how to recover slack line after a fish has been hooked, and on the importance of winding the line back on to the reel evenly, so that the trout may be played directly against the brake or check. I know of no more certain way to lose a big fish, than to adopt this procedure.

When playing any large trout, it is essential to concentrate on your quarry one hundred per cent. Take your eyes off the fish to recover slack line neatly on to the reel, and that is the moment he will either break you with an unexpected lunge, or come off because of the slackness of line. Even if one were to recover all the slack successfully, and to begin to play a big trout off the reel, a sudden burst of speed could snap the line like thread: the inertia set up by the reel and the check is often sufficient to cause this to happen.

I always play a big trout by hand, with finger and thumb controlling the fly-line. This method is very much more sensitive: it helps to give you complete control over the fish, and slack can be given or taken up instantly. The only slight disadvantage is the coils of loose line on the ground about your feet, but in practice the line rarely snags.

Now, how about large trout in lakes or reservoirs? Well, exactly the same rules apply to any trout up to about 6 lb that are hooked within a reasonable distance of the boat or bank. However, there are other factors that have to be taken into consideration in stillwater.

The occasional trout may be much larger, and, furthermore, it may be hooked in deep water on a sunken line or at very long range. It will therefore be necessary on waters that are known to hold large trout to increase the breaking strain of the point on your leader to 7 lb or even 8 lb test. In my opinion there is little to be gained in using a heavier test than this even for the largest trout, and in any case the average fly-rod would not be capable of handling a leader testing much heavier than this.

114

For those trout hooked near the bottom, or at long range, there is little one can do other than to apply the maximum strain your tackle will take and endeavour to employ as much side-strain as possible at the same time in an effort to turn the fish. Many anglers have experienced hooking a semi-wild rainbow of between 3 lb and 4 lb on one of our larger reservoirs. Trout of this size are usually in peak fighting condition and often take off for the far bank immediately. Many times I have been taken well into the backing on the fly-line under these circumstances, but I always apply as much pressure as quickly as possible because, should the trout decide to jump at very long range, a break is usually inevitable, particularly if you are using any form of sinking line.

Who Needs Barbed Hooks? 1980

It is now well over ten years since I have used a hook with a barb on it for fresh water fishing. In this period I have been extolling the virtues of using barbless hooks when I could and would like to think I have helped influence the growing number of fishermen that have switched to them. There is little doubt that the numbers are now rapidly increasing, and most admit they are only sorry they did not change over years ago.

It is most encouraging to note that today, apart from fly fishermen, many coarse anglers have also changed to barbless hooks – particularly match fishermen, although in their case they may have an ulterior motive. In matches speed is of the essence, and it was eventually realized a hook without a barb could be removed in a fraction of the time that it took to remove one with a barb. Whatever the reason I am only too delighted that this change has taken place.

I remember only too well many years ago when I used to do a lot of coarse fishing, I used to be shocked at the condition of most roach or dace I caught in rivers that were popular match venues. Mouths

Dressed on a barbless hook, to free the fish takes only a moment

that were ripped and cut, others raw with fungus growing and some with missing lips that had been ripped off by the match fisherman in his haste to remove the hook. Surely these facts alone must be the biggest indictment against the use of barbed hooks, as no matter how carefully a barbed hooked is removed some damage is inevitable, leaving a wound that will in most cases attract some form of infection. I understand that since the introduction of barbless hooks in match fishing circles the condition of fish in match venues has vastly improved. If you doubt the damage a barb does to the mouth of a fish I suggest the next time you remove one you examine the exit point carefully. I am sure then if you are conservation minded you will seriously consider changing.

On trout fishing waters where the rules do not permit the return of fish the change to barbless hooks may seem somewhat frivolous, but in fact nothing could be further from the truth. It is now rapidly becoming accepted that far fewer fish are likely to be lost when using a barbless hook. As I have pointed out many times, unless it hits bone a barbless hook will always penetrate up to the bend, unlike a hook with a barb, where the barb itself will often prevent penetration. When this happens three things are likely to happen: either the hook will become dislodged; it will (if a little soft) open at the bend; or if over-tempered, or if the barb has been cut too deeply, it will break off at the point. These three hazards which result in the loss of a lot of fish are more or less eliminated when using barbless hooks. Furthermore, contrary to popular belief a barbless hook definitely does not fall out when a fish jumps or is given a lot of slack line.

On those waters where it is desirable to return undersize fish or where catch and release is not frowned upon, trout can be easily and quickly released without removing them from the water. This factor alone is of great importance as the removal of a fish from its natural environment together with possible rough handling can often be injurious.

Barbless hooks are now widely used by fly fishermen in the USA and many different patterns of barbless trout hooks are available to them. Unfortunately at the moment they do not seem to be generally available over here, although it is possible now to order specially a limited selection from Partridge of Redditch and possibly one or two other manufacturers. However the fact that barbless hooks may be difficult to locate at the moment should not deter anglers as the barb on standard hooks can be simply and quickly flattened, with a small pair of flat-nosed model-makers' pliers. I normally do this after I have tied the fly onto the leader and it only takes a couple of seconds.

In the USA over the past decade or so considerable scientific research has been commissioned into various aspects of trout behaviour, including specific research into the use of barbless hooks. Initial research seemed to indicate that barbed hooks were less damaging to trout than barbless ones. However, further research seems to have proved otherwise as now on many catch and release fisheries in the States I understand you are not allowed to use a hook with a barb on it. American State Fishery Departments are now very conservation minded and I am therefore absolutely certain that they would not have introduced such a rule without being certain it was in the best interests of the trout.

In view of the above it is very sad to note that in a recent article in another fishing journal one of our leading big trout experts stated that in his opinion barbless hooks were actually harmful. The main point of the case he put forward was that a hook without a barb will penerate far deeper – down into the area where some nerve endings exist thereby causing more pain to the trout and possible infection when it pierces the true flesh. First of all I should like to know if this is just a theory or if it is based on scientific facts. If the latter I should like to know what his references were. In any case I find it very difficult to accept that the small hooks used by fly fishers in most catch and release situations could possibly cause such effects. Perhaps the author of this article only uses very large hooks. If this is the case then this may add a little plausibility to his opinion as the distance from the point to the bend on a hook size 8 or larger is quite considerable.

The Mayfly – A New Appraisal 1982

More has probably been written about the Mayfly than all the other species of upwinged flies put together. This is no doubt due to its large size, combined with the tremendous hatches which often occur during the Mayfly period and provide us with such exciting fishing on many of our rivers at this time. In view of this it would seem unlikely there are any new facts or secrets appertaining to its life-cycle (and consequent effects on our fishing) left to be discovered. I was therefore pleasantly surprised to find what appear to be a few interesting new facets, which came to light as a result of further research I carried out during the past two seasons. Before proceeding I should like to make it clear that this research has been confined to *Ephemera danica*, our most common species, so any conclusions I have drawn must be confined to this species only.

Ever since the first concoction of fur and feather was cast upon the water to imitate these large ephemerids, fishermen have speculated whether the life-cycle lasts one or two years. In the past arguments on this topic have waged fast and furious, but in recent years general opinion seems to have favoured a two-year cycle. Now just when it appeared the dust was settling, one of our most eminent authorities on fishing matters, namely Richard Walker, recently wrote in a fishing magazine that he was now of the opinion the cycle was yearly. His assumptions in this instance are apparently based on the fact that he observed Mayflies hatching out on a new lake that had only been excavated and filled with water the previous year. Although I am loath to query his conclusions, I feel I must, because I would require more positive and scientific evidence than this, as I think their apparent presence could be accounted for in many ways. Personally, I am now convinced beyond reasonable doubt that they have a two-year cycle, since last season I took many samples of silt from the riverbed

1 Male Mayfly dun (note the claspers under the penultimate body segment). The dun's wings are dull

2 A Mayfly dun caught in the act of transformation into a spinner

3 Here the transformation is complete with the bright, gauzy wings and beautiful body colours.
The cast-off skin or exuvia remains behind

4 Caught in the act! A pair of Mayflies are mating, the smaller male clinging to the female's tail with its clasper. A second male waits hopefully

in various sites containing the nymphs of the Mayfly. This was during late May at the peak of the hatch, and practically without exception the samples showed either large mature nymphs over an inch in length or small immature nymphs between 8 and 12mm in length. There were sufficient numbers of each to assume they were the result of two separate generations.

It was obvious that while the larger specimens were almost ready to hatch, the small ones could not possibly reach maturity until the following season. To check these findings I took samples also in November, and in this case specimens again in two groups were very tiny (less than 6mm) or of a medium size (over 15mm), which certainly seems to confirm beyond any reasonable doubt a life-cycle spanning at least two seasons.

The second interesting aspect that came to light concerns the imago (spinners). Now, I am sure most flyfishers, like myself, have always been rather puzzled over the inconsistency of spinner falls during the Mayfly fortnight. Some evenings, despite the tremendous swarms of male spinners along the banks, few spent females are to be observed floating along the surface, and consequently the evening rise is either sparse or absent. Conversely at other times, even when the swarms of males are small or insignificant, one often finds a steady trickle of dying females floating with the current, and reasonable sport is assured. On those frustrating evenings when nothing happens and the huge swarms of spinners eventually disappear, I always assumed (I think in common with most anglers) that the conditions were not conducive to mating and that they had all returned to the herbage till the next day. At first I assumed that if they did not mate in the evening, maybe they did so early the following morning, but despite being on the water soon after dawn on many such occasions there was seldom a significant spinner fall. The other assumption was that as the maximum life-span of the imago was thought to be about 48 hours, if they did not mate one evening they would have to do so the following evening, but as this did not always occur I realized that I would have to look for another answer to this intriguing problem.

After detailed experimentation, it soon became apparent that the life of the imago, particularly the males, was much longer than is generally supposed, and seemed to be days rather than hours. The other significant factor was the distinct predominance of males in most hatches. Adding these two factors together the answer quickly emerged, and certainly my consequent observations seem to confirm this.

Due to the predominance of males, and their ability to live for many days, there is a steady build-up of those unable to find a mate. Consequently, in the early evenings, when the weather permits, the huge swarms so often to be observed are composed entirely of males dancing in anticipation of arriving females. If they fail to materialize, the males will eventually return to the herbage till another day. As it takes approximately 24 hours for the freshly hatched duns, including a proportion of females, to transform into spinners capable of reproduction, the availability of these on any one day will depend entirely on the density of the hatch on the previous day.

In future, if you wish to anticipate a heavy spinner fall (weather, of course, permitting, as this can still affect mating) endeavour to be at the waterside the second evening after a heavy hatch of the duns. If this information is not available I have discovered an alternative which seems to be pretty reliable. Assuming one is fishing for the day, sometime during the late morning spend a few minutes examining the grasses or bushes. If they are liberally covered with Mayflies look for male *and* female spinners: if there is a fair proportion of females then you may anticipate a good spinner fall that evening, weather permitting.

Finally, as a direct result of underwater observations, I have noticed that the bodies of freshly hatched Mayfly duns floating along on the surface protrude into the film and can therefore be clearly seen by the trout in the mirror of the undersurface long before they reach the fish's window. This only applies to the relatively large and heavy Mayflies, as the smaller and lighter upwinged flies seem able to support the weight of their bodies on their legs above the film. This fact must have a direct bearing on the artificial Mayfly patterns we use, and indeed, since I have noticed this I have taken particular care to observe the effectiveness or otherwise of different patterns. Without doubt this confirms that those patterns that sit up and cock well on the surface, with their bodies clear of the surface, are less effective than those that are partly submerged. This would seem to account for the killing properties of such artificials as Barrat's Shaving Brush or the even more famous Grey Wulff.

The Killing Must Stop 1985

During recent visits to North America I have been surprised at the rapid growth of 'no-kill fisheries', as they are often called in the States. In many areas such fisheries are now more popular than stretches on which no catch-limits exist. It is a little difficult to understand why they have become so popular, but from my conversations with anglers over there, it seems it is partly due to the fact that most American anglers are more conservation-minded than we are, and because most catch-and-release stretches hold a heavier head of trout, including many larger specimens commonly referred to as 'lunkers'.

Over the last half-century many new products and trends from the USA have eventually become popular over here. Is this likely to happen with catch-and-release? Opinion among trout fishermen seems very divided. A few fishery-owners have experimented with catch-and-release fishing, and while some are still operating such fisheries, others have given up.

Why should there be such a division of opinion, and why are so many fishery-owners and managers reluctant to give it serious consideration? The main reason is probably that little or no scientific research has been carried out over here and so little positive information is available. However, considerable research has been done in the USA, and it is due largely to the favourable results of such scientific studies that this form of fishing is now so popular and widespread in North America.

From my own research in the UK, it seems that most fishery owners are opposed for two main reasons: first, that a large percentage of trout will die after being hooked and returned; second, that trout after being hooked once or twice will become impossible to catch.

Both research and practical fishing experiments in the States seem to prove beyond doubt that these fears are groundless. The weight of research over the past 20 years shows that less than 6 percent of trout returned die as a result of being hooked on a single-hook fly. Likewise, research over the same period shows that trout do not become too difficult to catch as a result of constant hooking. In one experiment, several tagged fish were caught four or five times in a controlled period. In another study, on one stretch of the Yellowstone River in Montana, it was established that most trout are caught and returned at least five times in each 12-month period.

The success of catch-and-release in the States can be gauged from the results achieved in the Yellowstone National Park. Records kept by the park authorities show that more anglers are now fishing than ever before, and it has now become one of the most popular venues for fly-fishermen in America. The park covers several hundred square miles and contains a host of rivers, ponds and lakes, and although only a small proportion of this water is catch-and-release, more than 90 per cent of all trout caught in the park are now being returned. Records show also that on the non-kill stretch of the Yellowstone River, the angling pressure is extremely heavy, coping with nearly 4,000 angler days per mile of river per season, which means approximately 20 fly-fishers per day on every mile of river throughout the season. Despite this pressure, the fishing is still excellent. The park authorities now seem to favour the use of barbless hooks, while they are also against the use of landing-nets as they feel physical damage to the trout from struggling in the net can result in increased mortality.

I am now in favour of catch-and-release over here on certain waters, provided that barbless hooks are obligatory and that no fish is handled or taken out of the water for the hook to be removed. This last is unnecessary with barbless hooks anyway. I would also suggest that on such waters fishermen should be advised that any trout deeply hooked in the gullet, gill arches or tongue should be immediately removed and killed, as any trout so hooked is most unlikely to survive.

Apart from all the research conducted in America on catch-and-release, other experiments have been carried out, and I am sure fishery managers and owners, as well as fly-fishers, will be interested to hear of one such experiment carried out on the Madison River from 1967 to 1971. This research was undertaken to show the effect of the stocking of catchable trout. The results are most interesting.

The study was conducted on the Varney section of the Madison and on the lower section of O'Dell Creek. During 1967 to 1969 the Varney section was stocked with catchable rainbows and the wild trout populations of brown trout and rainbows were estimated, as a result of tagging and netting, at 295 per mile. By the fall of 1971, after two years without stocking, the number of catchable trout to the mile had increased to 833, or by 180 per cent. In O'Dell Creek, where no stocking was done from 1963 to 1969, the average population of wild trout during the period was 354 per mile. By 1971, after two years of stocking catchable rainbows, the population decreased by 49 per cent, to 182 per mile.

This study shows that when hatchery-reared rainbow trout are added to self-sustaining wild trout populations, the wild trout decrease dramatically within the first two years after stocking starts.

Many years ago, when the River Test was stocked mainly with brown trout, there was also a thriving population of wild brown trout. Today, wild brown trout on the Test are a rarity. I had attributed this to increasing pollution, but perhaps it is due also to the present heavy stocking with large rainbows. This started several years ago, when it became inadvisable to stock with brown trout for fear of spreading UDN, which affected them but not rainbows.

CATCH & RELEASE FISHING AREA

A PORTION OF THE FRYINGPAN RIVER, FROM **RUEDI DAM DOWNSTREAM ALMOST 2 MILES** HAS BEEN DESIGNATED AS A 'CATCH AND RELEASE' FISHING AREA. ALL FISH CAUGHT IN THIS AREA MUST BE IMMEDIATELY RETURNED TO THE WATER. THE FRYINGPAN RIVER IS BEING EVALUATED AS A 'WILD TROUT' STREAM TO OBTAIN INFORMATION FOR THE FUTURE MANAGEMENT OF COLORADO'S FISHERIES. CONSEQUENTLY, NO ARTIFICIAL STOCKING IS DONE FROM RUEDI DAM TO THE ROARING FORK RIVER. FISHERMEN ARE ENCOURAGED TO NOTIFY THE DIVISION OF WILDLIFE OF TAGGED TROUT AND NUMBERS OF FISH CAUGHT AND RELEASED IN THIS AREA, USING THE REPORT FORM BELOW.

Could such signs ever be seen in Britain?

The American studies seem to indicate that it might be possible to preserve good brown trout fishing on many of our rivers without the need to stock them, particularly if catch-and-release rules were adopted. Fisheries would be much cheaper to run without the cost of stocking, and part of the saving could be passed on to the fly-fisher fishing the water. I have a suspicion that the first fishery-owner to offer such a deal would not suffer from lack of applicants. On the other hand, many owners may feel it is too bold a step to take initially. If so, a compromise could be offered in the form of reduced stocking with a brace or less per visit to be taken, and thereafter catch-and-release.

Another alternative to stocking rivers with mature fish is to stock heavily with fingerlings, or even yearlings, each season to supplement the stocks of wild trout. This is a longer-term plan as it will be two, possibly three, seasons before the survivors of the initial stocking attain a worthwhile size. In this period it will be necessary either to restrict fishing severely or to allow catch-and-release only. Each angler could be restricted to, say, one trout per day, and catch-and-release could be encouraged.

I know of one stretch of river in this country where this policy has been successfully adopted. It was implemented about eight years ago, and now the syndicate that runs the fishery has a superb wild-trout fishery producing a reasonable number of trout in excess of 3 lb each season. There are no rules, and although catch-and-release with barbless hooks is encouraged, the rods are at liberty to kill the occasional brace for the table, and everyone is happy. This is as it should be. I deplore the present approach to trout fishing in this country where the current disease of 'limititus' is unfortunately encouraged by many of our angling writers.

Twenty-twenty Vision? 1987

This is a subject that has fascinated me for many years as our knowledge of how a fish sees and what he sees is sketchy to say the least. While we may make educated guesses, one thing no one can say is how the brain of a fish interprets the message transmitted from the eyes. However, when it comes to *how* a fish sees we should be able to make some pretty accurate assessments, by combining known scientific facts with carefully controlled experiments and/or observations.

During the late 1970s when Brian Clarke and I were working on our book *The Trout & The Fly*, we were both involved in a tremendous amount of research and also carried out a lot of most interesting experiments, many on various aspects of fish vision.

After publication of our book I decided personally to pursue some of these aspects further and, as a result, have now reached certain conclusions which I hope in the fullness of time will prove to be correct.

One of the most intriguing aspects of a trout's vision is the fish's ability to scan an arc of 160 degrees or more on each side of its body while at the same time being able also to observe objects immediately ahead with binocular vision where the arc of the eyes overlap.

Obviously this area of binocular vision must be very important, particularly to a brown trout that spends a large percentage of its time searching for food on or near the surface. Would it not therefore be interesting from a fishing point of view, I asked myself, to find out the precise area that was covered by the fish's binocular vision?

On referring to all the books in my library that cover the vision of fish, little seems to have been written about this aspect. The only reference, which most of them repeat, is that a trout has a narrow arc or band of binocular vision some 45 degrees dead ahead, where the arc of the eyes overlap.

Now it seemed strange to me that a trout which spends much of its time searching the undersurface or mirror overhead would only have binocular vision immediately ahead. I therefore decided to study the structure and position of the eye in the head of the trout. The first point I noticed – and one which seems to have escaped the attention of other researchers – was that not only do the eyes slope inward slightly towards the nose, but they also slope inward to the top of the head. In effect this means that not only does the arc of the eyes overlap immediately ahead but also over the top of the trout's head, so surely this should mean that the range of binocular vision would be very much more extensive than previously suspected?

To find out what area this covered I took a series of close-up photographs of the heads of many trout – both from directly in front and also from overhead. I then measured the angles of the arcs formed by the inward angles of the eyes in front and overhead. While it was not possible with the equipment available to me to measure these angles

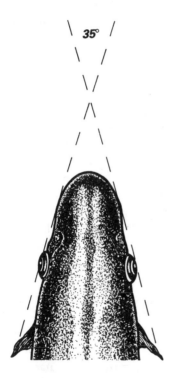

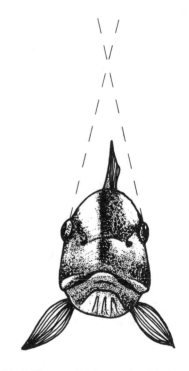

Fig. 5 The arc of vision immediately in front of a trout is 35 degrees and not, as commonly supposed, 45 degrees

Fig. 6 The arc of vision overhead is about 28 degrees

precisely, I am confident that they are probably accurate to within at least a few degrees.

To start with, I found that the arc immediately in front was about 35 degrees, and not, as previously supposed, 45 degrees (see fig. 5). The arc overhead was a little less and seemed to he about 28 degrees (see fig. 6). Due to the fact that the two arcs (or more probably elongated cones) of binocular vision appear to overlap considerably because of the two inwardly converging angles of the eyes, I assume that the overall area covered by binocular vision is about 125 degrees from in front to overhead. I also assume that the trout's binocular vision at each end of this arc would be less acute, and that its most acute vision would occur where the cones overlap – which would probably be at an angle between 35 to 40 degrees from the horizontal in front of the trout's head (see fig. 8).

From many hundreds of subsequent personal observations of trout in their feeding lies, I noticed that most trout seem to lie at a slight angle with their head up. This in effect means that this optimum angle of acute binocular vision is probably nearer to 45 degrees from the horizontal, which would enable the trout to observe not only the mirror above but also into the edge of its window. During the latter stages of my research into the above I once again contacted Professor W.R.A. Muntz in the department of biology at Stirling University. Professor Muntz is one of the world's leading authorities on fish vision and had been of considerable help to us when we were researching the fish-vision section of our book.

This time I asked him if he could provide some detailed information on the structure of a trout's eye with particular reference to its binocular vision and focusing ability. The information he provided was most interesting, as he was able to provide accurate details of how a trout moves the lens in its eye by means of a large retractor lentis muscle to adjust its focus. When at rest in the retina, the lens is so positioned that anything in front and overhead is in close focus, which to some degree seems to confirm my research. This lentis muscle when retracted moves the lens both inwards and towards the back of the retina in a straight line away from the nose, thereby providing focus to infinity directly in front and to some degree above.

As a matter of interest, during the vision research for our book we had established with the help of Professor Muntz that infinity occurred at about two feet. Having, I hope, established the approximate area of a trout's binocular vision I now wanted to establish, if possible, the width of water overhead and in front that this would cover. First of all we must take the two arcs first discussed: the one in front at 35 degrees and the one overhead at 28 degrees. A rough average would then be 32 degrees. This means that if the trout's eyes were focused at less than infinity he would be aware only of approaching food within a narrow arc no more than 13 inches wide at most. Even with its eyes focused to infinity and concentrating on approaching food within its area of binocular vision, the band of water above and in front covered would be less than 30 inches wide at the maximum distance, even in clear water.

Seldom is one able to confirm theories by practical tests or observations in the field, but early last season I was most fortunate to find a co-operative trout in a perfect lie in such a position that, with dense cover behind and partly over me, I was able to lower a dry-fly from directly above him and place it very accurately on the water a few feet in front of the spot where he was rising. To start with I was drifting the fly down to him at predetermined distances to each side, and by this method I quickly established that my theory seemed reasonably accurate, as with the trout lying only about 12 inches below the surface he completely ignored my fly if it were more than 18 inches to either side of his lie. I was about to retire and leave the trout in peace when to my astonishment he broke through the surface in the most perfect arc and took my fly in the air as it was hanging about 15 inches above the surface and about 20 inches upstream of his lie.

Now the only way he could have seen this fly in the air was over the edge and in front of his window, and as I was reasonably sure that he had not tilted upwards before jumping I realized that if I could persuade him to jump and accept the fly a few more times I might

Fig. 7 Eye seen from above with the nostril to the right In 'A' the lens remains equidistant from the retina at all times to give vision focused to infinity over almost 180 degrees. In 'B' with the lens extended and at rest, everything in front over an arc of about 125 degrees is in close focus, while about 45 degrees to the rear is still at infinity. With the lens retracted for forward infinity vision it appears that the trout's arc of binocular vision immediately ahead would be far less than 35 degrees.

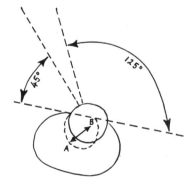

also be able to prove, or disprove, my first theory that they may indeed have cones of binocular vision to some extent overhead as well as in front. Never have I met such a co-operative trout as during the next 15 minutes or so as I persuaded him to launch himself into the air 17 times!

His reactions were absolutely fascinating as each time I lowered the fly and swung it down towards him I was in no doubt at all as to whether he had seen it. When he did, all his fins – particularly his tail – would start vibrating, and these vibrations would increase in intensity as I swung the fly closer until it was in range of his lie, when he would jump and try to take it in mid-air. I quickly established that he would first see the fly in the air if I swung it to within three or four feet directly upstream of his lie. Now of course what I wished to establish was whether or not the trout was observing this fly over the edge of his window through his ordinary vision, or through his binocular vision.

If my theory were to be confirmed, he would be unaware of the fly if I positioned it in the air between three to four feet upstream and more than 18 inches off-centre, and so it proved to be. If I swung the fly down to him anywhere near that centre-line he would see it every time, but I could swing it down right past him repeatedly if it were more than about two feet off-centre and not once did he seem to be aware of it.

Now what conclusions can we draw from the above – and how will this help the fly-fisher improve his chances of success? 1: A trout lying and feeding within, say, 18 inches or so of the surface will probably be concentrating through his binocular vision and therefore the approaching fly-fisher would probably not register unless he made any sudden movements. 2: A trout lying very close to the surface will probably be focused below infinity so any approaching objects, including the fly-fisher, will be even less likely to be seen. In both cases, however, accurate casting will be necessary, as the fish is unlikely to be aware of any fly drifting down to him either on or below the surface either side of his narrow arc of binocular vision. In view of this I am now beginning to wonder whether this may explain our difficulty in tempting trout during those infuriating evening rises on stillwater when every trout in the lake seems to be rising and yet any pattern we offer is ignored. At this time the trout are usually cruising along almost in the surface so would be unlikely to see any fly less than about 24 inches immediately in front or 12 inches on either side of them. Maybe during this evening rise we would increase our chances if we fished our team of flies much closer together. I certainly intend to try this during the coming season.

Finally, what about those trout that are lying and feeding at a much deeper level? All the angling books that contain a section on trout vision tell us that the deeper a trout is lying the further off he can see the angler as of course the deeper he lies the larger his window overhead.

While this is certainly true, the additional distance he will be able to see is at best marginal, so I am now inclined to think that the more likely explanation for his increased awareness of our presence is due to the fact that at this depth he is unlikely to be concentrating through his binocular vision so everything on each side of his head within the whole 180-degree arc of his vision will be clearly seen. This also means that when presenting a fly to such a trout even more care will have to be taken with your approach but at the same time accurate presentation of your fly will not be crucial as the fish will be aware of approaching food over a much wider area.

In conclusion, I would add that the detailed information provided to me by Professor Muntz on the structure of a trout's eye and exactly how he moves his lens to provide his focusing ability has thrown up a most interesting new fact. The lentis muscle is apparently so positioned that when it contracts to provide the necessary focusing adjustment to the lens, it moves in at such an angle that it leaves the front section of the lens equidistant at all times from the front section of the retina. This means that even when a trout is focusing at very short range on food immediately ahead of it, an arc of about 45 degrees on each side and to the rear of the fish is still focused to infinity.

This would indicate that a trout feeding very close to the surface and focused at short range would be less likely to see you if you were either opposite him or even slightly upstream, rather than well downstream, where you would come within the range of this 45-degree arc at his rear.

In confirmation of this point I am sure everyone has experienced evenings on a river when there has been a heavy fall of spinner and the trout are all lying so close to the surface that their dorsal fins are often protruding. During this period you can often approach a trout so closely that you are almost casting down on to him and yet more often than not he appears to be completely oblivious of your presence.

This season when the opportunity arises, try positioning yourself opposite or even slightly upstream of any trout rising very close to the surface and cast to him from this position as I think he will be less likely to see you, but do remember to avoid any sudden movements and where possible cast sideways with a wrist movement to avoid moving your arms.

Finally one other most interesting aspect of a trout's vision, which I do not think anyone has seriously considered, is whether a trout is able to focus one eye independently of the other. This is extremely difficult to prove or disprove but, while I think it is quite likely, I don't think that this facility would be of very great value to a trout, as most of the time when he is focusing on close-up objects he is utilizing his binocular vision, when both lenses would have to be focused together. As I have already suggested, it would appear that his vision on each side and to the rear is permanently adjusted to infinity so this would leave only a relatively narrow arc towards the front on each side where he could use such a facility – and I really cannot visualize many circumstances in which this would be required.

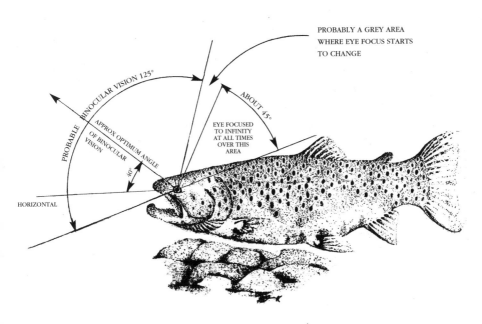

Fig. 8

Secrets of the Midge 1988

During the past two or three decades midge fishing (this now seems be the universally accepted term for fishing extremely small dry-flies, no matter what order of insects they actually represent) has become very popular in the United States. In some areas dry-flies in sizes 20 and upwards are considered the norm, and it is now possible to purchase an incredible range of different patterns of very tiny dry-flies ranging from size 20 to as small as a size 26.

These dry-flies now account for quite a large proportion of the trout caught in the States, and also take some very big fish as well. I have read many stories in the American fishing press of trout close to, and in some cases over, double figures being taken on them.

I have often wondered how the Americans are so proficient at this style of fishing when here it is, so far as I know, seldom if ever practised. In support of this I am sure that if a survey were carried out here, very few dry-fly boxes would contain any patterns smaller than size 18. I think the reason is because few, if any, of our dry-fly fishers have managed to perfect the technique.

Until last season I had never managed to crack the secret of how to hook and land large trout on tiny flies, though this was not for want of trying. I remember trying to catch trout on the Itchen over 20 years ago on a new American pattern called a 'Jassid' that was all the rage, but with little success. It was tied on a size 20 hook and required a very fine tippet to fish it correctly. The trout accepted this fly readily, but I found it difficult to set the hook, and on the few occasions that I succeeded I found I could not keep the trout out of the heavy chalk-stream weed with a 6x leader.

However, I persevered with tiny patterns. I was prepared to lose a few trout if only I could succeed in setting the hook. I tried striking quickly, and then slowly, and even saying the Lord's Prayer before striking, but with little success. Of those few trout that I did manage to hook I landed only a few of the smallest ones, so until the beginning of last season I doubted the accuracy of reports of the success our American cousins were enjoying with these very tiny flies.

I have visited and fished various areas in the United States, but until last season never for long enough to observe closely this method of fishing. In September last year I spent five glorious weeks fishing in Montana, Idaho and Wyoming. These states, particularly Montana, undoubtedly offer some of the best fishing in the whole of America, and the variety of water available is quite incredible. Large majestic rivers, like the Yellowstone and Big Hole, flow through awesome canyons, while fast boulder-strewn rivers, such as the Madison, meander across open plains, and such rivers as the Firehole and Snake River are known to fly-fishers all over the world. The Railroad Ranch stretch of the latter river is gin clear, full of trailing weed and is one of the few larger rivers in the United States that closely approximates to our own beloved chalkstreams. There are also many ponds, as well as large lakes, such as Lake Hebden, that hold some extremely large trout.

As can be imagined, with this variety of clear and largely unpolluted water, hatches of aquatic insects are often on a grand scale. In late May, June or early July many rivers produce incredible hatches of large upwinged flies similar to our Mayflies, as well as a species of stonefly that is called a salmon fly and is over two inches long.

As the summer progresses, hatches of extremely small species of upwinged flies – smuts and midges – proliferate, accounting for the preoccupation shown by many American dry-fly fishers with fishing tiny patterns.

In Montana there are a few lovely spring creeks like miniature chalkstreams, full of lush weed. On one of these I discovered the secrets of successful midge-fishing. My host at the time was one Herbert Wellington, an extremely competent dry-fly fisherman and recognized expert in the delicate art of midge-fishing.

During the morning we had been fishing the water with fairly small Sedge patterns and had caught the odd trout when at about midday there was a phenomenal hatch of upwinged flies so tiny I could not believe my eyes. They were a species of blue-winged olive and were even smaller than our caenis – the smallest of our upwinged flies.

My host called me over and insisted on presenting me with half-a-dozen tiny artificials. They were perfect representations, and had been dressed on size 22 hooks by Craig Matthews of Blue Ribbon flies, one of the best fly-tyers in the area. Within the next hour my host caught and released five lovely plump wild trout, while I failed to set the hook in a single fish. By this time, as you can imagine, I was feeling very frustrated, so I decided to seek my host's advice.

He asked to look at my fly, and then the revelation came. The answer was so simple I could not believe I had not thought of it years ago. After he has tied his fly on to his leader he takes a pair of fine-nosed pliers and offsets the hook. This simple operation increases your capability of setting these tiny hooks by at least 75 per cent. Within the next two hours, before the hatch petered out, I caught and released four nice trout and also hooked a big fish, which I estimated at over 6 lb, which eventually broke the 6x tippet.

Over dinner that evening I broached the question of how to land large trout on tiny flies and leaders as fine as 6x or even 7x. Then came the second revelation. Retrieving his reel from his fishing bag Herbert showed me where he had connected an eight-inch length of power-gum into his leader. It was tied in a little over halfway down, with triple-surgeons' knots.

He told me he had begun experimenting with this power-gum about five years ago. Up to this time he had rarely succeeded in landing any of the larger trout that frequented the creek. Since then he has caught and released many huge trout, including four well into double figures.

In the early days he experimented with this power-gum in many different positions on the leader, but finally settled on the following formula. He now uses a 7 ft Sue Burgess Airflo intermediate-tapered braid-leader and attaches to the end of this 6 in of 1x nylon, then 8 in of power-gum, followed by a further 6 in of 1x nylon, then 6 in of 3x and 6 in of 5x. This is followed With a 6x or 7x tippet of the desired length. He advises that the knots used to connect the power-gum to the nylon be treated with Pliobond adhesive, or similar, to safeguard them against slipping.

That evening I made up such a leader under his instruction and used this very successfully for the rest of my time in the States. Initially I suspected that the presentation of the fly with this power-gum built in to the leader would be very poor, as it would probably prevent a smooth and even turnover. However, in practice, probably due to its proximity to the braided section of the leader, it was quite satisfactory, though I did find presentation when casting into a strong breeze not too good.

The use of this power-gum in leaders is, of course, not new, for I believe salmon-fishers have been using it for some time now. I have not heard of its use before in connection with dry-fly fishing, however, though apparently quite by coincidence my good friend Brian Clarke has started to experiment with it and has been very impressed with its performance.

An Eye on the Fly Down Under 1988

One of the attractions of fishing for trout in New Zealand waters is that in most rivers, and even lakes, the fly-fisher relies on sighting fish before he casts to them. However, this is not always possible. Many of the streams flowing into Lake Taupo, for example, are far too fast and roilly for this technique to be practised. This is particularly true of the legendary Tongariro, which flows into the lake at its south end, near the town of Turangi. In addition to its boisterous nature, its water is also deep-green.

For this reason, until the late '60s the only method employed was wet fly fished across-and-down with a fast-sinking line. Earlier, traditional English salmon-fly patterns had been used, but gradually these were replaced with streamer flies developed in New Zealand especially for the conditions on local rivers. Today many of the streamer patterns used on the Tongariro are dressed to represent tiny silver fish called smelt, the main source of food for trout in the lake. Traditional wet-fly fishing is still popular with the older generation of fly-fishers, but the method is now used mainly on the lower, slower-flowing sections of the rivers.

In the last 20 years, at least on the faster middle and upper reaches, the heavily-weighted upstream nymph on a floating line has gradually taken over, but effective though this method is, it was soon realized that a lot of takes were being missed in the fast water. Many of the new breed of nymph fishermen started to experiment with various devices to improve the visibility of the butt-end of the leader, and then about six years ago a party of visiting American anglers were seen to be using big bunches of brightly-coloured wool on their leaders to indicate takes.

This method had been developed in the United States for fishing on many of their fast rivers, being generally referred to as 'indicator fishing'. It quickly became the accepted method in New Zealand, too, although it was not long before the Tongariro fly-fishers improved on the original concept and refined it to their own particular needs.

While strands of wool or a bunch of wool secured to the leader are still used by many fishers, the current vogue is to secure a small, round float at the end of the fly-line, and to use with this much heavier indicator two nymphs, one of them a large heavily-weighted nymph called a Bug Eye. Tied on to the bend of this large nymph is a piece of nylon between eight and fifteen inches long, on to which is tied a relatively small Pheasant Tail or similar nymph. This method was certainly an eye-opener for me. I had never seen it practised before and it was some little time before I mastered it.

A forward-taper fly-line is essential with this type of rig, and I found a weight-forward 8 or, better still, a bug-taper line ideal. It is also essential to extend the back-cast fully, otherwise the forward cast will put indicator and nymphs in an untidy heap. The ideal cast is upstream and slightly across into any likely pockets or runs, with the line being mended to keep contact with the nymphs as they drift down. Best results come when the large, weighted nymph is bumping bottom, and to achieve this in this really fast water it is necessary to have the distance between the indicator and the large nymph about twice the depth of the water being fished.

I soon realized that is is difficult to get the nymphs down to the bottom quickly in really fast water, but I achieved the desired result by checking my fly-line sharply when it was fully extended on the final forward cast. This caused the heavy nymph to backlash so that it fell fairly close to the indicator and then sank quickly before drag took effect.

 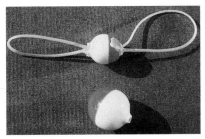

Left: A V-shaped wool indicator fastened to a leader; and a new clip-on wool indicator
Right: Two sizes of plastic-float indicator, one complete with securing loops

Norman Marsh's Blue Darter

A heavily-weighted Bug Eye

Craig's Night-time

The Glo-nymph

I found, too, that provided I mended my line sufficiently, I could fish my nymph for a considerable distance downstream as well as upstream. While most of the takes did occur upstream, I picked up quite a few nice trout down below, usually just as the nymph started to lift off the bottom. I also found that a firm strike was necessary to set the hook, particularly if I was fishing a long line.

I have never heard of anyone in this country fishing with indicators, but I am sure the method would prove effective on many of our faster, stony rivers. I have also found that fishing with an indicator and a single large nymph is effective on stillwater during the day, when the trout are often cruising at midwater looking for food.

The small, round indicator floats with central holes are made from brightly-coloured plastic, and in New Zealand they are available from most tackle-shops in two sizes, ⅜ inch and ½ inch. They have loops of braided line at each end so that they can be quickly linked between the end-loop of the fly-line and butt of the leader. But while they are efficient, I felt a little unhappy about using them, so I fished with a wool indicator for most of the time.

Bright crimson and yellow wool cut into strands about an inch long seemed to give maximum visibility under most light conditions, and these two inch-long strands secured into the butt of my leader with a double loop. I made one loop, then another, and pushed this up through the first loop, with the strands of wool then pushed under this second loop, the tightened leader then trapping the two strands.

When this is done correctly the wool strands are formed into a V-shape, with yellow and red on each side. They can then be trimmed if necessary. A wool indicator should only be large enough to be seen clearly, its size depending on the roughness of the water being fished. A soaking in 'Permafloat' will keep it buoyant.

Just before I left New Zealand, I was shown an alternative method of attaching a wool indicator which I shall certainly try. This made use of one of those tiny spring clips used to attach a lure to a swivel. If one of these is separated from the swivel, and some wool whipped round the bend, it can be clipped on to the loop at the end of the fly-line. The advantage is that several of these clips can be carried with different amounts of wool on each, to be quickly interchanged according to the type of water being fished.

Most indicator fishermen on the Tongariro seem to favour the Bug Eye pattern. This is dressed on a heavily-weighted wide-gape, down-eyed hook size 10 or even 8 and has two large silver eyes or balls tied on to the top of the shank immediately behind the eye. These are cut in pairs from chrome sink-plug chain which can be purchased in different sizes from most ironmongers.

It is an ugly-looking pattern, but it is simple to dress as the body and tails are formed from three or four strands of peacock herl. I used it extensively and caught as many trout on it as on the small nymph tied to its bend and swimming behind.

Most natural nymphs in New Zealand are dark-coloured, so it is not surprising that the ubiquitious Pheasant Tail Nymph is popular. The Hare and Copper is also widely used, but I found the most effective pattern of all was a relative newcomer developed by well-known New Zealand fishing author, Norman Marsh.

This is called a Blue Darter, and it can be dressed weighted or unweighted. The short tails are formed from a small bunch of the slightly longer fur found on a rabbit. The body is dubbed with buff-coloured seal's fur with fine gold wire, while the thorax is formed from dubbed black rabbit fur picked out on each side. The wing-cases are of a dark, shiny blue wing-feather from a New Zealand bird called the pukeka, but I shall soon have to look for a substitute.

Another fairly new pattern called a Glo-nymph is now becoming popular, at least on the Tongariro. This could prove effective over here, too. I like the look of it, and it is simple to dress. Lead-wire is wound around the shank of a long-shank, down-eyed hook, size 10 or 12, with a thorax formed with it behind the eye. Over this are wound four or five strands Of peacock herl up to the eye, with the tips extended to form the tails. It is then necessary only to tie-in a wing-case from a length of fluorescent orange wool.

I liked the look of several New Zealand lake patterns, but the one that impressed me most was a lure or attractor pattern called Craig's Night-time. I took some nice trout on this fly at dusk or after dark from Taupo, and it is probably the most popular Taupo pattern for night-fishing. It could well be a killing pattern on stillwater over here, either early in the season or later in the summer at dusk. This is the dressing:

Body: Black wool or chenille ribbed with silver tinsel.
Tag: Red wool.
Wing: Dark-blue pukeka breast-feather, tied in over the top of the body.
Hackle: Hen dyed yellow.

As a substitute for the pukeka, I suggest a breast feather from a coot or moorhen.

A lovely wild rainbow from the Tongariro River

142

A Fresh View of Summer Grayling 1992

For more years than I care to remember, towards the end of each trout season I have looked forward with keen anticipation to the coming autumn grayling fishing. Much as I love my grayling fishing, I have always concentrated on trout during the summer, casting to grayling only when my intended quarry have been in unco-operative mood. But come October, after a long, hot summer, to make a sortie for just a few hours on a bright crisp autumn day comes almost as a relief. This year, however, my attitude towards summer grayling fishing has undergone a drastic change, due mainly to my gaining access to some 'new' fishing water.

Living in the South of England, I have been privileged to fish at one time or another on most beats of all the major chalkstreams, but while grayling proliferate in all of them, their average size tends to be less than 1 lb. The main reason for this is that, unfortunately, many trout fishermen do not want them in the water, and each winter grayling are electro-fished or netted, together with unwanted coarse fish. Nevertheless, some of the chalkstreams, and particularly the Test, have a reputation for producing huge grayling, although on most beats they are few and far between and usually fish which live in deep holes and have escaped the nets.

Imagine my delight, then, when at the beginning of this last season I was fortunate to acquire a beat on the upper Test and found that the river was full of really big grayling. Chatting to the keeper, I soon realized the reason, for he is one of the few keepers I have met who believes in letting nature take its course. In the 20 years he had been keeper on the beat, he had never netted it. Despite this, the trout fishing was excellent and I caught a higher percentage of truly wild trout there than anywhere else I have fished on the Test. Other river-keepers, please note.

As usual, I concentrated at first on the trout, but I soon realized that, with so many large grayling in the water, I was missing a golden opportunity. By mid-season I had started grayling fishing in earnest, but while I caught some super fish, they were much more difficult to catch than the trout. Mind you, this didn't surprise me, because I have always found grayling much more difficult to catch in summer than in winter. I am not sure why this should be so, but in summer, once one or two fish are caught from a shoal, they seem to stop feeding, whereas in winter a larger percentage of a shoal can be caught before the remainder disperse. This may be due to the shorter day in the winter, with hatches of insects concentrated during the middle of the day.

By the end of July I found I was concentrating on the grayling almost to the exclusion of the trout – and thoroughly enjoying it. By now I had caught many fish of 1½ lb–2 lb and one superb specimen of 2 lb 5 oz, but I was still unable to catch them consistently. Mind you, we had more than our share of sunshine during July and August, and every time I went fishing it blazed down from a cloudless sky, making approaching the shoals of grayling without spooking them very difficult. Most of the time a shoal would disperse in panic as soon as the leader hit the water.

While many shoals of big grayling were in the main river, the carriers held even larger shoals of bigger fish, and these provided even more challenging fishing. The carriers were shallower and contained a lot more of the blanket weed which has been an increasing problem on most chalkstreams during the past four hot summers.

Fortunately, nymphs are allowed on this particular stretch of the Test from 1 August, so I was then able to vary my tactics. The grayling were still spooky as the sun still blazed down from a cloudless sky on my one day a week, even through most of September, but I did have two red-letter days when a little hazy cloud came over on two mornings. On the morning I was fishing alone on one of the shallow carriers, and on one particular stretch, less than 100 yards long but slightly deeper round a large bend, I landed more than 30 grayling with an

The PVC Nymph   The Gerroff

A lovely spring creek, South
Island, New Zealand

The Snake River, Jackson Hole,
Idaho

The Lochy River, South Island, New Zealand

The author landing a double-figure
brown trout, Lake Waikaremoana,
New Zealand

A crystal clear New Zealand
wilderness river

A lovely pool on the Mohaka River, North Island, New Zealand

Bernard Cribbins lands a nice trout
on the River Dever

The author with 5½ lb record size
Brook trout from the River Test

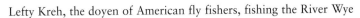

Lefty Kreh, the doyen of American fly fishers, fishing the River Wye

A difficult cast under trees on the River Kennet

Low water in late summer on the River Kennet

A pretty side stream on the lower River Test

Ron Clark plays a lively trout on the River Kennet

A big rainbow trout in crystal clear New Zealand stream

An impressive pool at the top of the Waimarino River, New Zealand

Herbert Wellington fishing at sunset on Odell spring creek, Montana

Gary Borger nets a fine trout on Du Puy's spring creek, Montana

All the famous fly fishing personalities below are friends of the author and feature in the text

The late Cliff Henry

The late Dermot Wilson

Brian Clarke

The late Charles Fox

Preben Torp Jacobsen

Peter Lapsley

Gary Borger

Bernard Cribbins

Charles Jardine

Tom Saville

The late Major Oliver Kite

Lefty Kreh

average size of more than 1½ lb. The smallest fish were more than I lb, and the bag included five of more than 2 lb, with the largest superb specimen nearly 2½ lb. At least half of these were caught on the nymph, but as midday approached and a reasonable hatch of small olives developed, so I changed to dry fly. To my delight, two of the larger grayling were taken on dry fly. This was, without question, the finest morning's grayling fishing I have ever had.

Two weeks later I had my good friend Bernard Cribbins with me, as he has a rod on the stretch on the same day. As the morning was slightly overcast, I took him to the same spot. To my delight, the shoal was still there, and we decided to take turns in fishing. Bernard elected to fish with a nymph, so I mounted a dry fly, and between us, within two-and-a-half hours, we landed nearly 40 superb grayling. Again, none of the fish was less than 1 lb, and we took five of more than 2 lb, the heaviest a fine fish of 2½ lb falling to Bernard's rod. This gave him a tremendous thrill, as it was the biggest grayling he'd ever caught. Most of the fish were returned.

We estimated at least two of the fish in this large shoal to be close to, or more than, 3 lb, so for the remaining weeks of the season we both tried to catch one of these. It was eventually my good fortune to succeed, more by luck than judgment, on the very last day of the trout season.

The weather was again bright and sunny, and the grayling were definitely not feeding. For more than an hour I persevered with a dry fly, but not a single fish showed any interest. Eventually, in desperation, I changed to a nymph, but this, too, was ignored. After another hour I was on the point of giving up when one of the smaller fish at the rear of the shoal took my nymph, a little later I took another of about 1 lb, so I decided to persevere for a little longer.

Bernard Cribbins about to release a big grayling on the Upper Test

145

It was now time for lunch, but we decided to give it another five minutes. As usual, most of the larger fish were at the head of the shoal, but one of these must have decided on a change of scenery, as, Eureka! I suddenly had a thumping take as I was lifting the rod to re-cast. This fish was one of the 'biggies', a fantastic fish of 2 lb 14 oz, beating my previous best grayling by 4 oz.

Normally, I rarely use a leader much longer than 10 ft for river fishing, but with these grayling, and in the bright conditions, I had to keep on extending the length until eventually I was using a leader of more than 18 ft down to a 6x or even 7x tippet. I also had to use much smaller nymphs than usual, as, due to the confounded silk weed, I found that the normal sizes I use for grayling were useless. A size 14 weighted nymph or a traditional Grayling Bug would pick up weed at every cast, so I finally settled for one of my own lightly weighted PVC Nymphs dressed on a size 18 hook. Another old pattern of mine, developed many years ago for fishing, under similar conditions, was also successful – The Gerroff. This is a shrimp-like dressing taking up less than half the hook-shank to give a small silhouette and tied unweighted on a size 14 hook. Bernard had most success with either a small PVC Nymph or a size 16 Grayling Bug he has modified by adding a short, bright fluorescent tail.

The fish we took on dry fly were nearly all to just one American pattern called a Sparkle Dun. It was developed by Craig Matthew and John Juracek, of West Yellowstone, to represent an emerging pale morning dun, and quickly became established as an effective pattern in the States when any small duns were hatching. I tried them on our chalk-stream trout and found them killing indeed. However, I soon established that the grayling found the pattern even more acceptable, and since then it has replaced Terry's Terror as my favourite grayling pattern. While it is a simple pattern, tying-in the flared wings of deerhair is a little tricky.

Sparkle Dun

Hook: Size 18 Roman Moser Arrow Point.
Silk: Grey.
Tail: Pale-yellow or gold krystal flash to represent empty shuck of emerging fly.
Body: Beaver fur dyed grey, or substitute. I use heron herl.
Wing: Fine deerhair tied in over the top of the eye flared and sloping slightly forward.

Midge Mimicry 1993

Despite the fact that these rather tiny members of the Diptera family are a major source of food for trout both on still waters and in many rivers, few fly-fishers seem to be aware of the truly vast importance of Chironomids, particularly on rivers. This is a great shame as if more fly-fishers were to fish patterns to represent them on the appropriate occasions, in either medium, I am sure their catch rate would increase dramatically. Now, before one can become successful at this style of fishing it is essential to have at least a basic knowledge of the Chironomid life cycle to know how best to present the fly.

There are more than 400 different British species which vary greatly in size from less than $1/8$ in to nearly 1 in in length. The body colours vary from black through green and brown to dark red. The adult female Chironomids, more usually known as buzzers or midges, lay their eggs in batches on the surface of the water where, within a few days, they hatch into tiny larvae. When fully grown the larvae vary from less than ¼ in to more than 1 in in length and also vary in colour through various shades of green and brown to bright red. The larvae spend their life on the river bottom, living in tubes of sand or mud attached to stones or other debris, or they make tunnels in the mud or silt.

The transition from the worm-like larva to the pupa which has a whitish caudal fin or tail, a segmented body and a small thorax with prominent wing pads – on top of which will be seen some quite prominent white filaments (tracheal gills used to abstract oxygen from the water) – takes several days. When the pupa is ready to transpose into the winged adult – both on running or still water – it leaves its tube or tunnel and swims to the surface, where it almost immediately adopts a horizontal position. The thorax splits and the fully-adult winged fly emerges and takes to the air.

This transposition is fairly rapid – usually taking well under 10 seconds – so the adult spends little time on the surface where the trout can feed upon it. The pupa, on the other hand, is also vulnerable as it is available to the trout the moment it leaves the burrow on its long swim to the surface, where it is available to surface-feeding trout for the several seconds it takes to transpose. On still water this transposition can often take many minutes instead of a few seconds, as on calm, windless days a film builds upon the surface which the pupa often has difficulty in piercing to emerge.

This movement of the pupa when a heavy film is present, is most interesting. Some will remain hanging vertically, with their head filaments just touching the film, while others swim spasmodically for short distances towards the bottom. Others spend most of their time swimming along horizontally, looking for a weak spot or crack in the film, only stopping occasionally to take up the more typical vertical position. On rivers this rarely applies, except in very slow areas or eddies where a film can form.

Pattern Variety

Now what can we deduce from the above life cycle when it comes to presenting a fly? First, we shall require a range of patterns in varying sizes to represent the three stages in the Chironomid's life cycle – larva, pupa and adult. The larval patterns should be fished as slowly and as close to the bottom as possible, where the trout look for them when they emerge from their tubes or tunnels. The pupal patterns should be fished, depending upon conditions, either descending or ascending from or to the surface, or, alternatively, either hanging vertically or horizontally in the surface film, but more of this later. Finally, one can occasionally fish a dry fly on the surface to represent the freshly-emerged adult or the returning egg-laying female.

When presenting your artificial to trout feeding on Chironomids, it should be noted that the size of any particular species varies during the three last stages of its life cycle. The larva is always larger than the pupa and in the final adult stage it is smaller than either the larva or pupa. In addition, the adult midge, when emerging from its pupal shuck, is in silhouette, and considerably larger than either of the previous two stages.

Before proceeding further I feel I should clarify the phrase 'midge-fishing' which is often quoted in the fishing press in the UK and generally refers to fishing various Chironomid patterns in still water. This phrase has generally been confined to stillwater fishing, as it is only comparatively recently that fly-fishers have become aware of the importance of chironomids and other tiny species on rivers. Prior to this, trout feeding on very tiny flies was usually referred to as 'smutting' fish and considered uncatchable.

In the United States midge-fishing has a completely different meaning. Over there it means fishing on rivers using very tiny artificials in sizes from 18 or 20 up to 26 or even 28 to represent not only members of the Chironomid family, but also many other tiny species of natural flies.

Few fly-fishers over here would be capable of fishing such tiny artificials with any degree of success, for midge-fishing is a very specialised style which many American fly-fishers have developed to such a degree it is now considered an art. On most of the rivers that I fish, hatches of Chironomids seem to be confined to the smaller species and are best represented by patterns dressed on hooks of size 16 to 20 – in fact these days I tend to dress most of my patterns on size 18 hooks as this has proved to be an excellent compromise. In my experience most river species are confined to body colours that vary from dark brown through to dark green.

On rivers, hatches are likely to occur at any time of the day or evening until it is almost too dark to see. While trout undoubtedly feed on the larvae on the bed of the river at times, and also on the ascending pupae, I seldom fish artificials to represent these stages. Apart from anything else it is usually too difficult to get such tiny patterns down to the level at which trout are feeding and it is easier to use small, standard-weighted nymph patterns which will usually be accepted just as readily. On rivers, therefore, most of my midge fishing is confined to those fish on the surface.

Trout always lie very close to the surface when feeding on Chironomids – whether these be the pupae, adults or, of course, any other tiny flies, such as black flies (simulium) or other small Diptera species. The rise form is usually unmistakable as it will be either a leisurely head and tail rise or, in heavier hatches, a sip rise when the trout is lying so close to the surface it only has to lift its head very slightly to take in the fly.

These sip rises are often repeated quite rapidly and are also acompanied by one or two air bubbles expelled through the gills as the trout sucks in the insect. Very ocasionally one may also observe trout lying a few inches below the surface and feeding on the ascending pupa just before it reaches the surface. The rise will then take the form of a slight bulge as the surface is not broken.

On rivers here and also in Europe, fishing with tiny Chironomid pupae or emerger patterns to smutting fish is a comparatively recent innovation and for those relatively few fly-fishers who have tried this tactic it has proved phenomenally successful. I will describe the various techniques to be tried later, when I list the best patterns for this style of fishing.

The hatches of Chironomids on still water are much more predictable than on rivers. To generalize, big hatches of the larger species tend to take place only in the early mornings or late evenings, while hatches of the smaller species – such as the Blagdon green midge or the tiny red or brown midge – take place during the afternoons. During the early summer some of the larger species – such as Grey Boy (Orange & Silver) or the large Red Midge do hatch spasmodically during the day.

The surface rise to the larger species is quite distinctive and takes the form of a leisurely head and tail rise. It is most likely to be observed under calm conditions in the early morning or late evening during fairly heavy hatches. Under calm conditions, when barely a ripple disturbs the surface, a heavy surface film develops and the ascending pupae have difficulty in finding a weak spot in the film. At such times, particularly during a heavy hatch, the under surface will be alive with pupae, either swimming horizontally beneath the film or resting and hanging in the traditional pupa manner with their whitish head filaments touching the film. At this time they provide easy pickings for the trout who will avidly feed on them.

The strikingly coloured blood worm larvae is hunted by trout as it emerges from its tube or tunnel

In the past, heavy emergence of these Chironomids used to provide some most spectacular rises on many of our big reservoirs, but these days, sadly, perhaps due to the increasing volume of purification chemicals introduced into the water by many authorities, much of the aquatic life in reservoirs has been reduced to an alarming degree. The only other time that trout rise in this manner on still water is when they are feeding on those rather rare occasions, on floating snail.

Surface Swimming

When trout are feeding on heavy hatches of the smaller Chironomids – usually the small brown or red during the latter half of the summer – the rise to these is what we term a typical sip rise where the trout is swimming very close to the surface and merely lifting its head to take in the insects.

This rise is often rapidly repeated and on calm days the trout tend to move in a circle, while under breezy or windy conditions it nearly always moves upwind. When this occurs, if one is fishing from a boat it pays to anchor and find a wind lane and cast to the feeding trout as they come towards you along these lanes. The only other time a substantial sip rise is likely to occur is during a heavy hatch of the dreaded anglers' curse, the caenis, a very tiny white-bodied, upwinged fly.

On many still waters, even today, Chironomids are still a major source of food for trout and unlike on rivers, where the angler is only concerned with trout feeding on the surface, on still water the issue is much more complicated. Here the trout are likely to feed on them at any time of the day beneath the surface, either on the larvae or the ascending pupa. It is therefore always a problem to know when to fish the many artificials available to represent these two stages in their life cycle, as one cannot see underwater on which species or stages the trout are feeding.

The fly-fisher can only be guided by local knowledge, or time of the year or day, or fishing by trial and error until the killing pattern is found. One other method which should never be overlooked when the opportunity occurs is to spoon out any trout caught and analyse its stomach contents.

Patterns to represent the larva should be fished close to the bottom on slow or fast sink lines – depending on the depth of the water being fished or the composition of the bottom – while patterns to represent the ascending pupa should be fished anywhere between a few inches below the surface, down to midwater or even deeper.

Today's fly-fishers are spoilt for choice with the fly-lines available, but success may depend on this very decision. When trout are feeding on ascending pupae it is usually at a depth predetermined by the trout – depending on the weather conditions or temperature. For this reason the fly-line is critical – be it floating, intermediate, sink-tip, slow-sink or even, on occasions, a fast-sink.

Leaders and Power Gum 1994

Over the years much nonsense has been written in the fishing press appertaining to the design of leaders. Many well known authorities have suggested various complicated formulas for achieving certain tapers or even in some cases, reverse tapers by joining various lengths of monofilament together with only one target in view – to achieve good turnover of the leader, and presentation of the fly.

Good turnover of the leader and presentation of the fly is far more a question of sound casting techniques rather than relying on the formation or taper of the leader to achieve this. Today many of our leading stillwater experts use leaders in excess of twenty feet utilizing a single length of 7 lb nylon, and they have no problem in presenting the fly correctly even under windy conditions.

However, to some degree, I do feel that a tapered leader offers some advantages, particularly in dry fly fishing, and therefore for many years now I have favoured the custom-made knotless tapered leaders now freely available. Until comparatively recently, I used for dry fly fishing a seven foot leader tapered to 3x or, for stillwater fishing, a twelve foot leader tapered to 1x, plus of course the tippet, but so far as I am concerned this has now all changed with the advent of a material called Power Gum. This is a synthetic material that has the appearance of rather thick monofilament but has the feel of rubber and stretches in the same way.

I was first introduced to this material about five years ago when fishing in Montana in the United States. At the time I was fishing on a spring creek for very large brown trout. My host, a very experienced dry fly fisherman, insisted I tie some of this into my leader as he had found it was the only way to land the bigger trout in this very weedy water. In this gin clear water where hatches of small fly were predominant, the only way to deceive the larger trout was to fish very tiny size 20 to 24 dry flies on a very fine 6x or 7x tippet, and on normal leaders it was impossible to grass any of these fish. The extra stretch in the leader provided by the Power Gum was sufficient to overcome breakages on the strike, and also gave you much more latitude while playing the trout. Initially he found out that the position of the Power Gum in the leader was critical, as in the wrong position it badly affected the turnover and presentation. He eventually perfected a formula which to a large extent overcame this problem, and he showed me how to tie in an 8 inch length of Gum on to the end of a seven foot tapered braided leader with 8 inches of 1x mono. On to the other end of the Gum he tied in 8 inches of 1x followed by 8 inches of 3x, and 8 inches of 5x on to which he tied his 6x or 7x tippet of about 3 feet. He also showed me how to offset the hook on these tiny dry flies with a pair of pliers. Without offsetting the hook it is all but impossible to hook a fish on small flies – in fact I now as a matter of course offset the hook on all my flies.

A year or two after my experiences with Power Gum in Montana I decided to try it on our chalk streams, but quickly came to the conclusion I would have to modify the original formula as the Gum, with its attendant knots was a little too near the end of the leader for my liking. In addition its overall length of well over twelve feet was too long for most of the streams I fish. Most of these are in wooded areas, and for accurate casting underneath bankside bushes and trees a leader over ten feet in length is too difficult to handle.

The new formula which I have now developed and have been using over the past two seasons has proved extremely successful. The turnover and presentation are excellent. In fact, I have let several well known fly fishers fish my rod with this leader and they were completely unaware of the Power Gum. I have now replaced the seven foot braided leader with four feet of 20 or 25 lb nylon which I have found gives a better turnover than the limper braid. To this I attach 12 inches of 15 lb nylon then 12 inches of 11 lb test Power Gum and another 6 inches of 15 lb nylon, followed by 12 inches of 6 lb nylon to which I attach a 3 foot (or longer) tippet. I was originally advised to use surgeon's knots treated with a touch of superglue to tie in the Power Gum, but this is a rather bulky knot, and I have now found an ordinary 4 turn double blood also treated to a touch of superglue is equally effective but provides a much neater knot. With this blood knot it is essential to use a matt finish monofilament as smooth shiny nylon slips and will not hold. When tying the blood knot leave plenty of overlap as, to start with, even matt nylon will slip quite a lot before pulling tight.

If you are going to fish for large trout with very fine tippets or with the relatively new very fine double strength low impact tippet monofilaments, which are so easily broken on the strike, do try this Power Gum. I now use it in the leader for all aspects of trout fishing. It has another huge plus factor. Over the course of a season, it can save you a lot of money. With these new double strength nylons, due to their low impact strength, if you catch a fly on any obstructions such as bushes, trees or grass behind you, you invariably lose your fly, but this never happens when you have Power Gum in the leader.

I have just returned from six weeks in New Zealand where I caught a lot of trout close to and over double figures using a 6 lb tippet. I used the same leader throughout the trip and was not once broken or had the knot on the Power Gum let me down.

In the Bleak Midwinter 1998

I have been fly-fishing seriously for grayling for more than ten years, and the longer I spend pursuing these delightful fish the more puzzled I become about certain aspects of their behaviour.

Most of my grayling fishing takes place on the chalkstreams of southern England, where the crystal-clear waters make it easy to watch the fish feeding.

I regularly fish a stretch of the upper Test which has an excellent population of good-sized grayling, thanks to our keeper, who insists that all big grayling should be returned, and who never electro-fishes the water. On a day when the fish are feeding well, I will often catch upwards of 40 or 50 grayling, while on a bad day I often struggle to catch a dozen. In the early days I used to put this down either to the weather or the lack of fly. Now, after three years of close observation, I am completely nonplussed, and have no idea what brings grayling on the feed. Of one fact I am fairly certain – neither weather nor fly hatches plays a significant part in the equation.

The other aspect of their behaviour which I do not understand is where they go in the winter. In most of the southern rivers I fish, the grayling become thicker on the ground as the summer progresses – until by late August, every run, pool or pot among the weedbeds holds its resident shoal.

September and October are usually the two most productive months, but by November, when the temperature begins to drop dramatically, they begin to thin out. No longer will they be found among the weedbeds. By mid-December they can be found only in the bigger, deeper pools, and once the first heavy frosts or snow arrive they become increasingly difficult to locate. So where do they go? An obvious answer would be that they migrate downstream to deeper water where the temperatures are more stable. Yet even in the depths of winter I still find the grayling just as difficult to locate in some of

When grayling are feeding hard, they are invariably hooked in the upper jaw

these lower stretches. Even if they do travel downstream for long distances, however, would they be able to negotiate the many weirs and hatch pools on their return to the upper reaches?

When they are feeding well, I've noticed the grayling lie a little way off the bed of the river, and these shoals are nearly always well spread out.

On the other hand, when the shoals are tightly packed and all the fish are hugging the bottom, you know you are in for a tough day. In the past ten years, I have discovered things about their feeding behaviour that have influenced both my fishing techniques and choice of fly.

Recently, much of my grayling fishing from July onwards has been with the nymph. There are two good reasons for this. On most of the streams I fish from July onwards, the hatches, of the upwinged species in particular, have been steadily declining over the past eight years. The past two seasons have been particularly bad, with daytime hatches either absent or very sparse, making the nymph one's only option.

If you want to catch the bigger grayling you really have to get your fly well down, since it is only during fairly heavy hatches that the really big fish will rise to take flies from the surface.

I have also noticed that, when the grayling are really on the feed and taking the nymph well, 90 per cent will be hooked in the centre of the upper jaw. On the other hand I find, when they are not feeding and difficult to catch, at least 75 per cent of those that do accept the nymph will be hooked in the scissors. I think the reason for this is that when hungry, and therefore on the lookout for food, they will either lift up to take insects passing overhead, or turn, chase and take them downstream – facing towards you – which in either case results in the artificial finding a hold in the centre of the top of the mouth.

When they are off the feed, grayling will seldom, if ever, take the artificial on the dead drift, and I have found that the only chance of taking the odd fish in these conditions is to cast your nymph well above the shoal, let it sink, and then give the nymph a good draw by lifting the rod tip.

If you are lucky, you will find that the odd fish in the shoal will sometimes be tempted to turn and take the fly as it crosses in front of him, a movement which nearly always results in the fish being hooked in the scissors.

Now, while it is not my intention to discuss either general fly patterns or fishing techniques, I would like to mention a couple of things that have increased my catches over the past season.

When the grayling are feeding indifferently, I have had most success using a small PVC Nymph dressed on either a size 16 or 18 hook. When off the feed, grayling seem to ignore larger patterns. When the grayling are feeding hard, however, I have found they will often take the artificial nymph as soon as it hits the water. When this happens, the fish are seldom hooked because by the time you see the leader draw as the fish takes it, you have too much slack line lying on the surface to set the hook.

Assuming that a grayling will react in this way, I have enjoyed some success by lifting the rod top smartly to make certain that the line is lying straight enough for me to set the hook.

PVC Nymph

Hook: Size 12-18
Thread: Brown
Tail: Golden-pheasant tail tips dyed olive-green
Underbody and thorax: Copper wire
Overbody and thorax: Three strands Of Olive/brown heron herl. The original used condor. Abdomen is wound with overlapping turns of 3mm-wide clear PVC.
Wing pads: Dark pheasant-tail herls.

Finally, I would like to suggest that if you currently use the now very popular Gold Head Hare's Ear nymph for grayling you may like to modify the dressing. For some time I have wondered why this pattern has proved to be so successful particularly when dressed on size 14 or 16 hooks with a 2mm or 3mm bead. I can only assume the fish see them as some type of sedge larva – even though, dressed on standard hooks they are really too short in the body to represent the average natural larva. So, with realism in mind, I now dress them on size 16 or size 14 longshank hooks and have consequently found them even more killing.

John Goddard with a good Test grayling

Think Big, Think Small 2000

I was fishing the Tekapo river in the central South Island of New Zealand when I first spotted the big brown. He was lying in fast water just behind the lip of a sill formed by the gravel and stones at the head of a long run of fast, white water flowing out of a large pool in the river. The water where he was lying was crystal clear and barely two feet in depth; despite this I would never have spotted him if he had not moved, as he blended in so well with the golden gravel on which he lay. He was not rising, but obviously feeding, as every now and again he would dart from side to side or sometimes just lift slightly. After observing him for some time I felt sure he was feeding on the nymphs of the medium to small upwinged flies that were occasionally hatching.

How was I to get a nymph down to him? This posed a problem, as the water above the sill was much slower than the very fast water flowing below it, so any artificial cast, even well upstream with a lot of slack line would be dragged to the surface by the fast current below. Eventually, I decided to try a very heavy leaded nymph cast a yard or so above him, which I hoped would get down to his level before the drag affected it. This seemed to work initially, as several times he moved to it, but would not take it. After that, he ignored it completely. By then, I felt sure size was the problem, so I changed to a smaller, heavily weighted pattern but with the same result. Now over the past two seasons I have been dressing my Goldhead Hare's Ear patterns on a long shank hook and have found those dressed with the smallest size 2mm ball on very small hooks - size 16 or 18 - have been incredibly effective, so I felt that one of these might fool this very wary trout. But how was I to get such a tiny, lightly weighted pattern far enough beneath the surface for him to see it? I then remembered that a few days before, my companion, Ron Clark, had given me a couple of these tiny longshank nymphs dressed with a 2mm tungsten ball which he said took the nymphs down much faster. Perhaps one of these might solve the problem?

And so it proved. On the third or fourth cast I saw the trout rise up in the water slightly and tightened and much to my surprise, and probably even more so to the trout, hooked him solidly.

I was immediately faced with the problem of keeping him out of the tumbling boulder-strewn white water below me, so had to hold him very tightly indeed, praying that my six-pound tippet would hold. This resulted in a breathtaking aerial display, as he jumped clear of the water six or seven times before I was able to persuade him into the quieter water closer to the bank. Several minutes later I was able to subdue and beach him.

These Tekapo trout are very handsome indeed: their flanks are bright silver, as opposed to the golden flanks of most New Zealand browns. This was a big trout for this particular river; when I weighed him prior to release I was surprised to note he turned the scales at 6fl lb. During our remaining ten days in New Zealand I rarely had a refusal to this tiny tungsten-headed Hare's Ear wherever I located a trout feeding in fast water. I am now looking forward to trying this in some of our deeper and faster water at home this coming season.

I've fished New Zealand waters for many years, and when fishing dry flies, I have, like many Kiwis, tended to fish quite large sizes most of the time. Most of my visits have been during February and March, as the weather generally is more reliable at this time. This period coincides with huge hatches of cicadas, a terrestrial which is often blown onto the water in numbers, so the trout generally are conditioned at this period to feeding on large surface flies. This time, and also on one previous visit during November and early December, I had noticed that the trout were consistently ignoring larger patterns, so I came well prepared with much smaller patterns. This proved to be a wise move, as our fishing during this visit was restricted to a few very hard-fished rivers.

When Ron and I arrived in Christchurch, our famous mentor and guide, one John Morton ('he who casts no shadow') met us at the airport and was upset to report that most of the South Island was experiencing the worst floods in living memory, so that it was quite impossible for us to fish many of the major southern rivers as planned. We therefore spent most of our visit in the McKenzie Basin around Twizel in the centre of the South Island which had been least affected by the heavy and consistent rain. The first week was very wet and the fishing far from pleasant, and we quickly realized that the trout were wary of any of the usual large patterns of nymphs or dry flies – Humpies, Adams, Royal Wulffs, etc. A couple of days after our arrival I was fishing one of the larger rivers where I found several trout rising reasonably well to some medium-sized duns that were hatching at the tail end of a shallow pool. I started fishing for these with a size 14 Adams, but could raise no interest at all. I then changed to a Humpy with the same result. It was not until I put on a size 18 Sparkle Dun with a heron herl body that I started to get positive takes. While I caught quite a few of these rising trout, which averaged around three pounds apiece, I also failed to hook several. This was due to the long casts necessary to cover these trout without spooking them in the shallow water, plus the fact that at this distance these tiny dries were all but impossible to see under the breezy conditions in which we were fishing. As a result of this experience, both Ron and I stuck with tiny patterns for the remainder of our visit and apparently fared much better than most of the locals, who were finding it very hard going. Apart from the Sparkle Dun I also had a lot of trout on a size 16 Winged Gold-ribbed Hare's Ear, as well as one of my own patterns, a size 18 Super Grizzly Emerger.

We spent the next three days fishing some small lakes (ponds) on the outskirts of Twizel, these were called Lakes Cameron, Merino and Poaka and were reputed to hold some very large trout. We fished all three of these gin-clear lakes on the first day and all had shots at several very big trout that were well into double figures. At the end of the day we had all blanked, and Ron reckoned that the trout in these waters were the most difficult he had ever fished for anywhere. By late in the afternoon he had all but given up as he had mounted a size 20 nymph which he cast at least 30 feet in front of a cruising trout and then waited until it approached. However, as soon as he lifted it in front of the fish it spooked and departed in obvious panic.

By the middle of the following day we were still fishless, and had tried every conceivable method we could think of, so it was in pure desperation that I again decided to try the tiny long shank Hare's Ear with the tungsten bead. I cast out, and let it sink to the lake bed in the vicinity of a weed bed that was being patrolled by a nice brown. I must have dozed off for a moment or so, as when I opened my eyes there was this big trout almost on top of where I had cast the fly. It was too late to lift it in front of him, so I just twitched the rod top

A magical pool on a typical wilderness river

which moved the fly but an inch. To my amazement he turned, dipped down and picked it off the bottom with confidence. This was a strong fish, well over 7 lb, and put up a spirited fight before being returned. The following day I returned and using this same pattern and technique attracted the attention of a dozen good trout. I found that if I gave it just the one small tweak – providing they saw the movement – they would turn and in some cases take it or at least have a look. However, I soon realized if I moved it again as they approached they would sheer off in panic. I finished the day well with three lovely browns all between six and eight pounds.

I now wonder why in New Zealand I had not tried very small nymphs and dry flies before, as at home here in the UK for many years now at least on rivers, apart from during the three weeks of the

Mayfly, I rarely fish any dry flies on hooks larger than a size 16. This now also applies to nymphs when I fish them in the latter half of the season; for the last three years or so I have caught most of my trout and grayling on a size 16 long shank GRHE gold bead or a size 18 PVC Nymph. If you use standard size dry flies and nymphs on size 14 or 12 hooks I am sure if your presentation is good you will still catch plenty of fish, but I am now equally sure if you persevere with very small patterns you will not only catch more, but you will also stand a much better chance of catching those much larger, better educated fish.

Net Loss, Net Gain 2001

One aspect or tradition adhered to by the vast majority of fly fishers is that one should always carry a landing net when fishing. Whilst I accept under some circumstances it may be prudent to consider this – if your quarry are very large fish such as salmon, steelhead and even large sea trout, or when trout fishing in stillwater from a boat, where it can be dangerous to lean over the side – I do not agree, particularly when fishing rivers for trout or grayling when covering a lot of water, where it is sensible to travel as light as possible. Apart from the weight aspect, landing nets when clipped to bag, or belt, or even looped over one's shoulder seem to act like a magnet to any tree, bush, fence or post in the vicinity and have to be constantly untangled. In addition to this, I am sure that more fish are lost at the net by mishandling than for any other reason. It is a long, long time since I last carried a landing net on a river, as providing you know what to do, it is a relatively simple matter to land any trout with your hand – even very large double-figure fish.

Distance release: the rod tip is slid down the leader towards the barbless hook when it can be seen on the outside of the trout's mouth

First of all, decide upon the area along the bank where you are going to land the fish. Ideally, this should be in a slack area out of the main current. Once you have played the fish towards the chosen landing area wait until you can get his head up above the surface and keep it there, then slide your finger and thumb down the leader, put the rod down or tuck it under your arm, and with your free hand grip the fish across his back, just in front of his dorsal fin and turn him upside-down. This seems to disorient the fish, as in most cases they cease to struggle and you can gently lift them out of the water and place them on the bank.

Over the years catch-and-release fishing has become increasingly popular, particularly on those rivers still holding stocks of wild fish, as it is now considered by many eminent authorities the only way to preserve the fishing for future generations. It has now been proved beyond reasonable doubt that – at least so far as the various species of trout are concerned – they can be caught and returned many times without affecting their well-being provided certain rules are strictly applied.

The Rules of Release

1. Always play a fish and release it as quickly as possible. Playing a fish too long and exhausting it builds up lactic acid in its body which may eventually kill it.
2. Do not practise catch and release during prolonged hot weather, which lowers the oxygen content of the water.
3. Always use barbless hooks.
4. Use a knotless landing net and release the fish from it while it is still in the water.
5. Release the fish by sliding finger and thumb down the leader with or without the use of a net.

Some authorities now advocate the use of a net, others prefer them not to be used. However, whichever of these methods is used, the time taken to get a fish close enough to release it counts against its survival.

I will now explain a method of release that will solve the controversy between these two methods and at the same time reduce the amount of time taken to release the average trout by nearly 50 per cent. This, I must admit, was a technique I discovered by accident rather than by design. When I first adopted catch-and-release tactics using barbless hooks in the early 1970s I found myself in a situation that I had never experienced before. I spotted a good trout rising in a mill stream at the head of a long, deep, brick-lined culvert.

The brick wall on either side was at least five feet high, so I must have assumed when I first started fishing that if I caught it I could play it downstream to a spot where I could release it. To cut a long story short, I did eventually hook it, only to discover to my consternation that there was no way of releasing it by any normal method, as there was a large pipe crossing the bottom end of the culvert only two feet above the water surface. Facing the probability that I would have to break it off, I decided to give it a little further thought. Realizing I was fishing with a barbless hook, I wondered if it was possible to release the trout by pushing the tip of the rod down the leader to get it as close to the fly as possible and then waggle it about, hoping the fly would drop out. Trying this manouevre, I must have slipped and pushed the tip of the rod down onto the fish's mouth. The next second, to my amazement, he was free and swimming happily away.

Giving it a little thought, I realized the tip ring of the rod must have acted like a disgorger, closing over the fly and removing it as I accidently pushed down. Since that day, I have never looked back and now release all my fish this way. The big advantage of course is that with this method you can release a fish very quickly indeed, in fact as soon as you have played it to within a rod length.

Bernard Cribbins with a fine brown trout. Turning the fish belly-up appears to disorient the fish and stop it from struggling

American fly fisher, Lefty Kreh about to release a trout

When my great American buddy, Lefty Kreh, first came over here to fish with me in 1983, I showed him this technique and he thought it was the greatest invention since sliced bread. He, and most of my friends over here, have now adopted this method, but there are certain rigid rules connected with the technique which one must follow to avoid breaking the tip off the rod. I have in the last 25 years broken two rod tips, but in both cases it was due to my negligence. In the first instance I slipped down the bank just as I had pushed the rod tip round the fly, and on the second I foolishly thought I could remove the fly from just inside the mouth of the fish, when he jumped and snapped off the tip.

Utilising the tip of the rod to release a fish

Distance Release by Rod Tip

If you follow these basic rules you should have no problems:
1. Never even think of using this method unless you are using barb-less hooks.
2. Never try this if the fly is well inside the mouth of the fish. In practice you will find that most fish are hooked where you can see most of the fly outside the mouth.
3. I advise that you only use this technique with small hooks, no larger than size 12, and never with longshank hooks, or bulky flies.

The procedure for releasing a fish is as follows:

When your quarry is within a rod length hold the fly line in the free hand and slide the rod down the leader until the tip ring encloses the fly, then if he is hooked in the scissors wait until his head is facing away and give the rod a little jab forward, but no more than an inch or so or you could of course break the tip. Usually the fly will come free on the first attempt, but occasionally it may be necessary to repeat the procedure.

PART THREE
FLY FISHING WORLDWIDE

We Lived on Norway's Wild Trout 1969

I have recently returned from a combined business and holiday trip to Norway and Sweden. From a holiday point of view we were extremely fortunate with the weather, hardly seeing a cloud during the whole of our stay. Needless to say, such unusually hot conditions were hardly conducive to good fishing; nevertheless, I did enjoy some very pleasant sport, mainly for brown trout.

During recent years I have travelled abroad fairly extensively and, in my opinion, Norway is certainly the most beautiful country I have yet visited. The scenery is positively breathtaking, particularly along the western part of the country among the fiords, while further inland the terrain is strongly reminiscent of parts of Scotland. The countryside is riddled with lakes and during the journey by car to our destination in the northern part of Norway, it became an almost irresistible urge to stop and cast a fly on each stretch of water as we came upon it, particularly as each lake we encountered appeared more tempting and attractive than the last.

I had arranged to meet some Norwegian friends who owned a log cabin in an isolated area high in the mountains to the north and west of Trondheim, near the Swedish border. This is almost into Lapp country and there are no roads. The terrain is very rugged and, consequently, the only means of access is on foot. My friend, Lauri Thaulow, and his wife Eva, had thoughtfully arranged for a local farmer with a horse to meet us at the point where the road ended and to carry our heavy gear up to the vacation cabin. This was a great relief, as we were faced with a nine-mile hike, and in this distance we climbed over 3,000 ft.

By the time we reached our destination my wife and I were in a state of near exhaustion, but a glass of the local beverage soon put us on our feet. The log cabin, with a typical Norwegian sod roof, was set in idyllic surroundings; sited between two small limpid lakes, it was ringed by lofty mountain peaks, some of which still held a trace of the previous winter's snow. Within a radius of 30 minutes' walking distance were at least a dozen lakes varying in size from a few acres to some which were over half a mile long.

All these lakes contained wild brown trout and although the average size was very small, going about three to a pound, they were a joy to catch as they would eagerly accept a dry fly or a nymph. This was fortunate as it happened, because we had planned to spend five days in our mountain retreat, bringing all the food required with us. Imagine our consternation when unpacking to find someone had forgotten to pack our supply of meat. Our host took this minor tragedy very calmly, so I thought, until he blandly announced: 'Not to worry. We have a very competent fisherman with us and I am sure he will provide fish aplenty.'

I must say at the time I did not share his confidence, as from past bitter experience I knew that fish were nearly always impossible to catch when one desperately required them for any particular reason. I had in the past frequently envisaged a situation occurring where it would be necessary to obtain trout for sustenance, but never dreamed I would one day actually be placed in such a situation. Now it was reality and I was faced with providing sufficient trout for five very hungry people for five days.

I have never fished so hard in my life – and I only succeeded in my task because of the assistance of my companion, plus the fact that the trout were extremely obliging, free rising and relatively easy to catch. During this period, each day we existed on trout for breakfast, bread and cheese for lunch, and trout again for the evening meal.

These small mountain trout were very pink-fleshed and extremely tasty and served as they were by our hosts, with chopped mushrooms cooked in a sour cream sauce, were absolutely delicious. These wild mushrooms were gathered by the ladies during the day from the mountain slopes, together with wild berries called, by the Norwegians, multer. Equally delicious, these were served as a sweet and in appearance were similar to our own raspberries, although far superior in flavour. These are reputed to be very nutritious as they apparently have a high vitamin content. They grow wild in the mountain regions and are eagerly sought. We were very fortunate to savour these succulent berries, as most summers they fail to ripen and it had been ten years since the last successful harvest.

Although most of the trout I took were small I did have a few nice fish in excess of a pound. But larger trout, which I felt sure existed in some of the lakes I fished, eluded me, the main obstacle being the eagerness of the smaller fish to take the fly. However, from discussions I had with various local fishermen in different parts of Norway, it seems quite apparent that there are certain lakes which not only contain a preponderance of large trout, but in some areas equally large grayling and Arctic char. In the time available I was unable to locate any of these.

For those fly fishermen who may be intending to visit Norway in the near future I would recommend small to medium-sized flies, with dark or even black dressings. Many of the insects and other fauna I had the opportunity to study were extremely dark.

Sedge flies were very common and two of the most prolific species I encountered were a dark brown sedge, very similar to our own Brown Sedge, *Anabola nervosa*, and a small very black sedge similar to our Black Silverhorns, and I am fairly certain this was from the same Leptoceridae family.

Many of the upwinged flies were also on the dark side, being similar in appearance to our own Sepia duns. The predominant colour among many of the beetles was also black, and even the corixa, which were exceedingly plentiful, had jet-black wing cases, as opposed to the brown which are normally encountered in England.

I found the most successful patterns were: Black Palmer, Medium Red Sedge, Pheasant Tail Nymph, Dark Corixa, Peter Ross and a Dunkeld.

Finally, one word of warning. Mosquitoes in Norway, particularly in the northern part of the country, are very large, vicious, and often swarm during the evenings so thickly that fishing is all but impossible, unless you have some form of protection, such as a strong repellent or a net face mask.

Trout in South Africa 1975

Most anglers probably regard the Republic of South Africa as a superb sea fishing prospect. It will therefore come as something of a surprise, perhaps, to hear that freshwater fishing – including trout fishing – is almost on a par. South Africa is a country of strong contrasts: semi-tropical weather on the east coast boardering the Indian Ocean, and the rainy, windy, often cold weather that is a feature of Cape Province. Likewise, the land also varies tremendously, from the flat lowlands of the Karoo to the high veldt of the Transvaal and down to the rugged mountains of the Drakensberg range. From this it will be appreciated that the rivers and lakes are equally varied, giving rise to a bewildering number of different species of fish.

I had never heard of many of these species when I went to South Africa two years ago, while others were more familiar. Both large- and smallmouth bass were introduced before the last war, and have now become well established in many still waters and rivers in the territory. Prior to this, European carp and tench were imported and quickly established themselves. The former are now widespread and common in many rivers, ponds and reservoirs, and in some areas grow to a very large size, specimens over 50 lb being quite frequently caught. Another very popular species is the yellowfish, a very powerful fighter, and although I did not catch any during my stay, I was shown photographs and have little doubt they are closely related to the British barbel. I understand that in some areas they exceed 40 lb, and they are reputed to accept practically any type of bait, both natural and artificial. I was also informed they would readily accept a wet fly, and in some rivers, even a dry. Various other species which grow to a large size are plentiful, and if you have strong enough tackle, and plenty of stamina, many of the larger rivers are reputed to hold catfish of monstrous proportions!

In addition to the 'coarse fish', both brown and rainbow trout are common and widespread in many rivers, lakes and dams, and in some areas the trout fishing is extremely good. Trout are not indigenous to the Southern African Continent but were introduced towards the end of the last century. Since then they have increased, both naturally and artificially, and are present in most of the major river systems. Most of the rivers where sport is good are swift-flowing and rocky or stony, and are reminiscent of many Welsh or Scottish streams. Consequently, the wet fly reigns supreme, but there is a certain amount of good dry fly fishing available in some of the rivers, particularly in the valleys of the Drakensberg Mountains, and in the upper reaches of the Orange River system, including Barkly East district near the Basutoland border. This area can be recommended because the water levels remain fairly constant throughout the year and for the most part they are less affected by such evils as soil erosion and water abstraction. There are many strong and active trout-fishing societies in the Republic, and nearly all of them control an abundance of good water which they are only too willing to share with visiting anglers.

In general terms flyfishing in the Republic is less sophisticated than in the UK. Both on rivers and still waters, anglers seem content with the older, traditional patterns that were popular in Britain in the first half of the century. Some progress has been made in recent years, mainly in the use of New Zealand fly patterns, many of which have been adapted for local conditions. During my tour I visited most of the popular places, such as Durban, Port Elizabeth and Cape Town, and although I passed by, or looked at, many rivers and dams in the areas, I unfortunately had no opportunity to fish them. However, during the last week of my stay in Johannesburg I was delighted to accept an invitation from Trevor Babich, President of the Rand Piscatorial Society, to accompany him and several other society members on a four-day trout fishing safari over the high veldt to visit some of the beautiful streams and rivers in the hilly country around Machadodorp, including the famous Elands and Crocodile rivers. This proved to be a most interesting and informative trip and provided me with a good insight into South African methods of fly-fishing and of the aquatic fauna to be found in the region.

There are several reasonable hotels in the area, but we took tents and sleeping-bags for mobility and were able to fish a lot of streams and rivers over a wide area. Some of these come under the jurisdiction of the society, but on others we had to seek permission from the local farmers which, I may add, was readily granted. Rainbow trout were most in evidence, but we spent one morning on a delightful stream flowing down one of the mountain valleys and which held a good head of browns. Most of these fish were between half a pound to a pound in weight, but on our light tackle provided good sport. The stream was fast and rocky and most of the fish were to be found in the deeper pools. All the members of our party fished wet flies downstream and they assured me this was the accepted method, using patterns such as the Silver March Brown, Teal and Red, Butcher and Invicta. I made a quick examination and discovered that various species of Ecdyonuridae-type nymphs (stone-clinging nymphs of upwinged flies) as well as shrimps, were much in evidence, so I decided to fish a deep-sunk

The author with a brace of rainbows from a small dam in the Eastern transvaal. And *below* is Patterson's Dam, in Eastern Transvaal.

nymph upstream in preference to a wet fly downstream, at which I am less skilled. As it turned out my choice was a happy one as I achieved as good, if not better results than the rest of our party, whether by luck or judgement I am not sure. My own weighted shrimp pattern produced the best results.

Next day we fished some of the larger rivers, including the Elands. Most of these were stony and very fast with few, if any, pools. Also they were rather coloured, particularly the Elands, which had a strong, milky appearance. On these the wet fly proved to be the only feasible method, and after some experimenting I found that dark patterns seemed to be best. My friends confirmed this as they favoured flies like the Connemara Black, Black Palmer, or Zulu, all dressed on very big (one or two sizes bigger than in the UK) hooks. These rivers were quite an experience to fish as many run through very thick, semi-tropical undergrowth in which small game, exotic birds, and even (to my horror) snakes abound. In many places wading in the only way it is possible to fish, and on one occasion, when I was up to my thighs in quite a deep run, a large snake either swam or drifted downstream between me and the bank. I must admit that after that wading lost much of its appeal! We caught several nice rainbows, some over 2 lb, and in the heavy water they gave excellent sport. The largest one I hooked was a beauty, well over 3 lb by the look of him, but he managed to throw the hook almost at the net.

Apart from the rivers, we also fished several lakes or dams on the veldt. The majority of these were on farmland and had been excavated and stocked with rainbows to provide fresh fish for the farmers. In most cases permission could be obtained to fish them for a small fee, and generally speaking, the fishing was good, the trout averaging about 1/lb. These ponds varied between two and five acres, but we did fish on a couple that were nearer 20 acres and on these we managed to catch some larger fish between two and three pounds. Without exception all the members of my party favoured a large matuka-type pattern called Walker's Killer, which they fished along the bottom on a sinking line. They assured me it had been the most popular pattern in the country for several years. Apart from this the only other artificials they used were all large New Zealand type lures or salmon flies such as the Silver Doctor, Jock Scott or Durham Ranger.

I found this very strange indeed because after taking many samples of mud and weed from the various dams we visited with my small collapsible insect net I discovered that the fauna was very similar indeed to that found in many British lakes and reservoirs. Various species of sedge and chironomid larva were much in evidence, as were damsel nymphs, shrimps, snails and even caenis nymphs, so I was at a complete loss to understand why imitative patterns were not in general use. I showed them some imitative patterns of this type that I had brought with me and they were all most surprised when I told them that these were the sort of artificials most popular in the UK. They expressed serious doubts as to whether they would be effective on their waters, and I was delighted to prove them wrong, as I promptly proceeded to catch fish on some of them. Both sedge and midge pupa proved to be real killers, and I also had a few nice fish on my PVC Nymph.

I also observed that frogs and toads of various species were prolific in many of the dams, and consequently found that an all-black pattern dressed to represent a tadpole proved to be extremely attractive.

On the last afternoon before our return I was to observe a sight the like of which I had never experienced before. This was an emergence of flying ants. Within minutes the air was full of them, and what ants they were! I can only describe them as gigantic; their wingspan was certainly in excess of four inches and they were more like dragonflies than ants. There was quite a strong breeze blowing at the time, and soon the surface of the dam was littered with these strange creatures as they were blown struggling on to the surface. Within minutes, it seemed, the water was boiling with trout rising to these tasty morsels. Sad to relate, I had nothing in my fly-box that even remotely resembled them so I just had to sit and watch, which I can assure you I found most frustrating. Strange to say, my hosts had no suitable artificial either, which I found most odd in view of the fact that they assured me this was not an uncommon occurrence.

And Now for the Good News 1979

Fewer than 10,000 anglers have caught an Arctic charr, according to an American statistician, thus making this species a more sought-after prize than even the lordly marlin. The reason is not due to their rarity, but because they are only to be encountered in rivers north of, or close to the Arctic circle. Until fairly recently access to areas where they are indigenous, such as Lapland, Greenland, Alaska and the northernmost areas of Canada, was extremely difficult. Cheaper air travel has now altered all this, and it is not only possible to visit most of these areas, but financially viable, although it may mean saving up for a year or so.

Of the many areas now being opened up, the south-western tip of Alaska would seem to offer the most exciting prospects as most of the rivers in this relatively vast and under-populated land have never been fished. Apart from the charr, Alaska also offers exceptional fishing for rainbow trout, various species of salmon and the beautiful Arctic grayling.

I had hoped for many years to fish for Arctic charr, so you can imagine how thrilled I was to receive an invitation from a very old American friend, Ron Cordes, to join him for 12 days' fishing in Alaska last August. Our host was John Garry, owner of Bristol Bay Lodge, who with his charming wife Maggie and a friendly staff, runs a superbly comfortable fishing camp during the 3 months of each Arctic summer. The lodge stands in a beautiful position at the head of a large lake that feeds into Bristol Bay, close to the Aleutian Islands. Two float-planes operate from the lodge and normally the 16 anglers accommodated each week are flown out each morning in groups of 4 to a different river or lake. This is an excellent plan as, apart from taking you to the best location for the particular species of fish you want to catch on that day, you are collected each evening and returned to the comfort and superb food provided by the lodge.

However, such comforts were not for us! For my visit Ron laid on something a little special – a 7-day 'float trip!' In my ignorance I had imagined this to be a 7-day tour of the area in one of the lodge's float-planes. Imagine my consternation on my arrival to be informed that a float trip on the American continent means floating down a river in a rubber boat and camping each night on the bank. To say I was horrified was putting it mildly. I had not roughed it in a tent, apart from a few days in South Africa, since I was a teenager, when I had a nice soft air bed and a sleeping bag.

On the evening of our arrival a superb barbecue was held in our honour, and it was diplomatically suggested that we make the most of it as it was likely to be the last square meal we would probably get for the next week! I now know how the Christians felt at their last feast before being thrown to the lions. Apart from Ron and myself, two other well known American anglers, Randall Kaufman and Jerry Wallace, were joining us on the expedition. The following morning the two float-planes from the lodge were loaded, one with we intrepid anglers and all our equipment, while the other took the two rubber boats, tents and, we hoped, a sufficiency of food and cooking utensils for the week.

The river chosen for our trip was the Good News and we were to be dropped on a small lake which formed the source, about 100 miles inland. The river is on top of the Alaskan peninsula and enters the sea between the Bering Straight and the Aleutian Islands. Little was known about the river, except that the fishing was excellent, because it had been navigated by boat only once before, due to its isolation. The plan was to row the boats with the help of the current, fishing on the way, and for the floatplane to collect us at the estuary a week later. For emergency use only, the larger of the boats was equipped with an outboard motor.

Once we were dropped we were strictly on our own because the floatplane could not land anywhere on the river between the lake at the source and the estuary. However, we were assured there was little danger. Although the river was fast and rough in places, there were no really bad rapids.

We did have one problem to face and this was the large number of grizzly bears indigenous to this area. Most rivers hold large numbers of salmon at this time of the year and are a great attraction to bears. The Good News proved to be no exception, as every campsite we chose showed bear tracks in profusion. Grizzlies are considered to be extremely dangerous animals, so we were provided with a rifle, and Jerry, an experienced hunter, was put in charge of it. We did see several large bears, and gave them a very wide berth, but we also had one rather frightening incident. On our second night, just after midnight, there was a crashing in the undergrowth behind the tents. We woke Jerry, who was snoring his head off and suggested it might be a good idea to load the rifle. One small problem! He had left it in the boat! Naturally, nobody was keen to walk the 50 yards to the boat, so for the next two hours we sweated it out while our furry friend rambled around the campsite.

The author with a fine silver salmon taken above the estuary of the Good News River.

The dark gunmetal hues and massive dorsal of the Arctic grayling are well illustrated

The flight from the lodge to the head-waters of the Good News was over what must be some of the most desolate yet beautiful terrain in the world: towering snow-capped mountain ranges interspersed with mile after mile of verdant green tundra, dotted with rivers and lakes sparkling like jewels in the bright sunshine of the brief Alaskan summer. Most of these lakes on the tundra were a bright, sapphire blue, while many of those nearer the mountains were filled with glacial water of frosty green. Even in summer the weather can change very rapidly and although it was quite warm and sunny when the planes departed, by the time we had all the gear safely stowed aboard the inflatables, ominous grey clouds were filling the horizon and soon it was lashing down with rain.

In retrospect, it was a most fantastic week and I would not have missed it at any cost, but by the end of the second day, after 36 hours of torrential rain, I would cheerfully have paid a thousand pounds to be air-lifted back to the lodge and some dry clothes and a warm bed. Despite the appalling weather, the fishing was fantastic. One of us fished over the stern of the boat, while the other on the oars manoeuvred the craft with the help of the current. I used one of my company's new 7½ ft built-cane dry fly rods with a slow-sinking line. The fish were very unsophisticated and while standard wet flies were accepted, the most effective pattern was a North American steelhead fly, Bill McGuire's Babine Special. A very garish dressing, the body of hot-pink fluorescent chenille is formed in two large distinct lumps, or balls, with a scarlet red hackle tied in between, plus a white hackle tied in front behind the eye. This is supposed to represent a couple of salmon eggs, which form the major source of food for all fish in the river at this time of the year. Fishing slightly down and across, we were hooking fish on every second or third cast: rainbow trout, grayling, charr and the odd pink or humpback salmon. The latter were ugly fish, especially the males. They averaged about 6 lb and were not particularly good sport, even on our light tackle. The rainbows, averaging about 3 lb, were grand sport, and took some handling in the fast water. In fact, a fair percentage of those over 4 lb we hooked were eventually lost.

However, the real cream of the fishing on the upper reaches of this river was undoubtedly for the charr. These were encountered in large shoals, when we would beach the boat and cast for them down likely looking runs from the shore. In the Good News they averaged about 2 lb, with the odd specimen approaching 4 lb. Fine fighters, like the rainbows, they spend much time in the air. I shall never forget the sight of my first Arctic charr, and as he lay gasping and quivering on the pebbles in the shallow water at my feet I marvelled at his fantastic colouring. This was a male in full spawning colours, and his back and flanks were a dark blue-grey liberally dappled with large, brilliant red spots, the lower flanks silvery white and the belly a bright, almost fluorescent orange. To complete the picture the fins were deep red, edged with white. As I removed the barbless hook and returned him gently to his natural element, I really felt that the 6000-odd miles I had travelled had been worthwhile.

The Arctic grayling were also a most exciting fish to catch, as with their high dorsal fin acting like a sail they were able to take advantage of every scrap of current. Spectacular looking fish, they are very different to the European grayling, which are bright silver. These Arctic fish are a dark gun-metal grey; in fact, some were almost black. Their bellies are cream and the fins are dark with purple stripes. The dorsal fin can only be described as huge and is covered with bright purple spots. Much larger than British grayling, the average was well over 2 lb. We took a few on the wet fly, but quickly realized they were free risers and would readily accept a dry fly. My own caddis pattern proved to be a killer, since on this fast water the body of natural hair floated beautifully.

What about the salmon fishing? There were masses of them in the upper reaches, but apart from the humpbacks, which we tended to discount, the majority were either very large kings or sockeyes, but as both species had been in the river for some time, they were mostly stale or spawning fish and all but impossible to take on the fly, even had we wished. However. the main run of coho or silver salmon was due to start, and according to the most recent information received there were already plenty of fresh fish in the lower reaches, and so it proved to be.

We made very good time down the river, and were able to spend the last three days in a permanent camp we set up some six miles from the estuary. I am not particularly keen on salmon fishing, but I must admit that these were three days I am never likely to forget. In this period the four of us must have caught almost 100 salmon averaging around 14 lb. The river here was more than 200 yards wide and very powerful; even so, we found we could handle these fish fairly comfortably on a 9 ft graphite rod. Apart from in some of the shallower reaches, where we were able to use a sink-tip line, we were obliged to use a fast-sinking No.8 line with 2 ft of leadcore line spliced to the tip to get the fly down to the salmon. On the first day we all used, and quite successfully, the Babine Special, but on the second day Jerry began experimenting and finally, out of curiosity, mounted a lead-headed jig. This was dressed with a silver and red body with a big spray of white marabou over the top, and it proved to be an absolute killer. Fortunately, he had a dozen or so of these, which he very generously shared between us. We found that by retrieving them with a quick steady sweep on the rod tip, followed by a brief pause, which caused them to flutter up and down, they proved absolutely irresistible. The take of these salmon was often quite gentle, but once you set the hook, all hell broke loose, and in this heavy water they would often take 100 yards of line on their first run, with several spectacular leaps thrown in for good measure.

Most of this fishing was accomplished by wading but we did locate a couple of superb runs below high, undercut banks. Here, we could clearly see the salmon hugging the riverbed, and using one angler as a spotter from the bank, we were able to present the fly directly to the fish. It was at the head of one of these runs that I experienced what must surely be one of the most incredible fishing experiences of my life. A large tree had fallen into the river and formed a small pool tight into the bank. This area held a solid mass of salmon, weaving and jostling for position in the current which even here was quite rapid. Fortunately, there were several large trees lining the bank over this pool, and I was able to position myself behind the trunk of one of these overhanging the water. Shielded by the trunk, I was able to poke the rod tip out over the head of the shoal and, probably for the only time in my life, I was able to 'dap' for salmon. Lowering the fly into the water, I was able to present it to the salmon of my choice, and tease him into taking it. Every time I hooked a fish I raced down the bank like a demented person to get the hooked fish away before it disturbed and scattered the shoal. My companions, observing this strange behaviour on my part, were soon in hysterics.

Several times I nearly fell into the river, as to play a salmon while running down the bank and not looking where you are going is very tricky, to say the least. I managed to extract well over a dozen fish from this shoal before they finally dispersed.

Finally, a word of warning should you ever decide to set up camp close to the estuary of a wilderness river: always check on the tide! We failed to take this into account and consequently, on the first morning in our new camp site we were rudely awoken at 5.30 a.m. with a torrent of ice-cold water pouring into the tent and surrounding us in our sleeping bags.

The Castaway 1980

Many readers will, doubtless, have heard of a float tube, even though it is a method of fishing confined mainly to American anglers. When reduced to basics, it is merely an old truck inner tube with a strip of canvas webbing suspended across the centre on which to sit, one leg on each side and both inside the tube. These craft for want of a better word, are on sale in most American tackle shops, and make no mistake they are very popular. Many of those on sale are extremely sophisticated, sporting a custom-made waterproof cover which envelopes the tube and this incorporates a multitude of pockets to take all your tackle, food or even cameras. They are widely used in the States for fishing both stillwaters and rivers, and despite their appearance are extremely safe.

On a recent visit to the States I spent a few days in Idaho and was coerced into joining a couple of American friends in these float tubes on the famous Hebgen lake to fish for 'gulpers'. These are trout, both brown and rainbow, which feed nearly every morning throughout July and August every year on hatches of tiny American upwinged flies called Tricorythodes similar in size to our own caenis. Hatching out in vast quantities, the trout cruise along with their mouths open sucking them down like vacuum cleaners with an audible gulp. This phenomenum is well known in America, particularly on this lake where the name originated, and it provides some of the finest and most exciting stillwater fishing on the American continent. It is a large lake even by American standards, fairly shallow and well weeded, at least around the edges, and the water is absolutely gin clear. At this time of the year in this area, most mornings up until mid-day are windless and often bright as well, so the fishing is extremely difficult. Local anglers use very long leaders in excess of 20 ft with a 7x leader or tippet and a single tiny dry fly dressed on a size 20 hook or even smaller. Many anglers fish from boats but the more experienced seem to prefer the float tube as under these flat calm conditions they create less disturbance when moving or casting, avoiding those alarming ripples that tend to fan out from an angler in a boat. In addition, you can approach much closer to rising trout, as being closer to the water you present a much lower silhouette. This is also a distinct advantage where accuracy is of the essence.

However, before I become too enthusiastic about the advantages of a float tube, I feel I should point out that it requires considerable expertise to fish from one successfully.

The day of my baptism dawned fine and calm and, as we arrived at the waterside, there were already several nice trout dimpling the surface. Now my hosts the previous evening had explained the robing ceremony and were most insistent that this be strictly adhered to lest I find myself drifting out into the middle of the lake minus some vital piece of equipment. First of all we placed the tubes at the water's edge, and then stowed our tackle and cameras, etc., in the various pockets. We then proceeded to don our latex chest waders and tape around our waist a life belt in the form of a half circle that fits around the back so it does not impede your casting. This is for emergency use, in case you puncture the tube, or in your exuberance drive a hook into it when casting. You are now ready to embark, but before actually stepping into the tube and wading out to a depth where you can sit down inside, you must fit your feet into your chosen means of propulsion. These are either fins fitted on your heels or standard skin divers' flippers. Opinions seem divided as to which are best, the former propel you forwards, so that you can at least see where you are going, but they take a long time to get you there, while the latter propel you backwards, but considerably faster. However, even with the 'speedy' flippers it takes the best part of an hour to cover a mile. Naturally, I chose the flippers as I felt speed was of the essence. In retrospect I am sure I made the wrong decision, as after half a dozen steps in my tube I fell flat on my face in about 18 inches of water. As I surfaced I heard one of my 'friends' say, 'I am sure I told him to walk out backwards.' A quick change of clothing and I tried again, and this time managed to launch myself successfully.

After about half an hour of hard paddling, we arrived in the area where all the action was taking place. My instructor, Tom Young, a real expert at this style of fishing, then indicated we could commence fishing. So started the most frustrating morning's fishing I have ever experienced. Tom, who stayed within talking distance, did his very best to get me into a trout but all to no avail. Most of the time I was too late to cover an approaching trout he had spotted, as by the time I had rotated the tube so that my back was towards it, paddled backwards close enough to cover it, and then rotated the tube again so I could cast, it was long gone. On those ocasions that a trout obligingly started to rise in front of me close enough to cover, I found to my utter chagrin that as soon as I commenced casting, the tube would start to rotate, until once again the wretched trout disappeared from my view. Tom was soon in hysterics at my peculiar antics but, eventually, took pity on me and came over and spent about an hour showing me how to manoeuvre and control the tube with the flippers. Unfortunately, by the time my lesson was over, the hatch was thinning out and there were far fewer fish rising.

I eventually succeeded in covering a couple of trout, one of which actually accepted my dry fly but almost immediately jumped and disdainfully threw it back at me. The time, by then, was past noon and Tom suggested we give it a rest, as a slight breeze was beginning to ripple the surface of the lake and he assured me this was the normal signal for the trout to stop feeding. This seemed strange to me as at home one would welcome a breeze after a flat calm as the fishing usually improves. Bowing to his superior experience I at first agreed we should head back but, being a little reluctant to give up without a fish, I requested one last try along a stretch of bank to our right which looked very inviting. Somewhat reluctantly, I thought, he agreed (I now know why) and said he would meet me back at our launching site. His parting words were, 'Do not be too long as the wind is sure to increase and we do not want to be late for lunch.' After drifting along this bank for some time I eventually spotted a good rise which, more by luck than judgment, I managed to cover. To my delight the fly was accepted and upon setting the hook the trout, which proved to be a brown, erupted in a magnificent jump. I estimated his weight at well over 5 lb, and it soon became apparent I was in for a tough fight, as I was soon being towed down the lake at quite a smart pace. The end of a perfect morning's fishing, or what might have been, came about ten minutes later when the hook pulled out and I realized I had been taken a further half a mile away from base. The banks here were high and rocky so there was no possibility of wading ashore and walking. To make matters worse the wind was now increasing and was, inevitably, dead against me. I struggled against wind and current for over an hour and I am sure I would have been on the lake for the rest of the day if my friends had not commandeered a boat and come to my rescue.

Despite all the trials and tribulations of my introduction to this new form of fishing I feel that once one has mastered the various techniques involved it could be a very rewarding method of fishing. It would certainly provide most of the advantages to be derived from a boat, without the current high cost of hire. Whether or not our water authorities over here would allow these on our reservoirs remains to be seen, although they certainly could not ban them on grounds of safety. I wonder who will be the first intrepid angler to launch his tube on Grafham or Rutland?

Bonefishing on 'Atomic Island' 1984

Where is the best bonefishing in the world? Unlikely as it may seem, one of the best candidates is Christmas Island in the middle of the Pacific Ocean. Though most people would consider this destination too far away and too difficult to reach, Christmas Island is certainly feasible for anyone considering a visit to Australia, New Zealand, the Far East, or the West Coast of the United States.

A tiny speck on the map of the world, Christmas Island lies about 1,400 miles/2,250 km south of Hawaii and just 119 miles/190 km north of the Equator. One of the largest true coral atolls in the world,

This big bonefish, about to be returned to the sea after an enthralling duel, displays the underslung lower jaw characteristic of this bottom-feeding species. Apart from the bonefish, Christmas Island has several other hard-fighting species to challenge the angler

Christmas Island is about 30 miles/48 km long by 10 miles/16 km across, enclosing a huge lagoon scattered with sand flats – the perfect natural conditions for bonefishing. The island is roughly oval in shape with an average height above sea level of barely 7 feet/2 m. Apart from the many thousands of coconut palms that have been planted over the years, the only other vegetation is a type of coarse grass interspersed with low bushes and mangroves.

First discovered by Captain Cook on 24 December 1777 (Christmas Eve), Christmas Island has had a very chequered history and has been occupied over brief periods by several nations. It has also been bought and sold by various companies interested mainly in the production of copra (the dried meat of coconuts). Christmas Island has never had a permanent population, and it was not until the Second World War that any form of civilization came to the island. After the entry of the United States into the war (December 1941) Christmas Island was developed as a staging-post between Hawaii and the South Pacific. A large runway was constructed, and hundreds of servicemen and construction workers occupied the island for several years.

After the war copra production was resumed and a small labour force returned to Christmas Island, but it was in the late 1950s that the attention of the world was focused on the island. On 15 May 1957, the first British hydrogen bomb was detonated 30 miles/48 km south of Christmas Island. During the next two years many more nuclear devices were tested, but in 1964 all military personnel left Christmas Island and copra production was once again resumed. The island has now been declared completely safe from any lingering radiation hazards.

For most of the century, Christmas Island was under British control as part of the Gilbert and Ellice (or Line) Islands; but in 1978 independence was granted to the Line Islands, and Christmas Island now forms part of the Kiribati Republic. Since gaining independence the new government has encouraged any propositions to provide employment for the growing population, and in 1981 funded the refurbishment of a small hotel complex to attract tourists. The buildings comprise a large single-storey dining area surrounded by modern air-conditioned sleeping units, plus a series of airy thatched bungalows stretching down to the beach. While it can hardly be described as five-star accommodation it is more than adequate, considering it lies more than 1,000 miles/1,600 km from the nearest civilization!

Christmas Island's new hotel can accommodate up to 40 guests and while most of these are usually anglers, a percentage of them are often bird-watchers. The island is indeed a paradise both for ornithologists and fishermen. Since the hotel opened a little over three years ago, several thousand anglers from all over the world have passed through, and so spectacular is the fishing that many of them are now regular visitors to the island.

Despite its close proximity to the Equator, Christmas Island enjoys a very pleasant climate, thanks to the constant trade winds which keep the temperature below 26°C/80°F. The annual rainfall is comparatively low; it usually occurs between December and March, and even then only in the form of showers. The island is indeed a fascinating place, with thousands of different sea birds nesting and breeding there. They are so unafraid of humans that one can move freely among them. The sea shore is littered with an incredible variety of shells, and within yards of the shoreline you can collect shellfish and even large clams which provide a delicious snack.

While many different species of fish are found in the lagoon and around the shores, the biggest attraction the one that brings anglers – from all over the world – is the vast numbers of bonefish that roam the flats which are now considered to be the most productive in the world.

The bonefish, or grey ghost of the flats as he is often called, is now a prime target - particularly for fly fishermen from the United States. While bonefish can be caught relatively easily on a bait-casting rod with shrimp or crab for bait, the ultimate challenge is to catch them on a fly rod. In areas where they are found, the bonefish come up on to the flats to feed as they are covered by the tide, which means that most of the time you are fishing for them in crystal-clear water seldom more than 15 inches/38 cm in depth. Their average weight is 3–4 lbs/1–1.8 kg, though specimens of 10–12 lbs/4.5–5.4 kg are not uncommon. These larger fish are naturally the prime target for the flyfisher but they are incredibly alert in this shallow water. To catch one on a fly you need eyes like a hawk, because until you become practised at spotting them they are very difficult to see. You then need to cast accurately, as you must be able to put your fly down lightly within 2–3 feet/60–90 cm of a feeding fish; any further away and he will not see it, any closer and you will frighten him off.

You can fish for bonefish in two ways – either from a flat-bottomed boat which is manoeuvered for you by a guide, or (where the flats have a firm bottom) you can wade and stalk individual fish. This is my favourite method as it becomes a direct contact between you and the bonefish, and you will have nobody else to blame for any errors you make.

For bonefishing, all you will need is a standard reservoir fly rod of 9-9fi feet/2.8-3 m length to take a 7 to 8 forward taper fine, a large capacity fly reel holding 200 yards/180 m of backing, and a bonefish fly (called a 'Crazy Charlie') in sizes No 6 and No 4, in three colours: pink, white or brown.

The bonefish of Christmas Island are slightly smaller than their cousins in the western hemisphere, but in my opinion they are even more powerful. The first run of a hooked bonefish has to be experienced to be believed, and woe betide the fly fisher who tries to stop this first panic-stricken run to escape from the flat. The hands should be kept well away from the fly reel, relying on the brake and line's drag weight in the water eventually to slow the fish until it can be brought under control. But this seldom happens until he has taken about 150 yards/135 m of line, as I can personally vouch.

For a long time I had felt that it should be possible to stop the average-sized bonefish within 20-30 yards/18-27 m, providing one could get his head up quickly; I regularly practise this successfully with large trout of 7-8 lbs/3-3.5 kg. On my last morning on Christmas Island, having hooked and released over 20 bonefish, I decided to try. The next bonefish to take my fly was a small one of barely 3 lbs/1.4 kg – ideal for the experiment. As soon as I hooked him I clamped my palm to the rim of the fly reel and held the rod as high above my head as I could extend it, expecting the fish to come up to the surface – but no. To my absolute astonishment he kept going and pulled the rod inexorably down until we parted company. This performance left me shaking my head in utter disbelief, as I was using a 10 lb/14.5 kg breaking-strain leader. Normally I do not use such a heavy leader as this, but on Christmas Island I found it necessary; most of the larger fish are found close to the edges of the flats, which are lined with coral. This can slice your leader like a razor if you are unable to stop the fish before he reaches the edge and plunges into the deep channels. It is a problem I have not experienced to any degree in other bonefish areas, but it is certainly acute on Christmas Island.

During my week on the island I hooked a number of superb double figure fish but lost every one on the coral. Unfortunately we had low tides throughout the whole of our week there, so the larger bonefish were not coming up into the heart of the flats. Had they done so I am sure that I could have stopped most of them before they reached the cut-off zone along the edge. One day I am sure I shall return, but when I do I will make certain of being there during a week of high tides!

Salt-water fly fishing, particularly for bonefish, is now rapidly increasing in popularity. While the latest hot spot is undoubtedly Christmas Island, there are many other areas in the world where the bonefishing is extremely good. Bonefish are distributed world-wide and are likely to be found in any areas where there are extensive sand flats covered by the tides in tropical seas. So far the main areas developed for this relatively new and challenging sport are in the Caribbean: the Florida Keys, the Bahamas, Bermuda, the Cayman Islands, plus the coasts of Mexico and Belize. But I am sure that other new locations will soon be discovered, particularly in the vastness of the Pacific Ocean.

Where Twenty-pounders Are Put Back 1985

Steelhead were one of the few species of fish for which I had never fished, so I was particularly pleased to receive an invitation from an old friend who lives in Vancouver to fish for these famed fish. Ehor Boyanowsky is an experienced and dedicated steelhead angler, and I knew I would be in good hands when I accepted.

Ehor had arranged for four of us to fish from a camp set up by the Totem Anglers' Club Vancouver on one of the many famous steelhead rivers in northern British Columbia. In addition to Ehor, my companions on the trip were to be Jay Rowland, of Vancouver, and Ron Cordes, an old friend and a well known outdoor writer and author from the States. Both were keen and experienced steelhead anglers. The Totem Anglers set up camp under canvas every year in August on this particular river for the five-week period of the run, and four anglers can be accommodated there each week. They allow occasional guests of members, so I was lucky to be asked.

These superb fish are undoubtedly the most sought-after species on the west coast of the North American continent. During the first half of this century they were prolific and widespread, and most rivers along the west coast had heavy runs. Sad to relate, during the last 30 years they have become almost an endangered species, due to a combination of over-fishing, pollution and the damming of many rivers for hydro-electric schemes. Fortunately, due to strict controls on both pleasure and commercial fishing, the situation is now gradually improving.

Steelhead range from the Russian River, north of San Francisco, in the south to Alaska in the north. They can be caught in some rivers all the year round, while most have either summer or winter runs, the latter being of wider distribution. Some anglers may be surprised to hear that steelhead are in reality our old friend the rainbow trout in its migratory form, spending most of their life in the northern Pacific and returning, like the salmon, to the river of their birth to spawn. Fresh-run fish are bright silver with tiny black spots along the dorsal surface, but as they ascend the rivers to spawn they become darker, the spots more pronounced, and the typical red band appears along the flanks. The largest steelhead recorded is one of 42 lb taken off Bell Island in Alaska, and the largest taken on a fly weighed a staggering 33 lb. However, these were exceptional fish. The size taken on fly from most rivers is in the region of 7–10 lb, while fish in excess of 20 lb are rare.

Most American anglers favour standard single-handed trout rods of 9–10 ft and capable of casting lines between weights size 8 and 10. Fly-reels are of large capacity, as at least 150 yds of backing is a necessity. Under favourable conditions steelhead may be taken on the dry fly, but most anglers use either slow or fast-sinking lines depending on the flow and depth of the river. At times heavy lead-core lines are necessary to get the fly down to the fish. Shooting-heads are extremely popular for steelhead fishing, no doubt due to the width of many of the rivers. In fact, shooting-heads were introduced specifically for steelhead on the Eel and Klamath Rivers in 1949.

We left Vancouver by light aircraft on a bright, warm, sunny morning in late August last year bound for Bellacoolla, a small airstrip in the Northern Province. Here it was necessary to change to an islander, the only aircraft capable of landing on the tiny dirt strip at the mouth of the river we were to fish. Shortly after leaving Bellacoolla the weather closed in and we had to fly below the low cloud base throughout the mountain passes rather than over, a hair-raising experience.

Jay Rowland about to release my 21 lb steelhead

One of our favourite pools on the Dean River

We were met at the airstrip by an old Ford pick-up and an even more ancient driver, and then driven about 10 miles upriver along an old logging track.

To reach the campsite on the river we had to trek nearly half-a-mile over very rough terrain, and it took three journeys to transport all our baggage, tackle and food for the week. While the others made light of this chore, I was totally exhausted, and for the first time came to the conclusion that I was getting too old for this sort of trip.

The camp-site was quite comfortable, but it took us the rest of that day to settle in. This mattered little, as the river was coloured and milky with glacial run-off from heavy rain the previous day, so fishing would have been a waste of time, anyway. This river, like so many steelhead rivers in BC, is of glacial origin, powerful, boulder-strewn and cold, so wading, unfortunately essential on this type of river, was both difficult and physically demanding. However, as we were soon to find out, this was of little consequence as the river was full of fresh-run fish.

The following day, within the hour, I was into my first steelhead. Never shall I forget this first fish. The initial run of more than 100 yards was quite unstoppable. Eventually, though, the fish slowed down. Then, as soon as I applied some pressure, it exploded out of the water, twisting, turning and shaking its head in an effort to dislodge the fly. After a further seven magnificent, heart-stopping jumps, and several more powerful runs, I felt a little confidence returning and started to think that I might even land it.

About seven minutes later – I am sure it was hours – I eventually beached the fish. For a few moments I was in agony as the pressure was released from my rod-arm, and then, as the pain eased, I was able to appreciate the sheer wild beauty of the great silver fish lying quietly on its side. Like a newly-minted silver coin, with tiny black spots, perfect fins and streamlined shape, I could not help but compare it with an 8½ lb rainbow I had caught from the River Kennet shortly before my holiday began. Really there was no comparison at all, in either the fish or the fight. After measuring the fish and removing the fly, it was gently returned to continue on its way, hopefully to spawn and reproduce. From the measurements taken, the estimated weight was a little over 14 lb – a truly memorable fish to mark my initiation.

The sheer power of these fish is quite astonishing. Pound for pound they must be the hardest-fighting species I have ever encountered. The take and first run is rather frightening, as it is so fast and savage. The spool of the reel revolves so fast the handles are but a blur, and woe betide the fisherman who instinctively puts his hand to the reel at this stage. With the best will in the world, in the excitement of the moment it inevitably happens occasionally, even to the most experienced angler, and we were certainly no exception. By the end of the week's fishing we were all suffering considerably from bruised and cut fingers.

The fishing was magnificent. In six days the four of us hooked 139 steelhead with an average weight of well over 12 lb. We actually beached 107 of these, which is a high percentage as the fish fight so hard it is normal for the hook to pull out on more than 50 per cent. The average weight was also high, and we all had several fish in excess of 18 lb. My best steelhead was 21 lb, but the best fish of the week was caught by Jay and at a little over 23 lb was the largest steelhead by far that he had ever caught.

We were lucky to have hit the river just right, and on our return we found out that our catch for the week was one of the highest recorded in BC in recent years, and certainly the top weight ever recorded from this particular river. We released 106 of the 107 fish we caught, killing one for supper one evening. It made delicious eating.

This type of fishing is physically exceedingly demanding, and as I stood in the river up to my waist in very cold water on the last morning, I was literally praying for the first time in my life that another fish would not take my fly. I had just released a steelhead of nearly 19 lb which took me more than half-a-mile downriver through two lots of rapids before I was able to beach it.

My prayers were not answered, as shortly afterwards I found myself fighting a losing battle with another powerful fish which craftily outmanoeuvered me and reached the rapids at the end of the pool. Trying to follow, I tripped over a large boulder and measured my length in the river, losing the fish in the process. Soaked through, I now felt I had a legitimate excuse to call it a day, so with a sigh of relief I deserted my fellow-anglers and returned to camp for dry clothes and hot coffee laced with plenty of brandy.

During our week in the wilderness we had many other adventures, including a rather frightening encounter with an ill-tempered bear. But that is another story . . .

In the Footsteps of Zane Grey 1985

The early settlers in New Zealand must have been very astute fellows. It did not take them long to realize they had a wealth of crystal-clear waters simply crying out to be stocked with fish of some kind. Fortunately for anglers all over the world they made the right decision and decided to stock with trout – both rainbow and brown – and at a later date, of course, with salmon.

So far as I am aware, the first batches of ova were sent from England in 1869, with further consignments arriving in 1870–71. It had also been suggested that some trout, or more probably ova, were sent to the South Island from Australia and were originally supplied to that country by Francis Francis, the well-known angling author. Unfortunately, some of those early consignments of ova were from sea-trout, not brownies, so that in due course the major strain for stocking the rivers was a cross between a brown trout and a sea-trout. This resulted in a type of trout that retained most of the characteristics if its more virile parent the sea-trout, so today most of New Zealand's brownies are migratory. All the rainbow trout in the country are also migratory, as all the ova for these came from American steelhead stock.

By the turn of the century most of the bigger rivers and lakes in both the North and South Island had been stocked with either rainbows, brownies, or both. In the unpolluted waters, with few predators and no competition from other species, the trout thrived and in some places reached enormous sizes. The peak was reached in the first quarter of this century, when Zane Grey mounted his first now famous expedition to the country in 1926 and described it as the 'angler's eldorado'.

Certainly the halcyon days of the 1920s – when double-figure trout were quite common – have disappeared. Today, apart from the spawning run up the rivers out of Lake Taupo, double-figure trout are to be found only in some of the more remote rivers. This gradual deterioration in the fishing is due mainly to the introduction of hydro-electric schemes and increased angling pressure from overseas visitors. However, the fishing is still fantastic and undoubtedly as good, if not better, than any other trout fishing in the world.

During the early part of this year I was privileged to spend nearly seven weeks touring and fishing both the North and South Islands. It turned out to be the greatest fishing adventure of my life!

We arrived in Christchurch in mid-February and after a day's rest set out for a tour of the South Island. Space does not permit me to cover our complete itinerary but suffice it to say that during the next three weeks my wife and I visited most of the larger towns and cities and also fished many of the major rivers and lakes. Sadly, some of the famous rivers were in raging flood and consequently unfishable, but this is something one just has to accept – particularly in the South Island. This is never really a serious problem, however, as when it happens one just moves on to another area. The scenery particularly in South Island, can only be described as spectacular, for the southern alps dominate this area and form a magnificent backdrop to the startling blue lakes which seem to be present in every large valley.

One of the great pleasures of fishing in this lovely country is the variety of the trout fishing. Within the space of a few days you can find yourself fishing in small clear ponds or deep, indigo-blue lakes, from slow-flowing gravel-bedded streams like the Mataura to rapidly flowing, boulder strewn rivers like the Edglington and on to incredibly fast-flowing rivers such as the Haast. Another of the great joys of fishing in New Zealand is that once you have paid for a visitor's fishing licence, which is less than £50 for the whole of your stay, all waters are open to you as there is no such thing as private fishing. You may at times have to seek permission from local farmers to fish waters on their land, but this is rarely refused. Apart from this the peace and solitude is unique, for rarely does one see another fisherman.

I found the fishing a tremendous challenge as, being there late in the season, I had to work very hard in some cases to find fish and I must confess I did have quite a few blank days. On the other hand I also had some highly rewarding ones! The trout fishing is very demanding, as the fish are truly wild and they will allow you only one mistake. On the plus side the average trout in New Zealand is big and during seven weeks' fishing I had very few weighing less than 3 lb. Brownies predominate in the South Island and in one afternoon alone I had seven between 4 lb and 8½ lb. As an example of the diversity of the fishing over there, four of these brownies came from a tiny stream barely five feet wide.

If you are prepared to accept slightly colder weather, the best time to fish the South Island is during late spring or early summer, which is November and December. At this time of year many of the rivers are full of fish and furthermore this is the best time for insect hatches, so the dry-fly fishing is infinitely better.

Fishing guides are freely available in both Islands and although, through choice, I managed without one in the South Island I would strongly recommend that, if you can afford it, you should engage one – particularly if you are there later in the season, when there are fewer fish about. A good guide knows exactly where the best fishing is to be found and can save you a lot of wasted time and effort. Like anywhere else the cream of the fishing is to be found in the more remote areas, and if expense is no object I would strongly recommend a stay at one of the many fishing lodges as they employ experienced guides to take clients into the remoter fishing areas either by four-wheel-drive vehicles or by light aircraft or helicopters. One of the top lodges in the South Island, and one I can thoroughly recommend, is Cedar Lodge, run by a charming character and excellent fisherman named Dick Frazer. This is near Makarora, below the Haast Pass.

A magnificent 11 lb rainbow from Lake Otamangakau

Alan Simmons, a top guide from Turangi, holds a huge super wild brown trout for the author

The North Island has a much bigger population and while it is more pastoral it is also mountainous and still has several active volcanoes. The fishing here is centred around Lake Taupo, which was once a huge volcanic crater. Covering over 240 square miles this must be one of the most impressive trout lakes in the world as well as being one of the richest, producing a yield of almost 500 tons of trout every season. A day on or along the shore of this splendid mass of water is always an unforgettable experience. The land is little removed from the wilderness and the whole area is fiercely volcanic: beetling lava cliffs dominate one shore while the others slope up to the surrounding mountains interspersed here and there with rivers flowing into the lake. One of these is the world-famous Tongariro, where many, many tons of trout are taken every year - especially during the spawning runs. On the banks of this river stands Tongariro Lodge, a mecca for visiting anglers from all over the world. While large brown trout are to be found both in Taupo and many of the surrounding rivers, the rainbows are the most prolific species.

Because of the vast size of the lake the only really effective way to fish it from a boat is by trolling. There are many operators hiring specially equipped craft on the lake, but I was particularly impressed by the company I used - South Pacific Sporting Adventures run by an extremely helpful and experienced angler named Simon C. Dickie. Based in the town of Taupo they run several large superbly equipped luxury launches and you can have a day out on one of these for about £25, which is wonderful value when you consider that this includes the use of all tackle with free beer or soft drinks as well as a superb barbeque lunch. You can either harl with a fly rod and fly, or you can troll a fly deep with a downrigger on a heavy rod with a good chance of catching a real monster.

John Goddard returns a 6 lb brownie

The most productive period for fishing the lake's tributary rivers is when the winter spawning runs take place. This is during their winter between May and August, but a good compromise would be October or November as a proportion of the fish from the lake will still be running up the river and by then the weather will be warmer. When the rainbows are running, some fantastic catches can be made and at this time it is not uncommon for one angler in a day's fishing to take 20–30 fish averaging at least 5 lb. Fishing from the shore of the lake can also prove excellent at certain times of the year – particularly in the many river mouths where they enter the lake. A lot of local anglers fish these either at night or very early in the morning as huge brown trout frequent these areas and double-figure fish are by no means uncommon. There is also excellent fishing in the many rivers of the mountains and hills to the south and west of the lake. However, many of these are difficult of access, so it is advisable to have a competent guide. One of the best is Gary Kemsley, who knows this area like the back of his hand. A few of these back-country rivers hold big brown trout but require a four-wheel-drive vehicle to reach them, and the only guide I know who has a licence to take you into some of these areas with such a vehicle is Alan Simmons, of Turungi. I can assure you a day with him on such an expedition is one of life's great experiences!

Finally, if you really want a trophy trout, take a tent and food for a two- or three-day trip to one of the remote mountain rivers. A helicopter will fly you in and pick you up at a pre-arranged rendezvous higher up the river. These rivers are gin-clear and full of superb pools. I shall never forget the sight of enormous rainbows and brownies cruising around some of these pools, in water so clear that they seemed to be suspended in the air. Some of them must have weighed more than 15 lb.

Fly Fishing in Mexico 1989

Tortillas, tacos and tequila – abject poverty, revolutions and the extreme wealth of many cities such as Acapulco on its Pacific coast. This can only be Mexico, a land of strange contrasts.

None, however, is stranger than the differences between its west coast bordering the mighty Pacific ocean, well populated and lined with opulent cities to attract the super rich holidaymakers from America and other countries from all over the world, and its south-east coast on the Caribbean. This is the Yucatán Peninsula, a vast under-populated and under-developed area the size of Florida.

Once, many hundreds of years ago this area was the centre of the ancient Mayan civilization and boasted at least a dozen large heavily-populated cities. By the end of the 15th century for some strange and as yet unknown reason this ancient yet highly gifted civilization had all but vanished, leaving their cities to fall into ruin and in many cases to be reclaimed by the jungle. The peninsula now forms one of the largest and most important archaeological sites in the Western Hemisphere.

My first sight of the Caribbean coast of the peninsula was a total surprise, as after a two-hour overland drive from the international airport at Cancun through arid scrub jungle, we arrived at Boca Paila on the coast, to be greeted by mile upon mile of bleached white sand bordered with majestic coconut palms bowing to the constant sea breezes which help to make the average 80 degree annual tempera-tures the perfect holiday climate. With the sparkling azure blue sea breaking over the coral reef which extends all along this coast, I was almost convinced that I had been transported in error to a tropical island in the Pacific.

The main purpose of my visit was to sample the magnificent sea fishing which was reputed to exist in this part of the world, and in this aspect I was certainly not to be disappointed. Originally the site of a small Mayan fishing community, Boca Paila now contains one of the best and most efficiently-run fishing camps that I have had the pleasure to visit.

It is now run by Pali Gonzales, whose late husband was the mayor of Cancun. Pali is a superb cook so if you like traditional Mexican or fresh seafood a real treat is in store for visitors to the camp. The central dining area overlooks the beach as do the individual sleeping chalets, and one can be fishing within two or three minutes of leaving the camp.

Although this camp caters specifically for fishermen, non-fishing wives who may wish to accompany their husbands will not be disappointed if they like the outdoor life. The swimming facilities are excellent and very safe along the beach on the inside of the reef, and for those keen on snorkelling one can spend hours but yards from the beach gazing down upon a bewildering variety of gaily-coloured reef fish that you only normally see in large aquariums at zoos.

You can also walk along almost virgin beaches for mile upon mile in perfect solitude, either beachcombing or shell collecting. In addition, this area is a paradise for anyone interested in ornithology as there are well over 100 species of birds in the area. These include many species of herons, brilliant white egrets, flaming pink spoonbills, eagles, ospreys and the scarlet-chested male frigate birds constantly soaring overhead.

Left The author with two fine snook taken on fly *Right* A fine tarpoon caught on an Orvis 9 ft fly rod at Boca Paila

As a special treat, a boat trip can be arranged to a nearby bird island which takes but half an hour. This ideally should be arranged for just before sunset, as at this time the maximum number of species will be seen as they return to roost in the trees for the night.

For those visiting the area for the first time, at least one day should be reserved for a sightseeing tour of at least two or three of the important Mayan sites that abound on the peninsula. Many of these are but a two-hour drive from the camp. The closest is the ancient coastal city of Tulum which takes less than 40 minutes to reach. These ruins perched on high cliffs overlooking the sea are quite spectacular and relatively well preserved as it is one of the last cities to be established well after the Mayan civilization had passed its peak. This apparently dates its origins from about 700 AD to possibly 1000 AD.

Another much older site within easy reach is Coba, which was built around several splendid freshwater lakes and covers a very extensive area. Although this very ancient typical Mayan city was first discovered in 1897, it was not until 1973 that it was opened up by the Mexican government after the worst of the jungle surrounding it was removed.

Excavation of the site is likely to continue well into the future. This site is so large that it would take many days just to walk, and apart from other buildings there are many hundreds of pyramids alone. The largest of these is the great pyramid of Nohoch Mul which towers 140 ft above the jungle floor, and is almost as impressive as some of the great pyramids in Egypt.

While other smaller sites may be visited in the general area if one has the time and the inclination, two other major sites can be reached. These are the world famous Mayan ruins at Chichen Itza and Uxmal, almost on the north coast of the Yucatán. The latter city was constructed somewhere between the 6th and 7th centuries, and even after all this time its massive stone structures are still awesome. Many of the wooden beams used in its construction are still intact, and most authorities consider that Uxmal contains some of the finest examples of ancient stone masonry in the whole of Mexico.

Many visitors to Boca Paila spend a day or so in Cancun either on the way in or out. This is one of only two modern cities on the Yucatán peninsula and from its inception just 16 years ago was purpose-planned as a holiday resort. The government very sensibly restricted the height and density of building here to ensure it will never become overcrowded, so it is a very pleasant resort in which to spend a little time.

There are many excellent restaurants and nightclubs, and water sports of all types are available, as the city is built on an island almost 14 miles long. If you want to catch a billfish such as a sailfish or a marlin, this is one of the best areas in the world for these majestic fish, particularly during May and June, which is probably the peak period.

These days few people can afford the cost for a charter of a fully equipped big game fishing boat for more than an odd day, so I think that this is the reason that more and more fishermen are turning to inshore species of fish that can give fine sport on light tackle at a fraction of the cost.

While the bulk of anglers are probably still using bait or spin casting outfits, an increasing number has become hooked on fishing for those species that frequent shallow water or the very shallow sand flats with flies and a fly rod. Most anglers who have fished for salmon, trout or bass with a fly rod take to salt water fly fishing, as we call it, like a duck to water. While it requires much more skill and patience, and also the ability to handle sometimes very large fish on a very light line and rod, it is quite amazing how quickly most freshwater fly fishers can adapt.

The fishing camp at Boca Paila is one of many camps that have now become established in many parts of the world in tropic or semi-tropic seas where in shallow crystal clear water it is possible to see and stalk various species that frequent these areas.

This camp particularly encourages fly rodders, and the guides are all very experienced in the demands required in this type of fishing. Papo, the camp manager, is a mine of information on the fishing, and will be only too pleased to assist you arrange your day's schedule.

Most anglers visiting the camp share a boat and a guide which helps to spread the cost. The flat-bottomed cathedral-hulled boats about 15 ft long and powered by outboards, are adequate for fishing in this area, which in my experience is quite unique. The camp has been built in the middle of a strip of coast probably 20 miles long and no more than a few hundred yards in width with the ocean on one side and a series of salt water lagoons all along the other side.

All of the fishing takes place in the comparative shelter of these shallow lagoons. These harbour an amazing variety of fish embracing all the more popular species to be expected in such an area from bonefish through to quite large tarpon.

All species of saltwater fish seem to fight harder than their freshwater cousins, particularly those species that frequent shallow water.

Pound for pound, the bonefish is probably the strongest fish that swims, and even a small specimen of a little over 2 lb will take all of your fly line plus a lot of backing on his first run before you dare try to stop him. These fish are comparatively easy to take on a bait casting rod, but on a fly rod success demands pretty accurate casting.

The bonefish in the Boca Paila lagoons although plentiful are rather small, and any fish over 4 lb may be considered a specimen. My best bonefish during my visit was close to 7 lb, and I understand that this was quite exceptional.

However, it is the other species of fish that frequent these lagoons that in my opinion make this one of the best all-round locations in the world for the dedicated and serious fly rodder. School tarpon, some up to 50 or 60 lb apiece, roam the lagoon throughout most of the year, and will take even an experienced fly fisher 30 or 40 minutes of exhausting physical effort to subdue.

Some of these are also found in among the mangroves and are great fun to hook even though there is little chance of landing them. There are probably more permit fish to be seen in these lagoons than in any other area I have ever visited, and some of these were very large, certainly in excess of 40 lb. The permit is a most handsome fish and is the biggest challenge of all to the fly fisherman as while they will

The fearsome barracuda shows its jaws – but was taken on fly

The author with fly-caught permit – one of the premier quarry at Boca Paila

often follow a fly they seldom take it. Only a very small percentage of fly fishers have ever caught one; indeed it took me over 10 years to boat my first specimen.

Fearsome looking barracuda are often encountered in the lagoon and I saw quite a few that I estimated to be over 30 lb. This species when caught in the open sea in deep water put up a poor fight, but hook one of these in shallow water on a light fly rod and you have a real battle on your hands.

The largest I boated during my stay was just over 28 lb. At the time I was wading one of the very shallow flats for bonefish when I saw this barracuda and cast my bonefish fly to it. He took savagely and I was lucky to hook him in the top lip, otherwise his razor sharp teeth would have very quickly cut through my nylon leader. Normally when fishing for this species, it is necessary to mount a short wire leader in front of your fly, as if you do not you are likely to be cut off from every fish you hook.

Various species of snappers can also be found in some areas, and at times these can often be tempted with a fly. However, in my opinion, the most interesting and exciting species of fish to be found in the Boca Paila lagoons are the snook. These crafty fish live in among the mangrove roots in many of the mangrove islands that dot the lagoons, and only come out into the open water to feed in the early mornings.

Fly fishing for them is very demanding as it is often necessary to cast your fly into gaps in the mangroves to cover feeding fish and as soon as you hook one he has but one goal – the sanctuary of the mangroves.

My friend Ivan Smith and I caught quite a few up to about 12 lb, but two much larger fish I hooked would not be denied their sanctuary and there was just no way I could stop them with the tackle I was using. My visit took place during April, but I understand that there are many more snook and tarpon present during October and November after the annual rains during September.

I would also point out that while stopping at Boca Paila daily trips can be arranged to Ascension Bay, where there is a number of huge, shallow, silver sand flats. Perfect for wading, these flats are alive with huge shoals of bonefish, mostly small.

However, I understand there is one flat which reputedly harbours very large bonefish as they have been caught in this area up to 11 lb. Ascension Bay can only be reached by boat and as it takes about two hours each way, a visit is only to be recommended on a calm day with little wind.

Paradise is Just Two Sleeping Pills Away 1990

There is a very old saying that once you have drunk the waters of the Nile a little bit of Africa enters your blood and you are bound to return.

I am now certain that this also applies to the world famous Tongariro river in New Zealand. It would appear that the green waters of this lovely river have certainly entered my bloodstream as I have now visited this most beautiful of countries five times in the last four years and cannot wait to return yet again.

Not so long ago a holiday in New Zealand, unless one was retired with unlimited time and money, would have appeared as an impossible dream, but today with the advent of the big long distance jets it is but 24 hours and two sleeping pills away.

While the air fare is relatively expensive, unless one is prepared to shop around, the cost of living in New Zealand is relatively low, so the overall cost of a holiday there is now within the budget for many. Hotels are few and far between, but clean and very comfortable motels proliferate and most of these for two occupants cost as little as £20 a night, or one can do as I do now and rent a holiday cottage for as little as £70 a week providing you are out of the main local holiday period which extends through December to early January.

During the past 25 years, I have been most fortunate to fish all over the world for anything that swims from trout to marlin but so far as I am concerned nowhere else compares even remotely with the quality and challenge of the trout fishing here. Mind you, since Zane Grey wrote of the vast numbers of huge trout he caught in these waters in the early part of this century, a myth has persisted to this day that even the tyro can extract double figure trout with consummate ease from any river he chooses to fish. Not so. What few people failed to realize at that time was that Grey spent most of his time fishing one river – the Tongariro and this was during the winter when huge numbers of trout leave Lake Taupo to ascend the rivers to spawn in the headwaters.

Even in New Zealand this situation is unique as few if any other rivers in this country have such large numbers of trout ascending such a fishable river for so long a period (May to August). During the mid twenties when Grey fished this area, trout fishing in New Zealand was at its peak and with few other fishermen in those days to compete with he must have had a ball.

From the thirties to the early fifties as fishing became more popular, both the numbers and size of the trout in this river deteriorated and the double figure trout that once were so common all but disappeared. Happily the

John displays a 10½ lb brown trout typical of North Island's Lake Waikaremoana

fishing has improved considerably, although it will never return to its former glory as, like so many large rivers all over the world, it now also suffers from water abstraction.

While there are many other rivers in New Zealand similar to the Tongariro, fast, and slightly coloured, that can only sensibly be fished with large heavily weighted nymphs upstream or the downstream wet fly, these are very much in the minority. Most of the fishing takes place in small, sandy-bottomed or gravelly gin clear streams or the pools of larger boulder-strewn rivers where the water is often so clear one can count every stone on the bottom.

Under these conditions it is essential to spot the trout before he sees you and as these are all wild fish, they can be very spooky indeed and difficult to approach. Most of this fishing, at least from mid-summer onwards, is accomplished with small nymphs, while in the spring and early summer when hatches of upwinged flies are most prevalent, they can often be taken on the dry fly.

The fishing is very challenging and even a reasonably competent and skilled fly fisher is unlikely to average more than two or three trout a day during the summer or autumn. However, by our standards, these are large and will all be between four and eight pounds. The fishing can also be very physically demanding as most rivers in New Zealand tend to run through very steep ravines or in gorges with sheer cliffs, and to reach the more productive sections of many of these rivers one literally has to climb down, then wade upstream often over boulders and against strong currents. There are of course many areas of easy access on most of these rivers and, while in the spring or early summer all will hold good trout, by mid-January the majority of these spots will be devoid of trout. Unfortunately for visitors most kiwis are avid fishermen and as they kill all they catch, by the time the annual holidays in December are over there are few trout left in any of the more accessible stretches of rivers.

I would therefore suggest that unless you are pretty fit and want good fishing, you should endeavour to fish New Zealand in the spring or early summer which is from mid October to early December. The problem with this time of the year though is the weather which is notoriously fickle in New Zealand, particularly early in the year. Wet weather is far more likely at this time particularly in the South Island which means unless you are lucky many rivers will be in flood and unfishable.

A typical New Zealand wilderness river

Apart from the Taupo area in the North Island, the best fishing in New Zealand is undoubtably between Invercargil and Queenstown in the South Island or along the West Coast. But, as both areas have more than 200 inches of rain a year, many of the better rivers fluctuate enormously. For this reason it is all but impossible to plan a fishing itinerary in advance. As a result of three fairly extensive fishing tours of the South Island, I have now come to the conclusion that one should be prepared to be very mobile. The heavy rain often proves to be local and by travelling perhaps 50 or 60 miles from one mountain range over to another, you can find rivers which are in good order.

While these are some of the problems associated with a fishing holiday in New Zealand, they pale into insignificance when compared to the actual quality of the trout fishing. To fish for hard-fighting, truly wild trout in gin clear unpolluted water in such magnificent scenery is my idea of heaven.

To anyone contemplating a fishing holiday in New Zealand I would offer this one piece of advice. If you can afford it, do seriously consider employing a good fishing guide for at least one or two days in each area that you intend to fish. While a good guide will cost you in the region of £75 to £100 a day shared between two or three fishermen, it is a relatively small sum to pay for the advantages gained. First and foremost he will know the stretches of rivers that are still holding good trout. Secondly, he will know the best access points to reach these areas and finally he will be able to advise the best methods and patterns to use.

If you do travel to New Zealand for a fishing holiday, unless you are able to spare five or six weeks, you must make a choice between the South or the North Island as it would be quite impractical to fish both in a shorter period. If you decide on the South Island, I would suggest that you fly either to Denedin or Invercargil and there hire a car and fish your way up towards Queenstown, and from there across the Haast Pass to the West Coast right up to Nelson in the north of the South Island. In the space of a short article it is impossible to list all the rivers and lakes one should fish on the way, but if they are fishable I will mention a few that should not be missed.

The Mataura river between Gore and Lumsden, a quite small but fine dry fly river. The Hamilton Burn to the south of Mossburn holds larger browns. The Orett to the north of Mossburn, is a much larger stony but clear and faster river than either of the others, where a large weighted nymph fished upstream will take brown trout that average well over five pounds. The Eglinton River which runs alongside Lake Te Anau is a large fast river that holds both big browns and rainbows. The Clutha in the vicinity of Cromwell, one of the largest rivers in New Zealand, often has good evening rises for both browns and rainbows, and from midsummer onwards very big browns can often be tempted by fishing the margins upstream with a big dry sedge late in the evening.

Try fishing the south end of Lake Wanaka along the margins for big cruising browns on a sunny day. The Makarora River flows into the north end of this lake; this is a large, fast stony river that holds large rainbows. It also has two excellent tributaries that flow into it, both of which are gin clear and have large deep holding pools where you can spot and stalk your fish. These are the Wilkin River near the mouth which can only be reached by jet boat or the Young River a little further up, which can be reached by wading across the Makarora if it is low enough.

After crossing the Haast Pass and travelling up the west coast there are few rivers of note until you reach Hari Hari. Here you will cross the La Fontain River, an excellent brown trout stream offering some of the finest dry fly fishing in the South Island. A little further north is Hokatika where inland from the sea lies a large fertile green valley that holds many small, clear spring creeks which hold very large brown trout.

Just to the north of this town, one crosses the Arahura River which is well worth fishing further inland. A few miles inland from Greymouth lies Lake Brunner where large brown trout can often be seen cruising the margins.

Current patterns popular in New Zealand. *Top row:* Craig's Nightime and Bug Eye Nymph. *Below:* the Blue Darter Nymph and a large Pheasant Tail Nymph

Paddle-tailed and ten pounds of solid muscle, this superb fish from Lake Rotorua, is a picture of what every rainbow should really look like

At the south end of Brunner, Bruce Creek enters the lake. This is a weedy but very clear and quite short river, reminiscent of our own chalk streams, that holds some very large brown trout. Between Lake Brunner and Lake Rotora there are many nice streams to fish and when you get to the top of the Island be sure to spend a little time on the Motueka river. The road from the little town of Motueka runs alongside this river for nearly forty miles and gives easy access to this fine river that holds a good head of brown trout and provides good dry fly or small nymph fishing.

Finally do not miss the little Rye River on the way to Picton. The water is so clear it takes on a strange blue green appearance in the deeper stretches and it provides excellent but difficult dry fly fishing for good sized browns.

So far as the North Island is concerned, the weather is generally much kinder with far less rain, particularly on the high central plateau where Lake Taupo lies. This lake is of course a legend in itself and I can still remember as a small boy gazing at photographs of the famous picket fence of fly fishers. This

John unhooks a hefty rainbow taken from the glass green waters of the Waimarino River

was a solid line of anglers but feet apart fishing the mouth of the Waitahanui River which runs along the shoreline where it empties into the lake. This is my current favoured area for fishing in New Zealand as you have a mass of excellent rivers within a two hour drive of Turangi at the south end of the lake which are rarely unfishable due to too much rain, unless you are of course unlucky enough to be there when the very occasional cyclone passes through. Even then the rivers are unlikely to be unfishable for more than a few days. In addition to all these rivers you also have the bonus of Lake Taupo itself and the rivers that drain into it, including the world famous Tongariro. Apart from January and early February, one can take good trout from this river all the year, although the best period to fish this river is during the New Zealand winter in late June through July and August when the huge runs of rainbows are passing up to spawn in the headwaters.

However, at this period the river is very heavily fished attracting fly fishers from all over the world as well as locals and it is often necessary to queue up to fish many of the more popular pools. For this reason my favoured time is late February through March as at this time it is little fished but there are always a few rainbows starting to run at this time and they are usually bigger fish. In addition to this it is undoubtedly the best period to catch some of the very big browns which run up the river to spawn in March.

On my recent visit at this time of year I had several lovely browns between seven and nine pounds and one superb brown of just over 10 lb. One can also at this time of the year experience some very exciting fishing at night in the many river mouths entering the lake. If you are well heeled you can also charter a helicopter (about £125 to take you in and a similar sum to come in and collect you) to take you into some of the back country rivers where I have observed both rainbow and brown trout in excess of 15 lb.

The tackle required for trout fishing in New Zealand is fairly unsophisticated, as for most of the fishing two outfits will suffice. An eight or eight and a half foot rod to take a No. 5 or No. 6 floating line, and a nine or ten foot rod to take a forward taper No. 8 floating line. You may also want to take a slightly heavier rod to take a No. 10 or even No. 11 sinking line for fishing a wet fly or lure in the deeper rivers and lakes. Suitable flies may be purchased locally but take a good number of weighted Pheasant Tail or Hare and Copper nymphs in sizes from No. 16 down to about No. 12 including some nice bushy high floating sedge patterns.

Both Alan Simmons and Simon Dickie, two of the top guides in the Turangi-Taupo area, both favour small well-dressed dry flies such as a Royal Wulff or a Coachman. During recent years, few if any really new patterns have evolved in New Zealand, but in the last year or so a new quite revolutionary pattern has appeared in the Taupo area which is rapidly gaining popularity. This is graced by the name the RTV fly. Take a long shank No. 6, 8 or 10 hook and whip along the top of the shank one of these permanently luminous little glass tubes, this is then covered with clear epoxy and formed into a fish shape with a long tail. When it has dried, this looks like a little transluscent fish and is meant to imitate the smelt that form the main basis of food for the trout in Lake Taupo. These may be worth trying on some of our big lakes when the trout are often preoccupied feeding on fry.

The Best in the West 1992

The USA offers some of the best trout fishing in the world but, because it is such a vast country, the visitor from abroad often finds difficulty in deciding where to go. Many of the famous rivers with world-wide reputations are in areas that have little else to offer. So where should one head? The middle of the country has many excellent rivers and lakes, but no great variety of water in any one area, so the choice lies between mountainous areas near the east and west coasts, both of which have a great deal of water from which to choose.

If I were heading for the east coast, I would probably opt for the Catskill Mountains, north of New York, which have varied rivers, streams and lakes in a relatively small area. In the west, I have no doubt whatever that I would choose Montana, Idaho and Wyoming, nestling among the Rocky Mountains. It is here that many of the largest and most famous rivers in the States have their sources.

These three states, particularly Montana, which is my favourite, offer an incredible variety of water, from small ponds to huge lakes, mighty rivers and small streams, as well as crystal-clear spring creeks. In addition, Montana boasts some of the most awe-inspiring scenery in the world.

I have spent several fishing holidays in Montana during the last 20 years or so, have come to know it well and have met many colourful characters. Early last year one of these kind friends insisted that I spend ten days or so with him on his ranch in Montana in the coming July. I accepted with alacrity, as he has the most beautiful spring creek running through his property.

I arrived in late June only to be told that the fishing was rather poor, as the summer was late and it was still too cold. For the first four days we had to work hard for those fish we caught, but on the fifth day the weather changed and became almost too hot. Despite this, we had some magnificent sport.

This is one of the prettiest yet most demanding spring creeks I have ever fished – gin-clear, with plentiful bright-green weeds, and running through open meadows. The clear water, combined with high banks and lack of background cover, made approach to any fish a major operation.

The creek holds a good head of wild brown trout and even a few rainbows. The browns average 2½ lb, and every year a few superb fish close to double figures are caught and released.

At first I put a lot of fish down because of my approach and length of leader. My host, an experienced fly-fisher, soon corrected my faults by lengthening my leader to about 20 ft and showing me how to approach the trout by crawling along like an Apache Indian or, where the water was shallow enough, to wade stealthily towards the fish, close to the high bank.

To catch these browns in the clear water, we had to use 6x or 7x tippets with dry flies in sizes 18–22, and to grass the larger trout of 5 lb and more needed much patience with such fine leaders in weedy water.

I vividly recall two particular incidents in our ten days' fishing. In the first, I saw what appeared to be a large trout rising close to the bank on a wide, shallow stretch of the creek with little current. It was in an area where the bank was only inches above the water. I decided my only chance of taking this trout was to crawl on my stomach as close to it as possible and cast while lying down. Gaining position took a long time. I found it impossible to cast while lying on my stomach, so I turned on my back. Casting was still difficult as I was surrounded by long grass and kept snagging my fly on the back-cast.

My host, who had been watching my manoeuvres, was almost having hysterics as he saw me spending more time retrieving my fly from the grass than in casting. But I had the last laugh, because I eventually covered the trout and succeeded in landing it – a superb 5½ lb brown.

The second incident involved a huge trout rising in a pool above a long, shallow rapid. This time the problem was that two smaller trout were rising immediately below the big fish. So first I had to hook and remove these as quietly as possible. I managed this, much to my satisfaction, and turned my attention to the big fellow.

After almost an hour of frustrating casting and having all my offer-

Left: A typical wild brown trout from a Montana spring creek   *Right:* Gary Borger, one of America's best known anglers, extracts a trout from under a bridge

ings refused, the fish eventually succumbed to a size 20 Black Gnat. I can still picture that glorious, golden fish leaping clear of the water as I set the hook. I estimated its weight to be 8–9 lb, and I was determined not to lose it.

Sad to relate, it was not to be. Despite all my efforts to stop the fish, it eventually managed to reach the fast water below me and we parted company.

I spent a further week in the West Yellowstone area, spending a day on the Madison River where I caught browns and some lovely, bright-silver rainbows. I also had a day on the famed Yellowstone River in the National Park, where it flows out of a lake. I succeeded in catching three of the big cutthroat trout which the stretch holds. I even managed a day on the legendary Hebden Lake, best fished from a float-tube. Despite the difficulty in handling this unfamiliar contraption, I tempted a couple of big rainbows.

The last two days of my holiday I spent with Gary Borger, one of America's best-known fly-fishers. He had arranged for us to fish another spring creek to the north of Livingstone. This creek was very different to the one on the ranch, as it ran through a lush, heavily wooded valley. The problem here was not lack of background cover, but relatively high fishing pressure.

The trout, a mixture of browns and rainbows, were spooky and difficult to tempt. Despite this, we both had a few nice fish in the morning, several of more than 3 lb. Following a substantial picnic lunch, we wandered further upstream where a reasonable hatch of small pale wateries developed. Despite all my efforts, I managed only a couple of small rainbows.

The main problem on this stretch was drag, difficult to overcome from the bank. Fortunately, Gary had on a pair of lightweight chest-waders so was able to wade into the stream, where he promptly caught seven or eight lovely browns, the best more than 4 lb.

The best time to fish in Montana is September when all the schools have re-opened. During July and August the area attracts fishermen from all over the States, and fly-fishers on some stretches are thicker than fleas on a dog's back.

The Monster of the Caledonian Pool 1994

For the past nine years I've spent a lot of time fly-fishing for big wild brown and rainbow trout in New Zealand. When Zane Grey fished there in the early 1920s he described the country as an 'angler's eldorado' – and in fact this was the title he eventually chose for the book he wrote about his experiences.

While the fishing is by no means as good as it used to be, it is still excellent by most people's standards and certainly on a par with the sport on offer in the Argentine or Chile.

But if the fishing is good it is also difficult – some would say very difficult, particularly on the rivers and streams which tend to run for much of their length through deep, bush-lined ravines. Access here is difficult and arduous – when you're not climbing along the edge of precipitous, overgrown banks, you're likely to be breasting your way up or across fast, deep, boulder-strewn water.

Wild New Zealand browns and rainbows average well over 4 lb, but you will be doing very well to catch four or five in a full day's fishing. Double-figure trout are often to be seen, but by the time they reach this size they are exceptionally difficult to tempt with a fly. This is particularly true of the brown trout. Numerous trips over the past nine years have resulted, for me, in just five brownies over 10 lb. My best weighed 10¾ lb.

So with nine years' experience, you can imagine how I felt when, last year, after only three days' fishing in the South Island I caught two more 10 lb-plus brownies – and both on fly.

We were fishing the west coast on the Grey, the Little Grey and the Rough Rivers. I was with Alan Simmons, a great friend who is a professional fishing and hunting guide; Ivan Tomka, a friend from Switzerland; and John Boyle, another local guide and a masterful fishspotter.

On the fourth day we were chatting over breakfast about where we should fish. Ivan wanted to try the Little Grey River again while I thought I'd opt for the Rough River. We compromised in the end when

John suggested we should all fish Larry's Creek. This is a big, very fast boulder-strewn river that had once been famous for its big fish. However, in recent years it has been subject to very heavy fishing pressure – largely because it is so easy to get to from the main west-coast highway.

I had fished it for a day on my first trip to New Zealand and hadn't even seen a fish, let alone caught one. The memory of that day made me wary, but in the end I agreed to give it a try. This time the big fish might be a little more co-operative.

Shortly after our arrival John spotted a good fish in a very fast run and suggested I try for it. Over the previous three days we had taken most of our fish on dry-fly, but this time I thought I'd try a heavily weighted nymph as he was lying at least 3 ft below the surface in a relatively fast current. Much to my amazement the cast was a good one and he lifted and accepted the nymph. As I set the hook he leapt clear of the water – a most magnificent brown trout. He took off on a long, terrifying downstream run, throwing in a couple of extra jumps on the way. I had no alternative but to follow him down. After ten minutes of electrifying acrobatics he was beached in the shallower water at the bottom of the run. In superb condition, he weighed well over 9 lb.

During the next couple of hours, Ivan had two lovely browns, one on a nymph and one on a dry-fly – both over 26 in – and Alan had an even bigger rainbow just on 27 in. I then hooked a giant of a fish, but after a couple of jumps we parted company.

John's decision to fish Larry's Creek had been fully vindicated and over lunch he told us that he'd heard from one of the top guides on the west coast (Peter Carty) that five huge brown trout had taken up residence in a large deep pool called the Caledonian, at the top of the fishery. Peter was particularly keen for me to have a go for these.

I knew from experience how difficult and frustrating deep, clear pools like this can be, but we decided to give it a go.

The bank on our side of the pool was high and tree-lined, providing a superb vantage point, with plenty of cover. The pool was huge and lined with soaring cliffs on the far side. Then we saw them: in the clear water were four of the biggest brown trout I have ever seen. They were roughly in the middle of the pool in the gentle current just below the surface, and as we gazed spellbound one tilted up to engulf an insect on the surface.

How on earth were we even going to get near them, let alone catch them? There were just two places from which we could cast. We could wade out into the river and cast a long way up the pool (in which case we would be fishing blind) or we could climb down the steep bank immediately below, wade out four or five paces and execute what looked to be a monstrously difficult cast from beneath the trees.

And there were other problems. John explained from previous experiences that as soon as an angler entered the water the reverse current along the nearside bank would carry his scent round into the pool. That tell-tale scent would mean that within 60 seconds all the trout in the pool would sink slowly out of sight.

We decided that our only chance would be to enter the water below as quickly and silently as possible and hope to get in maybe two casts before we put them down. The others generously insisted I give it a try so I tied on a small Cicada (Hopper) pattern that had been tied specially for me a few days before. Sliding gingerly down the steep bank I stripped sufficient fly-line from the reel to reach the nearest trout and gently entered the water. I took four paces, said a silent prayer and gave it my best throw. The gods must have been smiling that day because the fly, threading its way through the branches of all the trees, landed gently several feet upstream of the largest fish and drifted slowly towards him.

Up he came, down he went and, miraculously, he was on. In an instant he bored deep into the depths of the pool. I find it difficult to remember anything about the next few minutes, but I think I stopped him on three or four occasions just as he was about to reach the fast water at the bottom of the pool. I was aware that my lightweight outfit – Sage rod and No. 5 line - was woefully unequal to the task ahead, but I hoped the 10 in of power gum tied into my leader would give me at least a fighting chance.

An eternity seemed to pass but at last the trout began to weaken and I was able to get him into the shallow water under the trees. I looked for a place to beach him and seeing a patch of gravel under the bank nearby I shouted to John and Ivan to grab him as soon as his head slid on to it. The fish of a lifetime was mine.

The first thing was to measure him: at 30½ in long and 22 in round the shoulders he certainly weighed more than 16 lb.

From the moment I hooked him to the moment he slid up the beach Alan had kept the video running, which was just as well because disaster was about to strike. Just when we'd sorted out the camera for a few stills of the giant fish he gave an almighty wriggle and shot out of my hands like a bar of slippery soap. In an instant he had vanished into the depths of the pool.

We had planned to return the fish, but not quite as suddenly as this. Alan had managed to press the camera shutter just once, as we were both trying to lift the trout but that single picture will always remind me of the day I landed the monster of the Caledonian Pool.

Search for Rio Grande Silver 1998

Many years ago I prepared a list of world famous fishing venues that one day I hoped to visit. It included such countries as New Zealand, Alaska, America, Kenya, and South Africa, but high up on this list was Tierra del Fuego and the Rio Grande River, which since the early 1960s has had a growing reputation for holding the largest sea-run brown trout in the world. During the 1970s and 1980s I met many well-known American anglers who had been privileged to fish this river, and while I was very impressed by tales of the large numbers of double-figure sea trout being taken, I must admit I was less impressed at other aspects, mainly the prospect of having to fish the fly in the bitter winds that rarely drop below 30 knots throughout the year. Add to this the fact that to catch these fish one had to use large lures on fast sinking lines (not really my favourite method of fly fishing), I had more or less decided to delete this venue from my list.

All this changed two or three years ago when reports started filtering through that some of these huge sea trout were now also being caught on relatively small nymphs and even the occasional dry fly. Therefore, when several of my fishing buddies pressed me to set up a visit, I finally agreed. In early March 1998 three of my friends, Alfred Bond, Stuart McWilliams, John Sale and I took off from Gatwick bound for the southernmost tip of South America. After two very long flights via Buenos Aires over which I shall draw a veil, we arrived in the small township of Rio Grande which sits on the estuary of the river of the same name. There we were met by Steve Estela, manager and head guide of the Lodge Villa Maria, where we were to stay while we fished for the next six days. The very comfortable lodge is one of many buildings which make up the still working estancia (ranch) Jose Nenedez. This was the original estancia that owned and worked the whole of the island from early in the last century.

The island of Tierra del Fuego is very nearly as large as Wales and the Rio Grande River, which winds its way across fed from many tributaries in the high mountains of the Andes, is about 150km long. It is a very gentle river, and while we were there quite low, as on many pools with a really long cast you could cover the far bank. It has quite a brisk flow and has a bed composed of fine gravel which makes for easy and safe wading. There are no obstructions such as weed boulders and so on in this river, so few fish should be lost if they are played correctly.

The history of the sea trout in this rather barren freestone river is interesting. A little over sixty years ago the newly-appointed English manager of a meat-packing plant in the township, who was a keen fisher, marvelled at the fact that there were no fish of any note in its clear waters. He therefore decided to do something about it, and imported a quantity of either ova or fingerling brown trout with which to stock the river. These apparently did not thrive, so they were soon forgotten. Several years later a local thought he saw several large fish in the river, so fishing with a spinning bait he managed to catch one. This large silver fish proved to be a sea trout. In the ensuing years more and even larger fish were caught and it was quickly established that these were the progeny of the original brown trout that had been stocked. Finding insufficient food in the river, the young trout originally stocked had gone to sea, and had there found huge quantities of plankton and krill upon which to feed, only returning to the river to spawn early in the year. There is now a 60-mile exclusion zone from the mouth of the river where no fishing at all is allowed, so the future of this sea trout fishery is now assured particularly as the river itself is now designated a no-kill fishery.

The terrain is rather flat and rugged with very low rolling hills of pampas stocked with vast herds of sheep and also cattle, among which one can sometimes spot small groups of wild, nomadic guanaco which are very similar to but larger than the llama of Peru. There are few other wild creatures in this treeless landscape apart from odd beavers and many arctic foxes. However the bird life is most impressive with huge flocks of Magellan and other geese as well as caracara hawks with the odd mighty condor coasting in the thermals high overhead.

You soon become accustomed to the rather strange fishing routine. Breakfast is at 7.30 a.m. and shortly after you pair up and leave for the river with your guide in a four-wheel drive. Depending upon the pools you have been allocated for the morning session, the drive over

A fresh-run sea trout of 17fi lb, one of over 50 taken on a size
10 Goddard Caddis dry fly

a very rough bumpy track can last anything between 45 and 60
minutes. You then fish until about 1.30 p.m. and then drive to a large
mobile home parked by the river on one of the central beats, where
you meet up with the other anglers from the lodge for lunch. After
lunch, it is 'heads down' in bunks provided in the caravan until 4.30
when tea is served. You then change beats with other fishers from the
lodge and fish until it is completely dark. When we were there this is
around 9.30 p.m. so it was 10.30 p.m. before we arrived back at the
lodge. After changing and partaking of a few glasses of exceptionally
good Argentinian wine, it would be nearly midnight before we sat
down for our evening dinner. A punishing routine you may think, but
then the fishing is so spectacular time passes like lightning.

We arrived mid afternoon on a Friday, so after a quick bite to eat
we assembled our tackle and left for the river soon after. My companion for that first evening was John who elected to fish a hot spot
pointed out by the guide in the middle of the pool. I decided to start
above him at the head. Up to this moment in time, my largest sea
trout, landed from a Welsh river many years ago, was 5½ lb. After less
than a dozen casts I felt quite a gentle take, tightening immediately, I
felt the weight of a really heavy fish that surged off downstream strip-

ping my fly line off the reel until it was well into the backing. Taking a deep breath to calm my shattered nerves, I started to pump the fish upstream whereupon the most magnificient sea trout I had ever seen erupted from the water scattering droplets of water in all directions that looked like iridescent pearls in the dying rays of the sun. After several more spectacular jumps the now exhausted fish was scooped expertly into the waiting net of Steve, our guide.

This was a fresh-run hen sea trout; bright, bright silver with tiny black spots and which when weighed thumped the scales down to well over twelve pounds. Every fish caught is weighed and recorded by the guide and entered into the log back at the lodge. Shortly after this John was into his first fish which after a very dour fight proved to be a cock fish in super condition which weighed a little over 15 lb. What a start!

Even better was to follow as, before it got too dark within the next couple of hours, we both took three more good fish each of similar weights. That first evening I decided to fish in the conventional way, and used a large (size 6) Black Woolly Bugger on a sink-tip line. The following morning I decided, come what may, I would use a floating line and a nymph. This proved to be an excellent choice as alternating between a Pheasant Tail and an Olive Nymph dressed on size 10 hooks I landed four good fish in the morning between 8 and 11 lb and several more in the evening session up to 12 lb.

Before fishing the following morning I asked one of the guides whether it was worth trying the dry fly. He informed me no fish had been taken on the dry fly for a week or two, although several had been taken the previous month. The previous evening I had noticed a lot of large brown hairy moths flying about in the margins, so decided it might be worth a try. The closest representation I could find in my fly box was one of my own G&H Sedges or Goddard Caddis as they call them over there, dressed on a No. 10 hook. This seemed to be the answer, as by the time we had finished fishing that evening I had taken nine good sea trout including two super fish of 15 and 16½ lb.

During the rest of our stay I only used my dry Caddis – one morning alone I took 22 sea trout on it up to a staggering 19 lb. I fished this dry fly in various ways, but found that most takes came shortly after it landed, while it was on the dead drift, or as it started to swing and skate in the current. This was without doubt the best week's fishing I have ever experienced, which was confirmed by all the others in our group. We all had at least one fish over twenty pounds during the week – John Sale managed two while the largest sea trout of the week turned the scales at over 26 lb.

We were very fortunate with conditions, the river was quite low and the very strong winds which are normally such a feature of this area failed to materialize. In fact, we had three days of relatively light winds and sunny conditions, although there were quite heavy frosts in the mornings. The other days we did have quite strong winds and as these were blowing directly downstream most of the time over my right shoulder, it made casting with a single handed 9 ft rod extremely difficult. All the other members of the group were using double-handed 14 ft rods, which made casting very much easier under the prevailing wind conditions. Interestingly, the larger sea trout were mainly taken on sinking lines late in the evenings, with the three most killing patterns being a large CollieDog tube fly, a black or olive Woolly Bugger, or a monstrosity called a Yuk Bug which is dressed with six long rubber legs.

New World's New Zealand 2000

Many years ago, in fact when I first became hooked on fly fishing for trout, I made out a list of venues throughout the world I one day hoped to fish. High on this list was Patagonia, but for various reasons it has been up to now one of the very few places left that I have not visited. Over the past 14 years with 16 lengthy visits, New Zealand has almost become my second home, but with advancing years the prospect of very long flights is becoming less and less appealing. Now, while Esquel in southern Argentina is still a long way - twelve hours to Buenos Aires and a further three to Patagonia - it is still less than half the time taken to reach Christchurch. Having been assured by many of my American friends that the trout fishing in this area was the equal of New Zealand, I decided to set up a trip.

So with keen anticipation in early March this year (late autumn in this area) I found myself leading small group of six fly fishers out of the airport at Esquel where we were met by Michael Beale owner of the Ecuentro lodge that overlooks one of the major rivers in Patagonia - the Rio Futaleufo o Grande. The town sits on the edge of the pampa which is hot, dusty and flat, and extends for many hundreds of miles to the east, yet within minutes of leaving and driving westward we were entering a lush green valley approaching the foothills and finally the high snow capped mountains of the mighty Andes. Within an hour we passed through the small town of Trevelin which still harbours one of the largest Welsh communities in Argentina and whose ancestors first arrived here in 1865.

Half an hour later we arrived at the splendid and very comfortable lodge, overlooking the river. Built on the side of a very steep hill it sleeps six to eight guests and provides one of the most magnificent views I have ever experienced. Sitting on the verandah one looks down on to the fast flowing turquoise green yet crystal clear water of the Rio Grande, which at this time of the year is lined with tree-clad hills still in the full glory of their autumn colours. Imagine, then, lifting your eyes where the towering peaks of the mighty Andes range stretch up into the clouds.

The author plays a trout hooked on a dry fly from a creek in the foothills of the Andes

Shades of New Zealand: the lovely Rivadavia in the national park

Michael and his two guides, Diego and Nicholas, look after the fishing, while Jalle, his wife – also a very keen fly fisher – oversees the whole operation very efficiently. They have three boats with outboards for navigating the river, and you can either fish from these or from the banks, and they also have two four-wheel drives for taking you to the many other rivers and spring creeks in the area. The lodge is only six miles from the Chilean border and over this border – yet still in Patagonia and within an hour's drive – lies a large lake which I understand is full of very big rainbows with some in the four to five kilo range. The only reason we did not pay it a visit during our week's stay was because we were told that it takes at least two hours each way filling in forms to enter and again exit the border posts.

The scenery is magnificent and together with the extraordinary number and different species of birds to be seen alone would make the trip well worthwhile. But what about the fishing, and how does it compare with New Zealand? In the area around the lodge or in the national park to the south west of Esquel one could be forgiven for thinking one was in the South Island of New Zealand, but many of the creeks and spring creeks which are from an hour to two hours' drive from the lodge and in the flat, treeless pampas, one seems to be transported into an entirely different part of the world. In New Zealand, even if you are a competent fly fisher, apart from the few rivers where the trout are indigenous, one never expects to grass more than three or four fish in a day's fishing, but the average size is very high – in the region of four pounds plus with the prospects of a double-figure trout always on the cards. Now, in Patagonia, at least in the area where we were based, I must admit I never did see during the week any trout much over five pounds. On the other hand, apart from the Rio Grande, the number of trout – mainly rainbows – to be found

A fine brown trout from the Arroya Pescada – whilst the Patagonian trout were not as large, they were generally present in greater numbers than in New Zealand

in the other rivers and particularly the spring creeks – was quite aston-ishing. So, despite the lack of really big fish no way could we complain, as there are now very few places left in this world of ours where one can catch really large numbers of truly wild trout.

The river Rio Grande proved to be somewhat of an enigma, as it looked as though it should be literally not only stuffed with good sized trout but also with some monsters. Despite fishing it hard during several sorties which extended late into the evening until it was almost dark, results were very disappointing. We all caught fish but most of these were small rainbows between half a pound and two pounds and even these we had to work very hard for. We did have a few better trout, including a couple of nice browns, one of which caught by Hugh Salmon, which was close to three pounds. It is a big, sensational looking river over one hundred metres in width in places. It runs largely over sand or gravel with much luxuriant weed, and is full of very deep holes and runs. It is also crystal clear and even in nearly twenty feet of water one could see every stone on the bottom. Yet we saw no sign of any big trout. I am sure it must hold very large trout but we found the water very difficult to read and even more diffi-cult to fish. In many places the water was so deep you could not see bottom while in others the current was so fast you could not retrieve the fly line fast enough to keep in touch with the fly. We all tended to use floating lines and small nymphs or dry flies – maybe we should have been more successful had we used larger flies and sinking lines. Other factors which I am sure affected the fishing was lack of fly life (I understand they normally have excellent hatches), and – on the days we fished – a falling barometer.

On our second day we fished a wonderful spring creek the Arroya Pescada which provided some very challenging fishing as it ran through flat pampas and was a bright sunny day with but a gentle breeze. The trout – both brown and rainbows – were easily spotted in the crystal clear water, but were invariably spooked before you could get close enough to cast. Later in the day there was a good hatch of small midges, with plenty of rising fish. Initially we were unable to tempt any of these trout even on very tiny dry flies until I realised they were taking just below the surface. I quickly advised everyone to put on a small ungreased Super Grizzly Emerger and fish it in the film and we all started catching fish. Most of these were rainbows between a pound and a half and two and a half pounds, although later in the afternoon I did find a deeper section on the creek and managed to

Comfortable and convenient: the Encuentro fishing lodge overlooks the Rio Grande

catch five nice fish between three and five pounds, all on a size 18 P.V.C. Nymph. I also hooked two other fish which fought every bit as hard as the trout. They were both about one and a half pounds in weight and when I grassed the first one I initially thought it was a grayling. Fortunately when I landed the second one Michael was close by and he identified it as a species I think they call a Pjicaynu which is only found in this area.

On the last day two of our group, John Sale and Ivor Pattenden, returned to this spring creek. It was apparently very windy with a big ripple so the vision of the trout was very restricted and in addition, soon after they arrived, there was a huge hatch of a medium-sized upwing fly on which the fish started feeding avidly. This lasted most of the day so fishing mainly dry flies they estimated between them they returned almost a hundred trout, with the best fish of the day being taken by John – a rainbow weighing just over five pounds.

We also fished another creek which, while very small, formed frequent deep pools which held both browns and rainbows up to three or four pounds, but the fishing was difficult as again it ran through open pampas so there was no cover. The water was fairly clear, but it was very tricky to get close enough to spot any trout without spooking them. Later in the afternoon after quite a long walk downstream I did discover a few trees and bushes in a small valley and managed to extract several good trout from couple of deep pools.

The highlight of our visit proved to be the day we spent in the Alerces National Park which lies high up in the foothills of the Andes to the South West of Esquel. The drive through absolutely breathtaking scenery took nearly two hours but was well worth the effort. The park contains two very large bodies of stillwater, Lake Rivadavia and Lake Verde, neither of which we had time to fish, as our group spent the whole day fishing the River Rivadavia, connecting the two lakes. It is about 15 kilometres long, crystal clear, runs over gravel and the odd boulder, and is reminiscent of so many New Zealand rivers. This, according to some of the fly fishers in our party, did hold some very large trout, but none were caught: hardly surprising, as it was towards the end of the season and in a park that was probably fairly heavily fished. I am sorry to say I never did get around to fish the river as upon arrival we found ourselves on the most beautiful spring creek flowing into the river. This was full of trout – mostly rainbows of a good size – and proved to be so challenging that I spent the whole day on it. In the very clear water the fish were very spooky, and casting from the dense trees and bush which lined the banks was extremely difficult. I took the first trout on a small dry fly, but despite covering many other trout over the next hour or so, failed to rise another. Changing to nymphs I tried many patterns and sizes – all to no avail. Most of the trout would show interest in any nymph but the instant you moved it they would depart in panic.

Eventually I adopted a technique that I had previously found successful for educated trout. Tying on a very small long shank G.R.H.E. Gold Head, I allowed this to sink to the bottom well ahead of a cruising fish and then gave it but the slightest of tweak, as he approached. This proved to be the answer, as I finished up with four very nice rainbows between three and four pounds, plus a lovely brownie, which weighed over five pounds. Despite this I still regret not having spent at least some time on the river. Never mind, this may tempt me to return.

Trout to Pull Your Arm Off 2000

This year I was invited to spend a week in Northern Russia fishing for very large wild brown trout. My immediate reaction was one of incredulity – big trout within the Arctic Circle where all the rivers and lakes are frozen over during eight months of the year? No way. Always open to a challenge, I eventually decided to accept, after further assurance that large trout were really there.

We arrived in Murmansk in the middle of July and headed by helicopter for the Kola Peninsula where we were accommodated at a very comfortable lodge set up for the salmon fishermen who have been fishing the lower reaches of three large adjacent rivers for the past ten years.

This is truly the land of the midnight sun – during July it never really sets. Furthermore, we were there during the hottest summer ever recorded – while we were there we had cloudless blue skies with temperatures in the mid-seventies. This made the trout fishing very difficult, not least because although the rivers are crystal clear they are lined with huge boulders and stones covered in dark brown algae – which make it impossible to spot any trout, while they can see you only too clearly!

Although at times the trout fishing was very dour due to the very unusual weather conditions we experienced, we had a fabulous few days fishing in what must be one of the very few truly wilderness areas left on this planet. The only signs of civilization in this area are a few very small and poor fishing communities at the mouths of some of the rivers. The lower stretches of these rivers, which now provide some of the best Atlantic salmon fishing left in the Western Hemisphere, run through low granite hills and small ravines. But a few miles back in from the coast where the trout fishing starts, the land flattens out into open tundra interspersed with rocky outcrops and covered with literally thousands of lakes, some no larger than a football pitch, while others cover many hundreds of acres. During our week of fishing, the only signs of life we saw apart from the odd unusual bird were a couple of large eagles and two or three large but isolated herds of reindeer.

The rivers that we fished, the Kharlovka, the Eastern Litza and the Rynda, were all very similar and all are well over a hundred kilometres in length. These rivers are not for the fainthearted or physically handicapped. The wading can be rather difficult, in many cases over big boulders with deep water between, while the banks in some sections are marshy with deep holes that cannot be seen as they are covered in undergrowth. However, the lower and middle areas of these rivers have many miles of clear, easily-negotiated banks including many stretches where the wading is less hazardous. The further you travel up these rivers the more difficult the terrain. To start with you have long, shallow, boulder-strewn runs interspersed with deep pools, but then the pools become small lakes with shorter runs in between, until eventually in the higher reaches you find large lakes connected by relatively short stretches of river. In some areas the banks are covered for many hundreds of yards back from the water with dense undergrowth composed of scrub-willow, ash and birch trees in which it is only too easy to get lost.

I was accompanied throughout the week by Oliver Edwards, the well respected author and fly dresser. He is an excellent and very accomplished dry fly fisher, and we both had very high hopes of taking many trout on the dry fly. When we arrived, we were told that during the two previous weeks, under cloudy conditions, there had been good hatches of fly with a lot of rising trout – consequently four fly fishers over the previous two weeks had taken over sixty trout between them, all on the dry fly. These were mainly trout between two and five pounds with a few between six and seven. Mind you, they all camped out on the banks of the river and while there were hatches of fly and rising trout throughout the day, the best hatches occurred during the night when the sun was at its lowest. We had the choice of spending the week under canvas or fishing from ten to six each day after being dropped by the water from a chopper. We eventually opted for the chopper as we felt that we could cover and explore much more of the three rivers in this manner, or maybe our advancing years influenced our decision. In retrospect, I think in view of the weather we experienced we probably made the wrong decision. This was a classical case of 'You should have been here last week,' as we hardly saw a cloud during our stay.

During our six days fishing in bright, bright sunlight I observed but half-a-dozen rises and Oliver saw few more. This was hardly surprising, as apart from small hatches of large sedges, the substantial hatches of up-winged flies we had anticipated were notable by their absence. We therefore had to resort to speculative fishing in likely looking lies, most of the time using dry caddis patterns, size 12 or 14. Using this method and fishing the pocket water in the fast runs we did catch a lot of small trout of six to twelve inches, and also salmon parr which were a positive nuisance. All the bigger trout we caught were from the deep pools or lakes where they entered or left the river. We also tried various nymphs including gold heads but with little success, although we did catch some of the bigger trout on these. Bearing in mind this was classic trout water holding many fish, we were puzzled as to why nymphs were so ineffective. After examining the stomach contents of several trout we caught and returned, we found they were all packed with tiny snails. I therefore came to the conclusion that with such a huge and unlimited supply of these available, it was hardly surprising that they were uninterested in our nymphs.

Between us, we probably averaged between three and four good trout each per day, and most of these were between two and four pounds. However, we both caught some larger trout and one of these which I saw rise twice and subsequently managed to catch just tipped the scales at eight pounds. I also had another almost as large which jettisoned the fly as I was about to land it.

Pound for pound, the wild brown trout found in these rivers are by far the strongest I have encountered anywhere in the world. When we

Left: The middle section of the Kharlovka River above the falls *Right:* A superb brown trout from the Kharlovka

arrived we were advised not to use leaders of less than seven or eight pounds breaking strain, but even seven-pound test proved inadequate when I hooked a very large trout in one of the deep pools. I have over the years caught many large wild brown trout well in excess of ten pounds and seldom if ever have I been taken very far into the backing. This trout, which I am sure was well into double figures took forty or fifty yards of backing before I could turn him and even then after two or three minutes I had gained but little line before he managed to get downstream of me and into the fast current flowing from the pool. I knew then that I had to stop him before he entered the white water of the boulder-strewn rapids. Sadly when I applied maximum pressure he snapped the seven-pound leader like a piece of cotton.

PART FOUR
DEEP SEA AROUND THE WORLD

Portugal's Algarve Coast – Home of Fighting Fish 1965

Our long awaited fishing trip to the blue semitropical waters off the Algarve coast of Southern Portugal started from London Airport on 30 August. I was leading a small party of anglers on behalf of *Angler's World* and its sister publication, *Angler's Mail*, composed of David Stueart, the *Mail's* leading writer, John Denman, a well-known all round angler, and Barrie Welham, of Intrepid Reels.

Our main object was to find out from local sources the different species of fish likely to be caught at different times of the year, and also to 'have a go' and see what we could catch ourselves.

For our ten days' fishing we had booked a local boat based at Portimao. (Suitable fishing boats, it should be explained, are few and far between on this coast, and therefore I suggest to would-be holiday anglers that it is advisable to book a boat well in advance.)

The 'Sea Robin' is a superb craft built specially in America for big game fishing. She is fitted with twin 65 h.p. diesels which give her a cruising speed of nearly 12 knots. There is accommodation aboard to sleep six anglers, and she has a range of over 250 miles. Outriggers for trolling are fitted, and she has an echo sounder effective to depths of 300 fathoms.

A large tank with running sea water has been fitted in the aft cockpit for keeping live bait in. She is also equipped with four fighting chairs, two at low level in the aft cockpit, and two at high level at the back of the flying bridge. Her skipper has the very appropriate name of Terry Pike and hails from New Zealand. He is very willing and a keen angler himself. His crew consist of a cheerful and excitable Portuguese named Pablo, although the locals refer to him as Carlos, and Januvas, a very efficient cook.

Little is known of the fishing on this coast, up to now it has been virtually unfished except by locals. However, over the past few years we had heard repeated reports of large swordfish and sharks being seen, and it was these we were mainly interested in. Unfortunately for us though, we had strong northerly winds blowing for the whole of the ten days, which made this form of deep sea fishing extremely difficult.

All the time we were fishing we had to literally hold on with one hand, and apart from this, due to wind the rate of drift was such that we were quite unable to fish our baits at a suitable depth, for either the swordfish or mako sharks.

We had quite a few blue sharks up to 150 lb in weight, and on one or two days very small blue sharks were a positive nuisance, as we were unable to get our baits down to any depth at all for larger fish, before they were taken.

In this area are also to be found large hammerhead sharks, and during one afternoon we observed two of these on the surface, and had a third follow a trolled dead bait for some distance. We also caught a small porbeagle shark of 60 to 70 lb, and on the last morning of the trip when the wind abated for a couple of hours, we located three large broadbill swordfish basking in the sun.

Without a doubt, the most productive areas along the whole of this coast, are two rocky reefs on the edge of the Continental Shelf, immediately south-west of Cape St Vincent. These two large areas of rock lie in about 45 fathoms with a depth around them of between 70 and 80 fathoms. Also, a little further out in this direction and beyond the end of the Continental Shelf one comes to the Blue water.

This is quite a fascinating sight, one moment you are sailing through the blue green coastal water, and the next you are in the sparkling blue of the ocean. The dividing line between the two colours can be clearly seen. It was on the edge of this blue water we had hoped to locate marlin.

We were assured by locals that the strong northerly winds we experienced the whole of the time were most unusual, as it is apparently usual to have a period of flat calm nearly every morning up until about midday. Apart from the above personal experiences, we now have positive evidence that both white and blue marlin have been caught by commercial fishermen along this coast.

Our skipper assured us that on numerous occasions on calm days, he had seen many broad-bills on the surface. During one afternoon the week before we arrived he counted seven, at least one of which was estimated at over 600 kilos which is about 1,500 lb.

A played-out shark is brought into the side, ready for gaffing

From the above it would seem apparent that before long, this must become one of the premier big game fishing areas in Europe. Apart from the deep sea fishing, this area also has excellent inshore fishing from the rocks or a small boat at certain periods of the year.

Let us first of all consider the inshore fishing. This year it has been very poor, due mainly to the fact that the water temperature for many weeks has been 10 degrees below normal. This has been caused by the very bad summer experienced by the whole of Europe.

In normal seasons bass, averaging 5 to 7 lb, can be taken by the boatload, and many of these fish are in excess of 10 lb. Also mullet in very large shoals are present up to about six pounds in weight. Another species which can be caught close in are anchova, a fine sporting fish which attain a weight of about 15 lb. The best area for this inshore fishing is between the Cape and Lagos.

The offshore fishing for the larger species of fish found in this area, can be a little difficult. Due to the flat nature of the bottom, areas of rock are difficult to find. For this type of fishing, sturdy motorized commercial fishing boats can be hired for a day, and it will be necessary to fish between two and five miles offshore, in depths varying between 30 and 50 fathoms.

About five miles offshore between Portimao and Lagos, there is a very steep drop off in the bottom from 40 to 50 fathoms, and this should be a most productive area. Species to be found in this deeper water are large snapper up to 30 lb, various bream up to 20 lb, grouper up to 60 or 70 lb, palmeto between 30 and 50 lb, scabbard fish and large conger eels.

Another species of fish which is quite common in this area is the corvina or salmon bass. These grow very large, and average 40 to 50 lb, with odd specimens of 70 to 80 lb. They are mainly taken trolling just offshore in depths between 10 and 20 fathoms.

At certain times of the year large shoals of school tunny or albacore and bonito can be encountered, which vary in size from 10 to 30 lb. The best method for taking them is with a feathered jig trolled at a speed of about 6 to 8 knots. They usually appear in quantity during early August, and the best months are September, October and November. This year however, they had not shown up in August at all, and it was not until near the end of our trip during the second week of September that the first commercial catch of this species was made. We did run across one small school, and managed to take two nice Albacore of around 15 lb. apiece.

As previously mentioned, good fishing marks in the area are not easy to locate due to the uniformity of the sea bed, and it is therefore worth mentioning, that we did find one quite large wreck close inshore. This lies in about 15 fathoms of water, half a mile east of Sagres, about a quarter mile offshore. It is marked by commercial fishermen's cork floats, and is not too difficult to locate.

During the months of May and June, huge schools of very large tunny travel along the coast of Southern Portugal on their way to spawn in the Mediterranean. These pass very close inshore at Sagres, and again further along the coast at Faro. At these two centres these fish used to be caught in large numbers in fish traps, and there are many canning factories built along the coast solely for canning these fish.

It is not known whether these fish will feed as they pass through, and as far as we could ascertain no sport fishermen have actually tried fishing for them. If they can be induced to take bait, I am quite sure that this could become a new world centre for tunny fishing.

For a combined fishing and family holiday we now consider the Algarve to be at the top of our list. During our stay we hardly saw a cloud, and although it is very warm it is not unpleasantly hot. The coastal scenery is very lovely, and is very similar indeed to the Cornish coast. The rainfall is confined mainly to December; for instance during the whole of this year they have only had three days' rain. Naturally, as a result of this low rainfall, away from the coast the land is rather dry and arid, and green grass and trees are sadly missed.

The Portuguese people are a very happy and cheerful race, extremely friendly and very pro-British – nowhere else in Europe will you find people who will go to so much trouble to help you. Few of them speak English, but a smile will get you anything. The beaches are many and very safe for children, and if you have a car it is fairly easy to find small beaches that are very secluded and practically deserted.

For those people who like a bit of life in the evening there are three main centres along this coast: Faro, Albufeira and Portimao. The food is very good in most restaurants and hotels, and suitable for the English palate. Our only criticism was the lack of variety.

The whole of the Algarve coast from Faro to Sagres offers good fishing, but undoubtedly the nearer to Cape St Vincent the better the fishing.

As we were going to press we heard from Terry Pike, skipper of the Sea Robin, that the week after we left the weather moderated. During several days of calm weather he personally caught two mako sharks between 300 and 400 lb, and a swordfish – the first ever to be caught on rod and line off this coast.

Broadbill Swordfish. Drifting over depths of 75 to 300 fathoms. Either a live or dead bait fished between 40 and 60 fathoms.

Mako, Hammerhead or Porbeagle Sharks. Drifting over deep water 60 to 300 fathoms. Live or dead bait fished at various depths from 10 to 50 fathoms.

Blue Sharks. Drifting over deep water 45 down to 90 fathoms. Dead bait fished at 4 to 10 fathoms in conjunction with Rubby Dubby. Plenty of sardines can be obtained for this.

School Tunny or Albacore. By trolling with feather jigs over areas where birds denote shoals of fish. Another method is to fish a single sardine on a 6/0 hook tied direct to a 35 lb nylon line and let the current drift it away from the boat. Best months are September, October and November.

Bass (Rabalo). These can be taken spinning or trolling off the rocks, and average 5 to 7 lb. August to February.

Salmon Bass (Meagre). Reaching weights of up to 80 lb, they can be taken trolling in water varying between 10 and 20 fathoms, or can be caught on live squid fished a little off the bottom. From August to November.

Mullet. These can be taken just off the rocks with light float tackle or spinners. All year.

Scabbard Fish (Peixe-Espada). Reaching a length of nearly seven feet these are similar to Barracuda and on light tackle are good sport. Found in depths between 30 and 50 fathoms they can be caught on jigs or bait, using sardine or a strip of mackerel close to the bottom, or at night on spinners, close to the surface. Season from June to August.

Snapper (Pargo). These are caught up to 30 lb in weight and are taken just off the bottom on squid, over rock in depths between 30 and 50 fathoms.

The *Sea Robin*. A twin screw big game fishing boat used during the trip

Anchova. Can be taken spinning or trolling close inshore, and reach a weight of about 15 lb.

Palmeto. Taken up to 50 lb in weight. Will take a bunch of sardines fished mid-water, or sometimes by trolling a large spinner fairly deep.

Apart from the above there are, of course, many other species of smaller fish such as mackerel, shad and small bream, that can be caught in quantities.

Expedition to Madeira 1967

Leslie Moncreiff with a large bull-dolphin of 44 lb. This is the record on rod and line in Madeira waters

I shall always remember most vividly my first glimpse of the Island of Madeira as our Portuguese Airways plane approached the new landing strip on the south side. The ocean was as untroubled as a lake and from the shore where the surf gently lapped the rocks, the verdant mountains rose straight out of the sea dotted with little white red-roofed houses, thence soaring to the summits which reach heights of over 6,000 feet and are nearly always crowned with puffy little white clouds.

There and then I named it my 'fairy-tale isle'. It is barely 32 miles long and a little over 12 miles wide, and enjoys an incomparable climate rarely dropping below 63° in winter or exceeding 78° in the summer. The island lies in the North Atlantic approximately 500 miles from the coasts of North West Africa or South West Portugal.

Due to its geographical position the prevailing winds are from the north east throughout most of the summer resulting in wonderfully calm seas along all of the southern coast and also for quite a considerable distance out to sea. To the angler this is, of course, a most important consideration as it means few if any fishing days will be lost due to rough seas.

The Portuguese Tourist Office asked me to undertake a survey of the fishing in the seas surrounding the island. As a result we arrived in September for fourteen days' serious fishing. Our small party consisted of myself, Leslie Moncrieff, the celebrated sea angler, and Hymie Policansky (Polly to his friends), who spends his spare time designing fishing reels.

We arrived in Funchal, the capital of the island, on a Saturday, and early next morning we met the Director of the Madeiran Tourist Board, Senor Santa Clara Gomez, and a more courteous and helpful person would be difficult to find.

During the following few days his assistance in connection with the boat and supplies, and so on, was invaluable. He also appointed a very keen local angler, Avelino Camara, to act as our host for the duration of our stay.

After a leisurely lunch we decided to visit the Funchal museum. This includes a small aquarium and a very large and, indeed, excellent display of mounted fish all collected from the ocean surrounding the island. This is presided over by Dr Maul, a trained ichthyologist.

The doctor has been a resident of the island for many years, and has personally collected many of the specimens on display. He was, therefore, able to provide us with much useful data and information regarding the different species of fish and the areas in which they were to be found.

In the evening we were introduced to Dr Ribeiro, one of the only experienced big game fishermen on the island, and over a glass or two of mellow Madeiran wine he regaled us with tales of monstrous fish he had seen and caught in these waters. For any fisherman contemplating a trip to Madeira I would certainly recommend that they contact these friends of angling upon arrival.

Unfortunately, the Tourist Board's launch *Altair*, which had been reserved for us, had broken down and was not available. The boat provided in her place, the *Albacora*, proved to be a good sea boat, and ideally suited for the style of fishing we wished to undertake. She was placed at our disposal at very short notice, and we shall always be grateful to her owners, Senor Rua Mendesis and his two friends for this, and their many other kindnesses.

It was decided during the first week of our stay to try for the

A good day's fishing! Leslie Moncreiff, Hymie Policansky and John Goddard with a mixed bag of dorado and tunny

various species of surface feeding migratory fish which we had reason to believe should be found there in September. These included marlin, tunny and many other smaller species of game fish such as the dorado, wahoo, blue fish, bonito and barracuda.

From information we had been able to glean from the local sports and commercial fishermen, we felt our best chances of success would be provided by trolling, as this had never been tried before, and so it eventually proved to be. This turned out to be reasonably effective for at least some of the species of fish that we contacted and were fortunate enough to catch, and for the benefit of those readers who may be tempted to contemplate a trip in the near future to this area, I will describe the methods adopted for those species we located.

The Barracuda. The few of these we caught were mainly close inshore in the vicinity of rocks; these were taken on small lures and plugs, but it must be admitted that we did not try very seriously for them. Consequently, we are unable to offer any positive thoughts on this species.

The Dorado or *true Dolphin*. Hailed by many as the most beautiful gamefish in the sea, the dolphin is superbly streamlined and gorgeously coloured. Never shall we forget the sight of the first one we hooked as it was brought alongside, the long dorsal fin and back were an electric blue turning to a brilliant yellow and the sides gold-flecked green, turning to silver on the belly.

We were all most impressed by the fighting qualities of this species and were unanimous in our decision that they were definitely the fastest fish we had ever hooked. They are also spectacular fighters spending almost as much time airborne as in the water. We caught quite a lot of these fish varying in weights from five to over 40 lb, and we took nearly all of them on small feathered lures, usually three or more miles offshore.

These fish shoal in small numbers and are not easy to locate, and we had most success when trolling in the vicinity of stationary commercial fishing boats. We also found that a hooked fish often brought others in the shoal round the boat, and this gave one the chance of further fish on a fly-spinner or small baited spoon.

A big bull dolphin (fish) of 38 lbs about to be boated

Tunny. Although the month we were in Madeira was not considered a good time of year for these fish we were fortunate to boat several very good specimens. These were Atlantic Big Eyed Tunny, and two of these fish landed by Leslie Moncreiff and myself of 238 and 245 lb respectively were quite close to the world record for this species which stands at 295 lb.

We concentrated on these fish for several days but for the first day or so we were unsuccessful in attracting any to our lures. We tried trolling with different lures at various depths, but it was not until we varied our trolling speed that success came our way.

Polly had the first strike from a tunny when we were trolling at nearly eight knots. Subsequently, we came to the conclusion that between six to eight knots was the best speed for these particular fish, and the best lures were undoubtedly large Japanese feathers trolled right on the surface.

We were a little disappointed in the fight these fish gave us although the average time to boat one was about 1fi hours, the battle was not at all spectacular; however, they are tremendously powerful and do not give up until the moment the gaffs are brought into use. The fact that we hooked all these fish over very deep water may, of course, account for the way they fought. When hooked they sounded to great depths.

The big game launch, *Albacora* with Ponta de Sao Lourenco in the background

Apart from the Atlantic Big Eye, other species of tunny are common to these waters, and we were most excited to locate several shoals of the Giant Bluefin Tunny. Many that broke surface were in excess of 500 lb.

We spent the last two days of our first week trying to catch one of these monsters but with lamentable lack of success. It is generally recognized that the bluefin are particularly difficult to catch and these were certainly no exception.

The second week was devoted to bottom fishing and although we stuck it out and tried very hard indeed we must admit it proved unproductive. Small tope were a positive menace, and on several occasions we hooked these two at a time. The large pargo and grouper reputed to be present were conspicuous by their absence as were other large species of bottom fish.

In fairness, however, we must admit that our boat was not fitted with an echo sounder, and consequently the rocky bottom essential to this type of fishing proved very difficult to find. Also, the great depths of water around the island make bottom fishing very difficult, and on many occasions we were fishing in excess of 100 fathoms.

However, even though we did not find this fishing good, the local commercial fishermen seem to, as every night dozens of small fishing craft put to sea for a local species of fish called a peixe espada.

Considered a delicacy by the local people, these eel-like fish are caught in large quantities. Of fearsome appearance, they seem to be all teeth, and can only be caught at very great depths, usually in excess of 500 fathoms.

As a result of our trip, we feel that these waters have a great potential for certain species of fish, particularly some of the surface feeding game fish such as the tunny and Marlin. Unfortunately, in fourteen days were we unable to do more than scratch the surface, as there were many species of fish present that we did not have time to try for. For example, the mighty broadbill swordfish. These are caught regularly by the local commercial fishermen on their handlines when fishing for other species, and many were the tales they told of large specimens having to be cut loose as they find it quite impossible to handle these fierce fighters on their relatively puny handlines.

For the record, there are several suitable boats available for big game fishing in Funchal and the Madeiran Tourist Board are considering the provision of a proper sports fishing centre on the Island in the near future if results this year are up to expectations.

The Unforgettable Red Sea – Home of the Dog-tooth Tuna 1969

Fishing in the Red Sea! At one time even the suggestion would have appeared most improbable. Nowadays it is not only possible but quite feasible as a superb hotel, complete with its own airstrip, has been built, and it is possible to fly direct from London Airport to Hurghda on the Red Sea by United Arab Airlines in less than a day.

I have fished in many parts of the world during the past few years, but my first view of the Red Sea in the vicinity of the hotel on the day we arrived is one I am never likely to forget.

The water over the coral shallows was the palest of pale blue which rapidly turned to a deep green, and as the bottom dropped away this again changed from green to blue and then to a deep indigo blue over the very deep water.

The overall effect was quite astounding as I was presented with a kaleidoscope of blues and greens interspersed with gleaming white coral reefs.

It is perhaps just as well the sea itself is picturesque and full of life, as the coast here is drab and uninteresting being pure desert.

I was recently privileged to captain the England 'A' team for EFSA when we competed in the first Middle East Championship in this ideal location. At the time there was considerable adverse publicity from some of our members who were involved in an incident during the championships when three of the boats taking part on the final were boarded, searched and escorted to the Egyptian naval base at Safargo.

My colleague on this trip, Jimmy Hanley, and I were personally involved and although it was frightening and unpleasant, I felt that the resulting publicity was rather exaggerated and certainly unwarranted, as apart from this one incident I found the Egyptians most courteous, helpful and friendly, particularly their team members fishing in the contest.

Although the number and weight of fish caught during the championship was not particularly good, it was notable for the impressive variety of species landed, and when one considered that we were apparently there at the worst time of the year it certainly whetted one's appetite for a return trip during the peak of their season.

Many of the smaller coral fish up to about 5 lb were of fantastic shape and their brilliant colouration was, in some cases, quite indescribable.

Most of the larger species of game fish that were caught came either from the open water, or the deeper water alongside some of the outer reefs. Among these were many sizeable barracuda, wahoo, king-fish, Jack Crevalle and an unusual type of grouper with a formidable array of teeth, that strange to relate, often accepted a trolled lure.

Jimmy Hanley and I were most fortunate to take three reasonable tuna between us, Jim boating the largest, a dog-tooth tuna of 70 lb, the remaining two, a dog-tooth of 50 lb, and a yellowfin of 40 lb falling to my rod.

Unfortunately the two larger fish were taken the day before the event officially commenced. However, I was delighted to encounter these particular fish as in my experience they are pound for pound the toughest fighters of all game fish.

I was extremely excited over the capture of the first dog-tooth, as it was the first tuna of this particular species that I had ever seen, let alone caught. According to Francesca La Monte, editor of *Marine Game Fishes of the World*, these tuna are not often encountered and, furthermore, specimens of over 60 are uncommon.

There are, of course, many large species of shark to be found in this area, but none was caught during the time we were present. Several members of our party did, in fact, hook and lose extremely large fish which, they presumed were shark, but unfortunately the tackle they were taken on proved inadequate. Consequently none of these fish was actually seen and in any case, most of them were hooked at night.

The members of the Egyptian team were quite adamant that there were plenty of shark to be caught but they would only take during the hours of darkness. We found this difficult to believe as we were quite convinced that with this number of shark about it should be possible to take them drifting during the day providing a good trail of rubby dubby was laid.

We consequently wasted the best part of the day drifting in this manner with a simply beautiful trail and baits set at various depths, all to no avail.

This was a memorable trip in more ways than one as it was full of incidents, and one in particular I shall not forget in a hurry. One evening we were night-fishing and I caught a most beautiful looking fish of

Arab crewman looks on with professional interest as Jimmy Hanley displays
a Red Sea kingfish

about 3 lb. It was brilliant red overall and I was quite sure it was one of
the sea bream family. It was hooked deeply and both Jim and I handled
it at some length in an effort to retrieve the hook.

Jimmy Hanley with a fine dog-tooth tuna

Minutes later the Egyptian
team member who was fishing
on the other side of the boat
drew our attention to a fish he
had just caught and informed us
that this was the most deadly
poisonous fish in the Red Sea,
and on no account were we to
touch one if hooked.

Yes, you've guessed correctly,
it was exactly the same species
that we had just been wrestling
with. Reaction was immediate,
we stopped fishing and retired to
the cabin of the boat to calm our
quaking nerves with a couple of
double whiskies!

256

The Big Fish of Kenya 1971

Fabulous! Fantastic! These are the only two words I can think of to describe the deep sea fishing along the East African Kenya coast where Leslie Moncrieff and I were recently privileged to spend a little over two weeks sampling the sport at the main centres.

We started at Malindi, reputed to be one of the best areas in the world for sailfish – it is not uncommon for one boat to bring in four or five after just one morning's fishing. But despite the fact that we were there at the peak period, our four days at this location failed to produce one sail, due to the fact that the water was heavily coloured following very rough weather.

Although we were unlucky with the sails we did have some exciting general fishing, catching kingfish, rainbow runners, bonito, and so on. During our last day we had an interesting encounter with a shark. This was one of the surface feeding sharks called a blacktip which weighed about 250 lb and took a bait being trolled for sailfish.

I hooked it on my medium light outfit on 50 lb line and was most impressed with its fighting qualities – it took me all of 30 minutes to bring to the gaff. At this juncture I wrongly assumed it was finished, but as the gaff bit home the shark exploded into renewed life, broke the one-inch manilla rope attached to the gaff head and immediately sounded, taking our one and only gaff with it, and at the same time nearly jerking me overboard.

Five minutes later I had pumped it back to the boat where one of the crew had made a slip-noose in order to tail it. Our crew were far from experts at this job and three times they got the loop over the shark's head but failed to tighten it before it reached the tail. I was exhausted before, on the fourth attempt, they succeeded.

Les, who had been fliming the whole episode, was in hysterics. Each time the shark escaped the noose and dashed off he (very unkindly I thought) informed me that he had hoped the loose line would catch round the rod top and that I would follow the shark overboard like a cork out of a bottle!

I should explain that sharks on this coast are not caught by design. They are considered unsporting due to their poor fighting qualities. Maybe the shark we caught was exceptionally lively. If not I would disagree with this view held by local anglers.

Our next port of call was Kilifi where we spent an extremely pleasant four days at the Mnarini club. This is sited on high ground and provides a magnificent view of the bay and the encircling coral reefs. The atmosphere was informal and friendly, probably due to the fact that they have their own fleet of deep sea fishing boats for hire and are therefore used to the odd behaviour of anglers.

Kilifi is also a good area for sailfish and here our luck changed as the weather improved, and on each of the four days we had strikes' from these fish. The sailfish, like all billfish, are extremely difficult to hook and land, and we lost an awful lot, probably due to our inexperience, as neither of us had fished for this particular species before. Eventually fortune favoured us and Leslie boated two nice fish around 70 lb apiece on succeeding days, so we left Kilifi with happy memories.

We then spent a few days in the Mombasa area mainly inshore fishing, before departing for Shimoni – our final and probably most important destination. It was here in the Pemba Channel that we were to have a crack at the lordly marlin. While it is possible to catch these fish all along this coast, the Pemba Channel Fishing Club at Shimoni is undoubtedly the hot-spot.

Marlin are blue water fish and in this area the very deep water of the channel comes close inshore, so you are in marlin country within two or three miles of the clubhouse.

The club and accommodation are run by Pat Hemphill and his charming wife, and Pat is certainly the most knowledgeable and experienced marlin fisherman on this coast. Proof of this lies in the fact that most of the existing East African records for the larger species of fish have been taken from one or the other of his two boats.

The fishing is so popular here that it is necessary to book well in advance for the only two boats available. Our booking was done at short notice, and we were fortunate that Pat managed to fix us up with a friend's boat. She was the *Isurus*, a superb 35 ft catamaran fitted with two 90 hp diesels owned and skippered by Ted Holmes, a most friendly and likeable Kenyan.

Although I have fished for and caught marlin before, I think they are one of the most difficult fish in the world to catch, and the ensuing three days gave me no cause to alter my views.

On the first day we had several strikes, all of which we missed, while on the second day Leslie succeeded in hooking a grand marlin, but after a series of impressive leaps it eventually threw the hook. Later the same day I noticed the purple-blue shape of a large marlin approaching the teaser, or attractor, we were trolling. Without a second's hesitation he attacked it and shook it like a dog shakes a bone.

The skipper quickly pulled it away from him, but again he grabbed it. This happened several times so that when I was eventually ready to drop a juicy bonito to him he was so annoyed he took it without hesitation. On this occasion I must have had timed the strike right and next minute he was on.

I was using a fairly light rod with 50 lb line, and on this outfit it was great sport as he treated us to some grand aerobatics. In all he spent almost as much time in the air as in the water and also provided some fantastic tail walking for good measure. I played him for over 30 exhausting minutes before I eventually had him beaten, but then my luck ran out. I had him within ten yards of the boat lying on his side completely exhausted by the fight, when to our horror, the hook

Leslie Moncrieff with a big wahoo – the fastest fish in the ocean

pulled out and we watched him sink slowly out of sight into the depths.

However, lady luck smiled upon us eventually and on our last day I was fortunate to hook a fine striped marlin of 136 lb.

A nice striped marlin is brought ashore to be weighed

Tanzania and the Fabulous Fishing off Mafia Island 1972

Earlier this year, Leslie Moncrieff and I were privileged to visit the Tanzanian coast in East Africa to sample the sea fishing. We left Gatwick by Super VC10 and flew to Dar-es-Salaam on the coast via Nairobi. This is one of the oldest and most cosmopolitan ports on the East African coast and barely a century ago was one of the main Arab slaving centres. Even today, Arab trading dhows – unaltered in design for many hundreds of years – still ply their trade.

In common with Kenya, the whole of this coast offers exciting fishing, but unfortunately it has not been developed to the same degree, so at the moment there are only three areas open to visiting anglers. First of all, near to the northern border with Kenya lies the small seaport of Tanga. From here it is possible to fish the waters of the Pemba channel a few miles to the north, which is undoubtedly one of the best areas in the world for striped marlin.

Nearly opposite Tanga lies the island of Zanzibar, and along the southern tip of the island is a most prolific area for all species of game fish. Unfortunately there are no charter boats for hire here, but there are many suitable privately-owned local boats, and we understand it may be possible to arrange a private charter.

The southern part of the coast is a restricted zone. This only leaves Dar-es-Salaam on the mainland, and the fishing here is not so good as elsewhere along this coast due to dynamiting of the reefs by local Arab commercial fishermen. This illegal method of fishing has considerably thinned out the stocks of resident fish around the port itself, and due to the relatively shallow water extending over 20 miles out to sea, the larger migratory fish tend to pass well out.

However, at certain times, the fishing here can still be most rewarding and at least boats are no problem as Seafaris have a fleet of various-sized craft available for hire. One word of warning though –

261

Leslie Moncrieff holds a big, striped grouper taken on a deep trolled plug

tackle available for hire is very indifferent and we strongly recommend serious anglers to take their own. The best period for fishing is between November and February – unfortunately the hottest period of the year, but on the coast or at sea there are always cooling sea breezes which make the temperature bearable.

The third and least-known game fishing area is located on the very beautiful island of Mafia, 80 miles south of Dar-es-Salaam and 30 miles off the coast. Without doubt this is destined to become one of the most popular game fish centres in the world for European anglers – providing, of course, that it is managed efficiently. This is already developing along the right lines, as a most luxurious fishing lodge, capable of accommodating over fifty people has recently been constructed. Mafia is quite a large island but it is sparsely populated and its only industry is the cultivation of coconuts and the resulting export of copra. Considering that all supplies for the lodge, apart from local fruits, have to be flown in daily, the food is of a very high quality.

The lodge is very efficiently run by the manager Mr Douglas Haigh, ably assisted by his charming wife, Beryl. Locally-caught fish supplied by visiting anglers always feature prominently on the menu, and I can assure you barracuda or kingfish steaks take some beating.

Leslie gaffs a nice trevally for the author. These fish are known locally as karembesi

For the shellfish gourmet, the locally-caught mango crabs are out of this world and are the largest, juiciest, most succulent crabs I have ever encountered.

All rooms are air-conditioned and include a bath and shower in individual chalets. The view is breathtaking. The chalets have been located on a grassy slope among graceful coconut palms overlooking a beach of pure silver sand.

The lodge is situated on Chole Bay at the southern end of the island and access to the open sea through the Kinasi Pass takes less than 30 minutes. Once through the pass, within a mile of the coral cliffs which line these shores, the waters of the Indian Ocean plunge down to incredible depths over the edge of the great submarine plateau known as the Mafia shelf.

Leslie and I experienced some fabulous fishing either trolling along the edge of the shelf or along the outer edge of the coral reefs. We caught most of the species of game fish to be found along the African coast during our stay, with the regrettable exception of any of the bill fish. We were too late in the season for these. As for boats, the angler need have no worry providing they are booked in advance, as Seafaris run a fleet of boats from the Lodge.

For the angler with a family, Tanzania has a lot to offer. It is now only eight hours' flying time to Dar on the coast and from here several of the best game parks in the world are only a short distance. These include the Serengeti and N'gorogoro crater, which have no parallel.

Comfortable lodges are now a major feature of most of the parks and the cost for visitors is reasonable. After a few days in one of the parks, the family can return to the coast where the fisherman can get down to serious sport whilst his family can enjoy the superb beaches and warm waters of the sparkling blue Indian Ocean.

All forms of water sport are available to visitors, and for those interested in underwater swimming the coral gardens with their fantastic colours and myriads of exotic tropical fish are a never-ending source of amusement. In fact, some of the coral gardens off Mafia Island are now considered to be among the finest in the world. Normally, Leslie Moncrieff and I prefer to be on the water rather than in it, but on our last day on the island we were prevailed upon to don masks and flippers and visit one of these coral gardens.

It was a scene of such colour, beauty and movement that I shall never forget it. Neither shall I forget the sight that met my eyes when I surfaced – Leslie being swept away from the boat, blowing water from his snorkel like a stranded whale. Apparently, no one had thought to tell him it is all but impossible to do the breast stroke wearing flippers, and eventually we had to up anchor and race to his rescue. By this time, quite naturally, we were all paralysed with laughter, and it was only with great difficulty that we were able to get the boat under way.

The reef fishing along most of this coast is very good, with such species as barracuda, koli-koli, snapper and various species of rock cod. Many of the latter average 10 to 20 lb and have most exotic colourings.

In the deeper water, just off the reefs, are to be found large dogtooth tuna – in my opinion the hardest fighting of all the tuna family. Here also in mid-water lurk the large and powerful karambesi, a giant member of the caranx family, undoubtedly one of the most stubborn fighters to be taken by the game angler.

In the deep blue ocean water over the edge of the continental shelf, large yellowfin tuna and mako and other sharks are to be encountered during October and November, whilst in December and January sail-fish, striped and, occasionally, large black marlin will be taken. Apart from this, at most times during the year, medium-sized game fish are present, such as bonito, tuna, dorado, wahoo, kingfish, black and rainbow runners, as well as some large barracuda.

Finally, if you want a real thrill, try night fishing from a drifting boat in the vicinity of the reefs. We tried this one night after a session in the bar of the lodge while waiting for the moon to go down.

We were assured it was essential to success to have a pitch-black night. What a hilarious evening that turned out to be!

I rather foolishly elected to fish from the high bows of our boat to give the other fishermen more room, and consequently, I was on numerous occasions only prevented from departing overboard by a ridiculously low rail when I either snagged bottom or struck into a good fish. Playing a 40 lb grouper on a pitch black night from my insecure perch was exceedingly funny to everyone but me.

We certainly had a lot of sport though, and Leslie hooked one fish that nearly had him over the side of the boat before the hook eventually pulled out. Grouper in this area have been observed by experienced underwater photographers at well over 300 lbs, and to this day Leslie is quite convinced it was one of these giants that got away.

Where the Weather Starts 1974

The bright red balloon we were using as a float curtsied gently as an 8 ft blue shark far below mouthed the bait. Evidently sensing the movement above him, he ejected it and swam lazily upwards to inspect the strange object that had interrupted his meal. Conditions were ideal for photography, with a clear blue sky and a flat calm sea. Perched on top of the cabin roof with my camera I was in an ideal position to see every movement of the fish in the gin clear water.

The shark circled the balloon, butting it with his nose, until he decided it was inedible. He descended and once again picked up the bait. As soon as the bait disappeared down his large mouth I shouted to Les to set the hook. When he felt the prick of the barb the shark shot towards the surface. He turned in his own length and started to sound. When he had done so, I saw him swim through a loop that had appeared in the line. This gradually tightened and formed a dangerous-looking knot in the main line just above the leader. Les elected to give the fish slack line in the hope it would think the danger was past and stop sounding. Fortunately this worked, and he then began to lead the shark back up to the surface with the least possible pressure. Much to our surprise he came up as docile as a lamb. I am sure he did not know he was hooked, so I was now able to grasp the wire leader. At this stage we could have pulled him up to the gaff, but the thought of a green (fresh) shark thrashing about in the boat did not appeal in the least, so we decided to take a chance.

Instructing one of the crew to hang onto the leader, I undid the quick-release clip, took the knot out of the line and reconnected. The fight was then resumed on sound tackle and the shark eventually boated, but we were very lucky to get away with it.

This incident happened while Leslie Moncrieff and I were on a week's visit to the Azores. In mid-Atlantic, about 800 miles west of the Portuguese coast, this group of tiny volcanic islands is probably better known to most people for their starring role in many of our

A 150 lb plus blue shark on light tackle

weather forecasts, for it is in this area of the Atlantic that cyclonic conditions build up. There are nine islands in the archipelago, the largest of which is less than 40 miles long. They are all very beautiful and despite their volcanic origin they are green and verdant, supporting a profusion of flowers and vegetation of both temperate and semi-tropical zones.

At the time of the above incident we had just arrived on the island of Terceira. Local fishermen informed us that there were many large sharks a mile or two offshore in the vicinity of our base at Agra, capital of the island. So far as we could gather these were mainly blues, tigers and hammerheads, although we encountered only blues.

We acquired a suitable boat and began our drift about 2½ miles off-shore. Soon we had a good trail of rubby dubby going, and I spotted the first fish as already described. This was quickly followed by another of a similar size which we estimated to be about 150 lb. This was released after a disappointing fight. Up to this time we had been fishing with fairly heavy outfits, not knowing what to expect; but expecting that our next customer would also be a blue, I decided to have a little sport, so I mounted a bait on my light 30 lb test outfit. Sure enough, within 10 minutes or so Les saw another slightly larger blue swimming up our chum trail. It promptly accepted my bait. The ensuing battle lasted about 20 minutes. It was lively, particularly when the fish started to circle the stationary boat and I had to follow it, struggling around obstructions and loose gear.

I eventually brought him back alongside where he was subdued! But not without a struggle

At this point we counted seven other large blues which had suddenly appeared and were following my hooked fish with what appeared to be evil intent. One of these was a huge specimen, at least half as large again as the one on my line. I fought the fish to the side of the boat where the mate was able to grasp the leader. Then he and the captain sank in the gaffs. Unfortunately, the shark twisted savagely and the handle of one of the gaffs broke in half and they were forced to let the fish go.

I eventually brought him back alongside where he was subdued, but not without a struggle with only one gaff. After this we had to stop fishing as we had to be back at our hotel by midday. If we had stayed I believe we could have filled the boat with sharks.

I believe sharks are present all the year in the Azores. The average size of the blues is certainly high, and although we did not encounter either tiger or hammerhead sharks we were assured that they were fairly common. Some of the tiger sharks are said to be very large indeed. Sharks seem to be prolific around the island of Terceira, and on another day we saw three sharks on the surface fighting over a dead sea-bird. Later, in the evening of the same day, the wind blew an empty bait bag overboard and within minutes there were a couple of sharks circling around it.

Sport-fishing in the islands is largely undeveloped and local anglers have neither suitable boats nor heavy tackle to seek the larger fish. This is a great pity as there seems to be very good potential, and it is worthwhile being developed, in particular for visiting anglers. So far as I know at the moment there was only one boat available for hire and this is owned by the Club Nautique in Agra. She was about 30 ft long with a 50-h.p. diesel engine, and was only suitable for sharking or inshore work.

The inshore fishing during the summer is reputed to be very good particularly around San Miguel, another island we visited. Unfortunately, owing to the short duration of our stay we were unable to explore the potential ourselves, but according to local anglers at least three species of game-fish are abundant – amberjack, barracuda and bluefish. Amberjack reach a large average size and specimens of 60 lb and more are not uncommon. The locals told us that they were confident that several world line class records would shortly come to the Azores.

The main purpose of our visit was to evaluate the quality of the tuna-fishing, which was said to be very good, and this proved to be true because we were fortunate to capture several large tuna. But that's another story!

The Seychelles Potential 1974

The Seychelles archipelago – 86 islands – lies in the Indian Ocean midway between Kenya on the East African coast and Sri Lanka. The land area is less than 107 square miles, but the surrounding shallow underwater plateau covers an area of over 25,000 square miles. Most of the larger islands, including the main island of Mahé, are granitic and mountainous, yet the smaller coral islands are very flat but tropical, and of outstanding beauty.

Mahé, 17 miles long by 5 miles wide, is awe-inspiring as your plane circles it to land. Mountains over 3,000 feet high and densely clothed with tropical undergrowth, soar majestically down in many places, directly onto dazzling white coral sand beaches lined with palms.

The inhabitants are friendly and helpful, and unaffected by the influx of tourists since the international airport opened. Most tourists stay on Mahé, where most of the new hotels have been built. Two I can personally recommend are the Reef Hotel and the Beau Vallon Beach Hotel.

Despite being close to the equator, the climate is good, with average temperatures around 27°C (80°F) but sea breezes always make it bearable. The islands are out of the cyclone belt so high winds and thunderstorms are rare. There are two seasons, hot from December to May and slightly cooler during the period June to November. Annual rainfall is over 90 inches, and the wettest months are November to February. It is sensible to take lightweight waterproofs.

Fishing is possible throughout the year, except during July and August when it can be very windy and rough at sea. The two best periods are towards the end of the south-east trades (from mid-September to the end of October) and at the end of the north-west monsoon (from early March to the end of April). There has been much speculation regarding the fishing; some reports have been good, others poor. Having fished the Seychelles hard for two weeks I think it has considerable potential but there are difficulties. At present the only charter-boats available are based in Port Victoria on Mahé, which is roughly in the centre of the plateau. The average water depth over this plateau is around 40 fathoms, and most of the truly large big game fish, such as black, blue and striped marlin, mako shark, dogtooth tuna and the larger sailfish, are only to be found in the deeper water over the edge of the shelf. The aspiring big-game angler is faced with a long and expensive trip of at least 50 miles to reach this deeper water. Several boats in the local charter fleet offer special 24-hour charters to fish this blue water. You leave at five one evening and return at the same hour the following evening – about six hours actual fishing time in deep water. The boats are well equipped and the price includes cold drinks and all tackle and bait. The other, and in my opinion better alternative, is to charter for several days, and either camp out on one of the outer islands on the edge of the shelf, or arrange for accommodation on Bird Island. This is a typical coral island, barely a mile and half long by half a mile wide, and 60 miles from Mahé; it's right on the edge of the deep water shelf. It is one of the major nesting grounds in the Indian Ocean for the sooty tern, and the comfortable lodge on the island, composed of 10 individual palm-thatched chalets around a central bar and dining area, caters for visiting anglers and bird watchers. It has its own small airstrip so if you wish to avoid the long haul by boat you can fly by charter-plane from Mahé and arrange for a boat to meet you there.

Shore fishing from Mahé or any of the larger islands can be quite interesting using light baitcasting or spinning rods for such species as small snappers, caranx, mackerel and various brightly coloured and exotic coral fish. Other shallow water species, such as bonefish, permit, milkfish and pompano, are reputed to occur in certain areas, but despite a diligent search I was unable to locate any. The inshore fishing around Mahé, Praslin or La Digue is quite good and for those anglers interested in light tackle fishing there are quite exciting possibilities. Throughout most of the year there are large shoals of common bonito (little tuna or kawakawa) oceananic bonito (skipjack) yellowfin tuna, barracuda and wahoo. The latter are of a high average size here, and I recall we caught five over 40 lb apiece in one day around a small bank called the Pilot Patches barely two miles offshore. There are also odd sailfish to be picked up, as well as the possibility of black marlin, as this species sometimes comes into the shallow water. In fact the largest marlin caught (to date) in the Seychelles is a black weighing 528 lb, caught in 1972 in the lee of Mahé barely three miles off Beau Vallon beach.

During my visit in 1974 we had some wonderful sport during our five-day stay on Bird Island, a real paradise for the angler, catching an amazing variety of fish including sailfish, wahoo, kingfish, tuna (dogtooth and yellowfin), as well as many different species of caranx. We saw no marlin but I am sure this must be a good area for them, and when more is learnt about their movements and seasons in these waters I am certain we shall hear of some spectacular catches. The beachfishing from Bird is superb and anybody contemplating a visit should take a beachcasting or heavy spinning rod. The resident bar steward on the island, Les Hutcheson, specializes in this type of fishing and has had some very big fish: caranx 50 lb, sharks over 100 lb, and he also regularly hooks larger fish only to have them cut off on the sharp coral. His favourite method is freelining a live mackerel. I understand the owners of Bird Island may buy one or two suitable boats to be based there for charter. There is an excellent fleet of charter-craft based in Port Victoria and these may be booked in advance through the Marine Charter Association, Box 169, Port Victoria, Mahé. The Association has about eight boats for hire from 20 to over 40 feet.

John takes good care to keep his hand behind the choppers of an Indian Ocean barracuda from the Seychelles

It is never cold in this area, even at night, and only light clothing need be taken. Heavy tackle available for hire on the charter-boats is adequate, but I would advise visiting anglers to take their own light tackle.

Leslie Moncrieff caught this huge wahoo just three miles off Mahé

South African Adventure 1975

The Republic of South Africa attracted more than 140,000 tourists from the UK alone last year. The fishing can only be described as fantastic, no matter whether your interest lies in coarse, game or sea fishing.

During March of last year I visited South Africa mainly to sample the sea fishing, and what a trip it turned out to be! From Durban I fished my way around the coast to Cape Town. The fishing varies greatly from area to area, due to the conflux of two great ocean currents off the Cape of Good Hope, the cold Benguella which flows along the west coast, and the Aghulas which flows along the south coast. Not only is the quality of the fishing exceptional, but the variety of species to be caught is very wide, many of them indigenous to South Africa alone.

In Durban I was immediately introduced to the main tool of the South African offshore angler – the ski-boat, the comparatively small, flatbottomed, extremely fast craft powered by large outboard motors which, over the years, have been specially adapted or designed by anglers from the original speedboats used by water-skiers. They average about 17 ft and look far from safe for offshore or deep sea work, specially in the rough seas often experienced around their coasts. These boats are used by the majority of the Republic's anglers because they can be launched off any beach, as deep water harbours for larger, more conventional sport-fishing boats are practically non-existent. Despite their looks, these tiny boats are very stable and safe, even in rough seas, as I can now personally confirm, and furthermore, due to the safety equipment carried and stringent regulations imposed by all the ski-boat clubs, accidents are very rare. However, I can assure you the ride out and return from the fishing grounds in a choppy sea can be quite an uncomfortable experience until one learns the correct technique. The first day I remained seated and as a result was unable to sit down again for the rest of the week! The second trip I stood all day and wished I hadn't, as I received several nasty bruises. Eventually I found the answer was to relax the body and ride the waves with the boat.

During March the most prolific species off Durban is a fish locally called a barracuda, which in fact is the barred mackerel of the Pacific, the tanguigue, commonly called a king mackerel in other parts of the world. Next to the wahoo they are probably the fastest fish in the ocean, and the first run after they are hooked has to be experienced to be believed. I had several days exciting sport with these fish over the offshore reefs outside Durban with Dusty Miller, one of the local ski-boat kings. We also caught several other species of fish, including Spanish mackerel and even a small hammerhead shark.

From Durban I flew down the coast on a local S.A.A. flight to Port Elizabeth where I was met by Doug Wheafley, president of the local angling club, who had very kindly arranged for some local ski-boat owners to take me out tunny fishing. The most common tunny in this area is the yellowfin and during my visit they were averaging around 30 lb, so we were very fortunate to run into one school of fish close to 100 lb apiece. Pound for pound these are one of the toughest fighters in the sea, and on my light tackle I was hard-pushed to handle them. The blue water where these fish are found is more than 25 miles offshore, but this can vary depending on wind and currents, and I recall on one particular day we had to travel directly out from land for more than 40 miles before we found it and commenced fishing. I was most perturbed but my companions assured me that it was quite safe as we were in the company of two other boats and also in constant radio contact with the coastguards.

From Port Elizabeth I travelled overland to Cape St Francis, where I was treated to some most spectacular fishing. This is a very isolated area and life here is centred around the Hotel Cape St Francis, constructed in a delightful setting among the sand-dunes overlooking the beach. I heard that the surf fishing here, and also a little farther into the bay towards the estuary, is at certain times of the year quite fantastic with elf or bluefish, leerfish, sharks and large kob – a type of salmon-bass – making up the bulk of the catch. The latter species alone attain weights in excess of 90 lb. There are two fully equipped deepsea craft here which can be booked at a very reasonable cost through the hotel, so during my short stay I decided to concentrate on the boat fishing. Accordingly arrangements were made for me to fish from one of these, the *Spray* owned by Leighton Hulett, an experienced local angler.

The first day we concentrated on leerfish, a handsome silvery fish rather flat in the body, but great fighters, spending almost as much time in the air as in the water when hooked. We trolled slowly with small lures on the surface, locating the shoals by spotting flocks of gulls. I had a good bag with the fish averaging between 20 and 30 lb apiece.

The second day was most memorable as for the first time ever I was to fish for the legendary red steenbras. The most sought-after species in the Republic, they are comparatively rare, particularly larger specimens over 50 lb. They are a bottom-feeding species, found in deep water over rock, and Leighton is a recognized expert on these fish. We used fresh fillets of mackerel fished on a flowing trace just off the bottom, reminiscent of the cod fishing at home, except that the bites were very delicate and the timing of the strike was critical. We caught upwards of a dozen, including two magnificent specimens of 54 and 47 lb, the former which provided me with one of the hardest battles I have ever experienced on my 30 lb outfit. They are without doubt the hardest fighting bottomfeeding fish I have ever encountered. I was most reluctant to leave this delightful spot, but the bright lights of Cape Town were calling.

In Cape Town I was looked after by Kerry Malt, angling correspondent for the *Cape Times*, and Hymie Steyn, president of the Cape ski-boat club, two international anglers and fine sportsmen. In the past, fishing for the giant bluefin tuna in False Bay was exceptionally good but, sad to relate, for the last two or three years they have failed to appear in any numbers, so at the moment most local deep-sea anglers concentrate on the shoals of longfin and yellowfin tuna passing around the Cape during the summer months. These tuna average between 20 and 50 lb and provide exciting sport on light tackle.

I spent two interesting days in the rough waters of the Cape, this time fortunately in a large tuna boat, the *Hunter* (skipper Frank Wittwen) based in Simonstown. We trolled six sets of feathers at a time, and on several occasions we had a full house.

One of the most popular fish with South African anglers is the famed yellowtail. Closely related to the amberjack of the Atlantic they are an inshore species similar in shape to a tuna. A very sporting fish, they are usually to be found over deep-water banks or reefs and can be taken either by trolling or on bait or spinners from a drifting boat.

My last three days on the coast was spent at Struis Bay fishing over the six- and twelve-mile banks, two of the hottest spots for this species along the whole coast. We used spinning tackle with shiny 4 and 6 oz lures, and what sport we had! The strike of a large yellowtail is electrifying, and immediately he feels the hooks he heads for the distant bottom, and I soon found to my cost it was essential to stop them before they gained the sanctuary of the sharp rocks lining the bank. Yellowtail often attain weights well over 50 lb, averaging between 15 and 20 lb, so I was very lucky to tempt several fine specimens around 30 lb.

It would be unfair to leave South Africa without a brief mention of the shark fishing, although South African anglers are not keen on this branch of the sport, probably due to their being so prolific and easy to catch. Most boat anglers consider them vermin and cut the line if one is accidentally hooked. On the other hand, in certain areas shore anglers do fish for them, and sharks often of a staggering size are beached after superhuman battles lasting many hours.

Throughout my tour I had been keen to get to grips with at least one big shark, but as my fishing was predominantly from boats, every time I mentioned it my request was politely refused. However, on the last day, when fishing for yellowtail over the six-mile bank, an opportunity arose which was too good to miss. One of my companions had just hauled in a plump yellowtail when a huge shark suddenly appeared behind the boat and I persuaded my colleagues to let me try for it. All my heavy tackle was back at the hotel, but by chance there happened to be a heavy rod aboard with a 9/0 Senator loaded with 80 lb line. I only carried one shark hook on a 15 foot wire trace (which was barely long enough) but it would have to suffice. Lip-hooking a dead yellow-tail of about 15 lb I quickly lowered it over the back of the boat, and while I was still paying out the trace the shark, which had been leisurely circling, slowly turned and completely inhaled the bait in one gulp.

Picking up the rod I waited for the line to tighten and then struck as hard as I could – immediately all hell broke loose. If you have never hooked a really big shark from a small, crowded ski-boat with nowhere to sit and no harness to don, then my advice is not to try. My opponent took off for the far horizon, jumping and ejecting my bait as he broke surface (see photograph) but fortunately by this time the hook was set firmly in his jaw. I would rather forget the following 10 minutes. Then the skipper was appealing on the radio for any nearby boats with a harness on board to come to our rescue. Within minutes

Here's a superb yellowtail that gave John
a memorable battle on his 30 lb outfit.
Berkley Regulation rod and Policansky
Monitor No. 4 lever-drag reel

help arrived in the shape of a slightly larger ski-boat, all of 18 feet, and
her skipper-owner kindly invited me aboard. What luxury: not only
did he have a harness but also a fighting chair! Mind you, swapping
boats in a choppy sea with an angry shark on was a hazardous operation, and I received several nasty bruises.

Now properly equipped, I really went to work on that shark and
with expert co-operation from the skipper handling the boat I had
the fish alongside in just over the hour. One of the anglers in the boat
gripped the trace, another the gaff, and I heard them both gasp as the
full length of the shark slid into view, and I realized for the first time
the colossal size of my adversary. We estimated his length at well
over 12 feet, and our imminent danger was immediately apparent:
one blow from his powerful tail would have been more than sufficient to wreck our flimsy craft. Easing off the brake on the reel I
urgently signalled for the trace to be released, as I decided to put a
little distance between us as quickly as possible. After consultation
with the skipper and crew, who all wanted him cut off, it was reluctantly agreed I could fight the shark for a further period to exhaust
him thoroughly and we would then try tailing and towing ashore.

During this discussion my attention must have been distracted and the issue was settled for me, as he must have taken a turn of the short wire trace around his body and cut through the line with his tail. I am sure everybody else was secretly delighted, although I was a little sick at the time. It was a mako shark, certainly the largest I had ever seen, and I am quite convinced it must have weighed well over 1,000 lb.

Before returning to the UK I visited Johannesburg for a few days where I was introduced to Trevor Babich, president of the Rand Piscatorial Society. As a result my last three days in the Republic were spent on a trout fishing safari in the Eastern Transvaal. This proved to be an interesting and entertaining trip and I was very pleasantly surprised at the quality of the trout fishing. We fished several small dams and lakes on farms in the high veldt stocked with rainbows averaging around 1½ lb, but the fishing I enjoyed most was the brawling, rocky streams in the mountains on the edge of the escarpment. Local anglers fish the wet fly downstream, but I found the most successful method was to fish the pools and eddies with a weighted upstream nymph, which brought me several nice trout, up to and including one superb rainbow of just over 3 lb.

The author with a huge red steenbras at 54 lbs. This was the largest to be caught off the South African coast in 1975

Fishing in Central America 1978

Have you ever heard of a Cubera Snapper or a Roosterfish? No? Well I am not surprised as they are both relatively little-known species, although both are true game fish. The latter is only to be encountered in the Eastern Pacific ocean, between Mexico and Peru, so it is only in the past ten years or so since the Americans have set up exploratory fishing camps along this coast that reports of encounters with this fabulous looking fish have appeared. Ever since I saw the first photograph of a roosterfish I had set my heart on catching one, so when I received an invitation to fish off the pacific coast of Costa Rica I accepted with alacrity as I knew this was an area where this species was likely to be found.

Costa Rica is the smallest of the Central American republics. It is sandwiched between Panama and Nicaragua, and despite the fact that it has no army, it is a very safe country with a fairly stable economy. My first reaction was that it is a hell of a long way to go for a week's fishing. However. if like me, you can arrange to have a week's fishing in America either before or after, it is reasonably accessible.

From Miami the capital of Costa Rica, San José, is but a 2½-hour flight, and the fishing camp on the north-west coast can be reached within an hour. The camp, which has been literally carved out of the jungle, is owned and run by a very jovial and keen American angler, Henry Norton. The accomodation and food are excellent, particularly when one considers that the camp, called Bahía pez Vela, is many miles from the nearest town. The translation from the Spanish means The Bay of Sailfish, and this camp was originally set up to take advantage of the superb billfishing that is to be found in this area. It is without doubt one of the world's hot spots for sailfish, and while these are present throughout the year, the peak period is from May to September, and at this time it is not uncommon to raise 20 to 30 sails during a day's fishing. The heaviest concentration of sailfish are to be found in the vicinity of the Bat Islands, which are on the far side of the Bay of Pappigius, and form a natural corridor for most migratory fish running up and down the coast. Many large blue and black marlin have been caught in this area, but the potential for these has not yet been developed as blue water is further offshore and is very rarely fished. Certainly there are marlin in excess of 1000 lbs as many have been seen.

This is one of the most exciting areas I have ever fished, and I think the potential is immense. It is a very isolated area, and is only fished by the boats from the camp. These are the nearest to virgin waters that I have yet come across, as there are but few commercial fishing boats working in this area. Offshore, apart from billfish, one can catch wahoo, dolphin fish and many species of tuna.

However, as good as the offshore fishing is, it really does not compare with the inshore fishing which can only be described as fabulous. Max King, my fishing companion on this trip, and I spent the first three days of our visit inshore fishing in the white water along the rocky shoreline. Our main quarry was of course the roosterfish, and I shall never forget my first sight of one of these incredible looking fish as it rolled, exhausted, on the surface after a long and bitter fight. The black bars stood out from its silver flanks, which were dominated by the high and regal dorsal fin which looks for all the world like a cock's comb, and it is this feature which doubtless accounts for its common name. They are a true gamefish, and are caught either in midwater or near the surface, and in my opinion pound for pound are the hardest fighting fish I have ever had on the other end of a rod. In this area this species reaches a large average size. The smallest we caught was about 25 lbs while the largest was a superb specimen of over 70 lbs. In addition we caught many other interesting midwater species, including amberjack which averaged 60 lbs, and Cubera snapper which averaged 40 lbs. The latter are also a hard fighting species who have a most fearsome looking mouthful of teeth. After this first three days, we had caught so many large fish our arms were almost dropping off! We also spent one morning bottom fishing, but we lost so much tackle on unseen fish which took our baits that we eventually gave up. Most of these fish were quite unstoppable on the tackle we were using, and we can only assume they were very large sharks or huge grouper.

For those anglers considering a visit to Bahia pez Vela, I would proffer the following information. The accomodation at the camp is excellent; detached chalets have been strategically located overlooking the beach, each sleeping two persons, and showers with plenty of hot water are provided. The camp caters for a total of twelve anglers fishing two to a boat. The boats, 25 ft long and capable of speeds in excess of 30 knots, are well equipped. with a tuna tower, fighting chair and outriggers, as well as top quality rods and penn international reels. Each boat carries one 80 lb and two 30 lb outfits as well as plenty of hooks and spare line. Live bait is widely used and is very effective for most species likely to be encountered. The weather in Costa Rica is excellent as temperatures rarely drop below 75° or exceed 90°, so it is only necessary to take light clothing with perhaps a light sweater for evening wear as the evenings are mostly cool. During the rainy season from June to October, heavy showers may be encountered early morning or late evening, so it is advisable to take light waterproofs. The only tackle you need take is a selection of large deep diving plugs and spoons for trolling, on those odd days when live bait may be in short supply. If you are a light tackle enthusiast you will have to take your own tackle. We took 12 lb and 20 lb outfits, and had some great sport with these, particularly the latter, which we used most of the time, even for sailfish as well as large roosters and snappers, although these proved to be quite a handful.

These huge Cubera snapper are only one of the hard-fighting fish to be found on the inshore fishing grounds

John's companion on the trip, Max King, plays out a big roosterfish

The guides hold a 'rooster' of specimen proportions. It was one of several
caught to over 70 lb

A superb Pacific sailfish. This was an average fish for the venue –
about 100 lb in weight!

The 'Kenyahead' Teaser 1992

Early this year a few friends and I travelled to Watamu, Kenya, on the east African coast, with the hopes of catching some sailfish on a fly. During our two-week stay we hooked many sails and succeeded in landing several. In fact, I was fortunate enough to land the first sailfish ever taken on a fly off Kenya that would qualify under IGFA rules.

Aside from the skill of the angler, the most important parts of fly fishing for sailfish are the effectiveness of the teaser used to bring the fish within casting range and the skill of the teaser handler. For the first few days we used a Panama teaser, made from a strip of fresh bonito belly sewn into a cone shape. This makes an excellent teaser, since the shape of the rig causes it to dive and surface attractively. However, it has an annoying habit of quickly falling apart, even when trolled at slow speeds.

How could I overcome this problem? For several days I made attempts to improve the teaser, all of which failed. I had almost given up when I stumbled upon a possible solution. Why not use the hard cartilage behind the gills of the bait to form the front of the teaser? This should result in a durable, curved face like the front of a Konahead lure.

I tried it and it worked! I now had a teaser that ducked, dived, and swam in a realistic manner. Even better, I found that one teaser would stand up to an entire day of trolling, even after being ravaged by several hungry sailfish.

At the end of our Kenya visit we had two days of marlin fishing. Although the local skippers there prefer to troll artificial lures for marlin, we convinced them to let us run two of my new creations in the spread. This time, however, I mounted a large hook in front by sewing it into the bait. The hooked versions worked great, and it was hard to distinguish them from the plastics running beside them. However, the fish seemed to know the difference, and in two days we hooked, landed, and released two marlin and a large sailfish that each time chose one of our baits over the plastic lures. Our skipper was most impressed, and I wouldn't be surprised if the new bait replaces plastics along that stretch of coast.

The following instructions show you how to prepare the teaser and hooked versions of what I have come to call the Kenyahead, in honour of its birthplace.

1 The first step is to cut the belly section from a freshly caught bonito (or similar species), including the hard cartilage behind the gills that forms the start of the body.
2 Make an inch-long slit in the bottom front of the belly.
3 Make a loop in a length of 50-pound mono leader and push it through the slit.
4 Place this loop over the front, pointed part of the belly section.
5 Pass the end of the mono leader through this loop and pull tight.
6 The bait is then sewn with strong thread over the gill edges and three quarters of the way along the top. Slit the last two or three inches of the belly at the end to form two tails.
7 To make a one-hook bait, pass one large marlin hook through the front of the bait in the nose of the gill section. Then sew the bait together as above and bind the 'nose' in front of the hook with 30-pound Dacron to stop it from pulling out. The hook is then free to swivel in the bait and will reverse when taken by the fish.
8 To make a double-hook bait, wire two medium-sized books together and insert them through the base of the belly, one near the front and the other as near as possible to the end of the tails. The bait is then sewn up along the top and around the gill sections. Finally, sew the nose of the gill section around the shank of the first hook with 30 pound Dacron to keep it from pulling out.

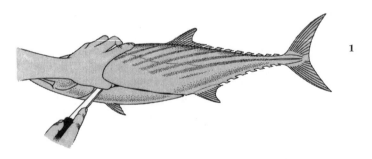

1

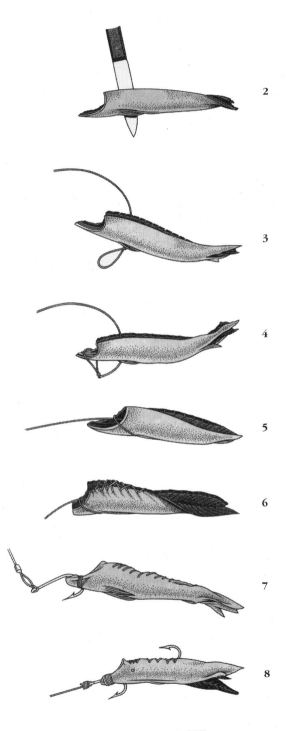